Mesos in Action

Mesos in Action

ROGER IGNAZIO

MANNING
SHELTER ISLAND

Manning Publications Co.
20 Baldwin Road
PO Box 761
Shelter Island, NY 11964

Development editor: Cynthia Kane
Technical development editor: Jerry Kuch
Copyeditor: Sharon Wilkey
Proofreader: Melody Dolab
Technical proofreaders: Chris Schaefer, Yogesh Poojari
Typesetter: Dennis Dalinnik
Cover designer: Marija Tudor

ISBN: 9781617292927
Printed in the United States of America
1 2 3 4 5 6 7 8 9 10 – EBM – 21 20 19 18 17 16

For Sarah

brief contents

contents

foreword

If you ever want to see a man's head explode, walk up to somebody whose job it is to manually configure and provision scores of servers inside a datacenter, and say the following: "Wow! It must be so easy, and so much fun, to keep track of what's running on which machines."

Or find a person who has spent years carrying a pager and responding to server outages and say, "Sounds like a stress-free job. At least it guarantees you get a good night's sleep."

The truth, of course, is that managing servers and other datacenter infrastructure has historically been difficult, tedious, and full of sleepless nights for the poor men and women charged with configuring all these machines and responding to failures whenever they strike. As companies started relying more heavily on information technology during the past 20 years, often housing one application per server (or, in recent years, virtual machine), the practice grew increasingly difficult. A few servers grew to dozens, dozens grew to hundreds, and hundreds sometimes grew to thousands.

Then the web blew up, fueled by incredibly popular services such as Google, Facebook, and Twitter. The mobile web, fueled by billions of smartphones, tablets, and other devices, followed shortly thereafter. Old ways of computing could no longer cut it in a world where millions of users might be on a site or app at any given time.

Inside datacenters, single-server databases (single-server everything, really) were rapidly replaced by distributed systems that could handle previously unimaginable volumes of data and traffic. Often, complex monolithic applications were replaced by microservices—collections of single-purpose services managed separately, then connected via API to construct end-user applications. Scalability demands increased, but so did the learning curve for building these systems and the complexity of managing them.

Google famously solved this problem inside its own datacenters with a system called Borg, which ostensibly let most employees—systems administrators and developers alike—manage hundreds of thousands of servers like one big computer. Several years after Borg simplified operations at Google, the open source Apache Mesos project hit the scene and changed the lives of its users in similar ways. All of a sudden, the process of deploying, running, and managing complex distributed systems became much simpler; everything shares the same set of machines, and Mesos handles the legwork of matching workload requirements with available resources.

I experienced this shift firsthand as a software engineer at Twitter, where Mesos helped conquer the infamous fail whale and helped Twitter reach new heights of scalability and reliability. When I moved on to Airbnb in 2012, then a fast-growing startup just four years old, Mesos once again helped us grow our infrastructure—but not the complexity of it—along with our user base. I was so impressed with Mesos and its promise that I decided to start a company, Mesosphere, dedicated to making Mesos usable by mainstream enterprises.

As Mesos grew in popularity and Mesosphere grew in size, we set our sights on hiring the best Mesos engineers and practitioners around. When we saw the work Roger Ignazio had done building out a Mesos-based continuous integration platform at Puppet Labs, we knew we had to have him. Running scalable production systems at established companies is always valuable experience, and since joining Mesosphere, Roger's experience has been a boon to the quality of our Mesos-based Datacenter Operating System technology and to our customers' experiences with it.

With *Mesos in Action*, Roger lets anyone who is interested in Mesos and its ecosystem of technologies take advantage of his experience. The book is a great guide to getting a Mesos cluster running and installing your first frameworks, but also delves into more-advanced topics such as mastering powerful Mesos frameworks (including Marathon for container orchestration and Spark for big data analytics) and even building your own framework.

Whether you're preparing to deploy Mesos or already have it running and want to improve your knowledge, you would be hard-pressed to find a better guide than Roger and a better book than *Mesos in Action*.

FLORIAN LEIBERT
COFOUNDER AND CEO, MESOSPHERE

preface

Apache Mesos began in 2009 as a research project at the University of California at Berkeley, led by Benjamin Hindman. Ben and his team wanted to improve datacenter efficiency by allowing multiple applications to share a single computing cluster, just like multiple applications can share the processor, memory, and hard drive in your laptop or workstation. But they wanted to do this across the many servers that make up a modern datacenter. After an initial implementation of 10,000 lines of C++ code, they published the paper *Mesos: A Platform for Fine-Grained Resource Sharing in the Data Center* in 2010.

Not long after, Ben joined Twitter and used Mesos to better scale its infrastructure, largely bringing an end to the era of the "fail whale" that became infamous as Twitter was rising in popularity and its servers couldn't handle the demand from users. Although Twitter doesn't publicly disclose the number of servers in its expansive infrastructure, online sources and firsthand knowledge from presentations put this somewhere in the ballpark of 10,000 Mesos nodes per cluster.

In December 2010, the Mesos project entered the Apache Incubator, an arm of the Apache Software Foundation that provides a means for projects to gain the full support of the ASF's efforts. The Apache Mesos project graduated from the incubator in June 2013 and is now a top-level project.

In 2013, Ben—along with Florian Leibert and Tobi Knaup—founded Mesosphere. Mesosphere's flagship product, the Datacenter Operating System (DCOS), commercializes the success of the open source project by providing a turnkey solution to enterprises looking to deploy applications and scale infrastructure as effortlessly as other companies using Mesos, such as Airbnb, Apple, and Netflix. Mesosphere continues to be a major contributor to the open source Mesos project and provides Mesos packages and tools to the open source community.

My foray into the Mesos ecosystem and large-scale infrastructure began in 2014 when I started looking at using Mesos to share resources among multiple instances of Jenkins, the popular continuous integration framework. At the time, it seemed like Mesos was reserved for those who already knew about it; a lot of resources were available online but were hard to find, and there wasn't a single canonical source of truth. There also weren't any books covering Mesos. I wrote a couple of blog posts about my experience, and it seemed like other people were in the same boat I was in: wanting to know more about this project but not knowing where to start.

In January 2015, Manning reached out and asked if I'd be interested in writing a book about Mesos. Having never written a book before, the request seemed overwhelming at first. But I also saw it as an opportunity to write the book that I wished I had when I first started using Mesos. Fortunately, the team at Manning gave me the freedom to do just that.

I hope that you find *Mesos in Action* a valuable resource for deploying and administering Mesos clusters and improving the overall efficiency of your infrastructure, and that it allows your team—and your customers—to deploy applications to production quickly and easily.

ROGER IGNAZIO
PORTLAND, OREGON

acknowledgements

You're reading the result of a yearlong effort to produce an in-depth book on the Apache Mesos project and ecosystem. Despite my name being on the cover, many people contributed to the final publication, people who would otherwise remain anonymous if I didn't thank them here. I'm sure that my family, my friends, and my wife already know how much I appreciate their support through this endeavor.

First, I'd like to thank the Mesos community. In every interaction—at conferences, on the mailing lists, on IRC—everyone has been extremely helpful and kind. As of this writing, there are over 100 individual contributors to the Mesos code base, and even more people who volunteer their time on the Mesos mailing lists and chat rooms to answer questions and provide help. In addition to all the people I've had the pleasure of talking to at conferences and working with on a daily basis, I'd like to thank Ben Hindman, Florian Leibert, Thomas Rampelberg, Dave Lester, Christian Bogeberg, and Michael Hausenblas for all of their help. And I'd like to thank Florian for writing the foreword to this book.

Next, as if writing a book isn't already a stressful and time-consuming task, I changed jobs about two-thirds of the way through writing. At Puppet Labs, I'd like to thank Scott Schneider, Colin Creeden, Cody Herriges, Eric Zounes, and Alanna Brown for their support. Before I even signed with Manning, I recall a moment when Scott asked if I really thought you could write an entire book about Mesos; as it turns out, you can!

Many people behind the scenes helped review the book at various stages and provided feedback, including Al Rahimi, Clive Harber, John Guthrie, Luis Moux Domínguez, Mohsen Mostafar Jokar, Morgan Nelson, Nitin Gode, Odysseas Pentakalos, and Thomas Peklak. A special thank you goes out to Jerry Kuch and Chris Schaefer for their technical reviews, and to copy editor Sharon Wilkey for making a countless number of fixes to the original manuscript.

Last, but certainly not least, I need to thank my amazing team at Manning Publications. My editor, Mike Stevens, helped me get from "That sounds like a lot of jargon!" to a formal proposal and signed contract. Development editor Cynthia Kane ensured I was always providing the right amount of context (in both text and graphics), and helped me become a better writer and communicator. And finally, to my publisher Marjan Bace, who not only helped shape the book during the editorial board review, but also ultimately gave me the freedom to write the book that I wish I had when I first got started with Mesos. Thank you!

I'm grateful to all of the people who helped get the book to this point, and I apologize if I've forgotten to mention anyone here.

about this book

Mesos in Action is a practical guide to learning about and deploying Apache Mesos in a real-world setting. I provide a complete tour of the project—from a basic introduction that introduces Mesos and containers, to production-ready deployments that include high availability and framework authentication. I also provide real-world usage of popular (and open source!) Mesos applications that allow you to deploy applications and scheduled jobs on your Mesos cluster.

Although *Mesos in Action* is tailored for intermediate-to-advanced systems administrators, it's well suited for various audiences. I've written the book in such a way that systems administrators, DevOps, application administrators, and software engineers alike will feel at home throughout the text. Although some knowledge of application deployments and software development is desirable, I've provided enough background that it isn't strictly required, instead opting to teach you new skills that you can use to make teams—your own included—work smarter, not harder.

Roadmap

If you are a systems administrator or DevOps person looking to deploy your first Mesos cluster, you'll want to pay particular attention to chapters 1 through 8. These chapters cover everything you need to know to get a cluster up and running, and cover a few ways you can use it to deploy applications and scheduled jobs. Chapter 10 may also be beneficial in helping you to understand how to write your own Mesos-enabled applications. Otherwise, this book is divided into three parts.

Part 1 introduces the Apache Mesos project, compares containers to virtual machines, and presents a real-world use case for deploying a Mesos cluster.

- Chapter 1 introduces the Mesos project. I cover key terms and components used throughout the book, introduce the architecture, and explain how deploying applications in containers is different from deployments in a traditional datacenter.

- Chapter 2 builds upon the introduction provided in chapter 1 by running an Apache Spark data-processing job on the Mesos cluster. You'll see a real-world workload running on the cluster and observe how the cluster behaves. You'll also get a sense of how Mesos allows multiple applications to share cluster resources, leading to improved datacenter utilization.

Part 2 examines the Mesos fundamentals in detail, including installation and configuration, high availability, and monitoring.

- Chapter 3 provides a soup-to-nuts approach for deploying Mesos on your own servers, whether they're in your own datacenter or running on a cloud provider such as AWS or Azure. You'll learn how to install and configure ZooKeeper, Mesos, and Docker, and should have a highly available cluster up and running by the end of the chapter.

- Chapter 4 examines the fundamentals of the Mesos project. You'll learn about the scalability, fault tolerance, high availability, and resource isolation that Mesos provides.

- Chapter 5 provides a tour of how Mesos handles logs and how you can debug issues when they arise. I cover topics including the Mesos web interface, CLI, log file locations, and logging configuration.

- Chapter 6 covers topics necessary for running Mesos in a production environment. This includes information about monitoring the Mesos and ZooKeeper clusters, as well as security and access control for users and frameworks alike.

Part 3 provides you with real-world uses for Mesos.

- Chapter 7 introduces the open source Marathon framework, which allows you to deploy applications and long-running services in Linux and Docker containers across the cluster simply by specifying the amount of resources and number of instances you'd like.

- Chapter 8 introduces the open source Chronos framework, which allows you to deploy scheduled jobs on the cluster using ISO 8601–formatted timestamps. Chronos allows jobs to run on a schedule, or allows them to be dependencies on other jobs, and supports tasks running in both Linux and Docker containers.

- Chapter 9 introduces the open source Apache Aurora framework, which— similar to Marathon and Chronos—allows you to deploy both applications and scheduled jobs on a Mesos cluster. Where it differs, however, is that Aurora has support for multiple users out of the box, and a sophisticated configuration language to match.

- Chapter 10 provides a tour of the Mesos APIs, and includes an example (written in Python) of how to develop your own Mesos applications.
- Appendix A provides a case study on Mesosphere's Datacenter Operating System (DCOS), an enterprise-grade Mesos distribution, as well as a walk-through of how to set up a continuous deployment pipeline using DCOS, Jenkins, and Marathon.
- Appendix B provides a list of Mesos-related projects known at the time of writing. These projects range from Mesos applications, to language bindings, to load-balancing and service-discovery tools. Each entry is accompanied by a short description and a link to additional information online.

Source code

The code for the examples and configuration files used throughout this book is available on GitHub, located at github.com/rji/mesos-in-action-code-samples. The code is also available from this book's website, located at manning.com/books/mesos-in-action.

Much of the code for parts 1 and 2 of the book consists of configuration fragments designed to support or enhance the text. The code for part 3 includes examples of applications and data-processing jobs that are used to illustrate how you might run these workloads on your own infrastructure.

Typographical conventions

- *Italic* typeface is used to introduce new terms.
- Courier typeface is used to denote code samples and commands.
- Code-line continuations are indicated by ➥.

Online and community resources

Many online and community resources are available for the Mesos project. First, and perhaps most important, you can find the latest documentation online at http://mesos.apache.org/documentation/latest. For those interested in Mesos development and where the project is heading, it might be best to consult the project's issue tracker, located at https://issues.apache.org/jira/browse/MESOS.

In addition to using these two resources, you can communicate and interact with other people in the Mesos community in the following ways:

- *Mailing lists*—Several mailing lists relating to Mesos exist, but perhaps the two most important are the users and dev mailing lists. More info can be found on the Mesos project's community page at http://mesos.apache.org/community.
- *IRC*—Developers and users alike chat in the #mesos channel on irc.freenode.net.
- *Planet Mesos*—An RSS aggregator for members of the Mesos community, Planet Mesos contains writings and presentations from project maintainers, contributors,

and conferences. The aggregator itself is available at http://planet.apache.org/mesos. The team also operates a Twitter account that automatically updates when the RSS feed does; it can be found at https://twitter.com/PlanetMesos.

- *Twitter*—The official Twitter feed for the project is located at https://twitter.com/ApacheMesos.
- *MesosCon*—Started in 2014, MesosCon is an annual conference organized by the Mesos community. It has hosted talks from some of the largest internet companies on how they use Mesos to solve scaling problems. More information is available at http://events.linuxfoundation.org/events/mesoscon.

Author Online

Purchase of *Mesos in Action* includes free access to a private web forum run by Manning Publications; you can make comments about the book, ask technical questions, and receive help from the author and from other users. To access the forum and subscribe to it, point your web browser to manning.com/books/mesos-in-action. This page provides information on how to get on the forum after you're registered, what kind of help is available, and the rules of conduct on the forum.

Manning's commitment to our readers is to provide a venue where a meaningful dialogue between individual readers and between readers and the author can take place. It's not a commitment to any specific amount of participation on the part of the author, whose contribution to AO remains voluntary (and unpaid). We suggest you try asking the author some challenging questions lest his interest stray!

The Author Online forum and the archives of previous discussions will be accessible from the publisher's website as long as the book is in print.

about the author

Roger Ignazio is an experienced systems engineer with a focus on distributed, fault-tolerant, and scalable infrastructure. He is passionate about improving productivity through better automation, tooling, and reporting. He's currently a technical lead on the engineering team at Mesosphere, and lives in Portland, Oregon with his wife Sarah and their two cats.

about the cover illustration

On the cover of *Mesos in Action* is "Girl from Petrovo Polje, Dalmatia, Croatia." The term "Polje" derives from the Slavic for "field" and is used to denote a large flat plain. Petrovo Polje is located in Dalmatia, a historical region of Croatia on the Adriatic coast. Dalmatia was once a province of the Roman Empire, and over its history has been fought over and controlled by the Goths, the Byzantines, the Venetians, and the Austro-Hungarian Empire. The illustration is taken from a reproduction of an album of Croatian traditional costumes from the mid-nineteenth century by Nikola Arsenovic, published by the Ethnographic Museum in Split, Croatia, in 2003. The illustrations were obtained from a helpful librarian at the Ethnographic Museum in Split, itself situated in the Roman core of the medieval center of that town: the ruins of Emperor Diocletian's retirement palace from around AD 304. The book includes finely colored illustrations of figures from different regions of Croatia, accompanied by descriptions of the costumes and of everyday life.

Dress codes and lifestyles have changed over the last 200 years, and the diversity by region, so rich at the time, has faded away. It is now hard to tell apart the inhabitants of different continents, let alone of different hamlets or towns separated by only a few miles. Perhaps we have traded cultural diversity for a more varied personal life—certainly for a more varied and fast-paced technological life.

Manning celebrates the inventiveness and initiative of the computer business with book covers based on the rich diversity of regional life of two centuries ago, brought back to life by illustrations from old books and collections like this one.

Part 1

Hello, Mesos

What is Apache Mesos? How does Mesos compare to traditional datacenter architecture? How are containers different from virtual machines? Why might you use Mesos? These are questions that I begin to address in part 1. You'll learn about the Apache Mesos project and its use of containers by comparing and contrasting these relatively new technologies to that of a traditional datacenter. You'll also see a practical example of Mesos in action in the context of running an Apache Spark data-processing job on the cluster.

Introducing Mesos

Traditionally, physical—and virtual—machines have been the typical units of computing in a datacenter. Machines are provisioned with various configuration management tools to later have applications deployed. These machines are usually organized into clusters providing individual services, and systems administrators oversee their day-to-day operations. Eventually, these clusters reach their maximum capacity, and more machines are brought online to handle the load.

In 2010, a project at the University of California, Berkeley, aimed to solve the scaling problem. The software project, now known as *Apache Mesos*, abstracts CPU, memory, and disk resources in a way that allows datacenters to function as if they were one large machine. Mesos creates a single underlying cluster to provide applications with the resources they need, without the overhead of virtual machines and operating systems. You can see a simplified example of this in figure 1.1.

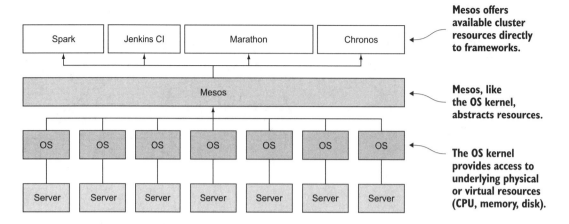

Figure 1.1   Frameworks sharing datacenter resources offered by Mesos

This book introduces Apache Mesos, an open source cluster manager that allows systems administrators and developers to focus less on individual servers and more on the applications that run on them. You'll see how to get up and running with Mesos in your environment, how it shares resources and handles failure, and—perhaps most important—how to use it as a platform to deploy applications.

1.1   Meet Mesos

Mesos works by introducing a layer of abstraction that provides a means to use entire datacenters as if they were a single, large server. Instead of focusing on one application running on a specific server, Mesos's resource isolation allows for multitenancy—the ability to run multiple applications on a single machine—leading to more efficient use of computing resources.

To better understand this concept, you might think of Mesos as being similar to today's virtualization solutions: just as a hypervisor abstracts physical CPU, memory, and storage resources and presents them to virtual machines, Mesos does the same but offers these resources directly to applications. Another way to think about this is in the context of multicore processors: when you launch an application on your laptop, it runs on one or more cores, but in most cases it doesn't particularly matter which one. Mesos applies this same concept to datacenters.

In addition to improving overall resource use, Mesos is distributed, highly available, and fault-tolerant right out of the box. It has built-in support for isolating processes using containers, such as Linux control groups (cgroups) and Docker, allowing multiple applications to run alongside each other on a single machine. Where you once might have set up three clusters—one each to run Memcached, Jenkins CI, and your Ruby on Rails apps—you can instead deploy a single Mesos cluster to run all of these applications.

In the next few sections, you're going to look at how Mesos works to provide all of these features and how it compares to a traditional datacenter.

1.1.1 Understanding how it works

Using a combination of concepts referred to as resource offers, two-tier scheduling, and resource isolation, Mesos provides a means for the cluster to act as a single super-computer on which to run tasks. Before digging in too deeply here, let's take a look at figure 1.2. This diagram demonstrates the logic Mesos follows when offering resources to running applications. This particular example references the Apache Spark data-processing framework.

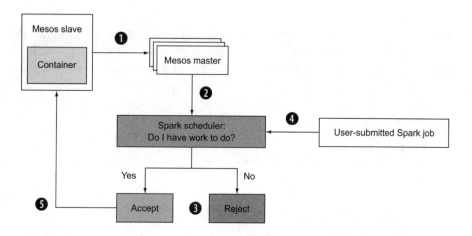

Figure 1.2 Mesos advertises the available CPU, memory, and disk as resource offers to frameworks.

Let's break it down:

❶ The Mesos slave offers its available CPU, memory, and disk to the Mesos *master* in the form of a *resource offer.*

❷ The Mesos master's *allocation module*—or scheduling algorithm—decides which *frameworks*—or applications—to offer the resources to.

❸ In this particular case, the Spark *scheduler* doesn't have any jobs to run on the cluster. It rejects the resource offer, allowing the master to offer the resources to another framework that might have some work to do.

❹ Now consider a user submitting a Spark job to be run on the cluster. The sched-uler accepts the job and waits for a resource offer that satisfies the workload.

❺ The Spark scheduler accepts a resource offer from the Mesos master, and launches one or more *tasks* on an available Mesos *slave*. These tasks are launched within a container, providing isolation between the various tasks that might be running on a given Mesos slave.

Seems simple, right? Now that you've learned how Mesos uses resource offers to advertise resources to frameworks, and how two-tier scheduling allows frameworks to accept and reject resource offers as needed, let's take a closer look at some of these fundamental concepts.

> **NOTE**   An effort is underway to rename the Mesos *slave* role to *agent* for future versions of Mesos. Because this book covers Mesos 0.22.2, it uses the terminology of that specific release, so as to not create any unnecessary confusion. For more information, see https://issues.apache.org/jira/browse/MESOS-1478.

RESOURCE OFFERS

Like many other cluster managers, Mesos clusters are made up of groups of machines called *masters* and *slaves*. Each Mesos slave in a cluster advertises its available CPU, memory, and storage in the form of resource offers. As you saw in figure 1.2, these resource offers are periodically sent from the slaves to the Mesos masters, processed by a scheduling algorithm, and then offered to a framework's scheduler running on the Mesos cluster.

TWO-TIER SCHEDULING

In a Mesos cluster, resource scheduling is the responsibility of the Mesos master's allocation module and the framework's scheduler, a concept known as *two-tier scheduling*. As previously demonstrated, resource offers from Mesos slaves are sent to the master's allocation module, which is then responsible for offering resources to various framework schedulers. The framework schedulers can accept or reject the resources based on their workload.

The allocation module is a pluggable component of the Mesos master that implements an algorithm to determine which offers are sent to which frameworks (and when). The modular nature of this component allows systems engineers to implement their own resource-sharing policies for their organization. By default, Mesos uses an algorithm developed at UC Berkeley known as Dominant Resource Fairness (DRF):

> In a nutshell, DRF seeks to maximize the minimum dominant share across all users. For example, if user A runs CPU-heavy tasks and user B runs memory-heavy tasks, DRF attempts to equalize user A's share of CPUs with user B's share of memory. In the single-resource case, DRF reduces to max-min fairness for that resource.[1]

---

[1]   A. Ghodsi, M. Zaharia, B. Hindman, A. Konwinski, S. Shenker, and I. Stoica. "Dominant Resource Fairness: Fair Allocation of Multiple Resource Types." NSDI, vol. 11, 2011.

Mesos's use of the DRF algorithm by default is fine for most deployments. Chances are you won't need to write your own allocation algorithm, so this book doesn't go into much detail about DRF. If you're interested in learning more about this research, you can find the paper online at www.usenix.org/legacy/events/nsdi11/tech/full_papers/ Ghodsi.pdf.

RESOURCE ISOLATION

Using Linux cgroups or Docker containers to isolate processes, Mesos allows for *multi-tenancy*, or for multiple processes to be executed on a single Mesos slave. A framework then executes its tasks within the container, using a Mesos *containerizer*. If you're not familiar with containers, think of them as a lightweight approach to how a hypervisor runs multiple virtual machines on a single physical host, but without the overhead or need to run an entire operating system.

> **NOTE** In addition to Docker and cgroups, Mesos provides another means of isolation for other POSIX-compliant operating systems: posix/cpu, posix/ mem, and posix/disk. It's worth noting that these isolation methods don't *isolate* resources, but instead monitor resource use.

Now that you have a clearer understanding of how Mesos works, you can move on to understanding how this technology compares to the traditional datacenter. More specifically, the next section introduces the concept of an application-centric datacenter, where the focus is more on applications than on the servers and operating systems that run them.

1.1.2 *Comparing virtual machines and containers*

When thinking about applications deployed in a traditional datacenter, virtual machines often come to mind. In recent years, virtualization providers (VMware, OpenStack, Xen, and KVM, to name a few) have become commonplace in many organizations. Similar to how a hypervisor allows a physical host's resources to be abstracted and shared among virtual machines, Mesos provides a layer of abstraction, albeit at a different level. The resources are presented to applications themselves, and in turn consumed by containers.

To illustrate this point, consider figure 1.3, which compares the various layers of infrastructure required to deploy four applications.

VIRTUAL MACHINES

When thinking about traditional virtual machine–based application deployments, consider for a moment the operational overhead of maintaining the operating systems on each of them: installing packages, applying security updates, maintaining user access, identifying and remediating configuration drift; the list goes on. What's the added benefit of running applications atop an entire operating system when you're more concerned with deploying the application itself? Not to mention the overhead of the operating system, which consumes added CPU, memory, and disk. At

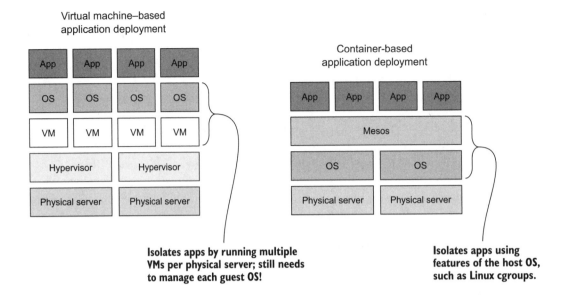

Figure 1.3   Comparing VM-based and container-based application deployments

a large-enough scale, this becomes wasteful. With an application-centric approach to managing datacenters, Mesos allows you to simplify your stack—and your application deployments—using lightweight containers.

CONTAINERS

As you learned previously, Mesos uses containers for resource isolation between processes. In the context of Mesos, the two most important resource-isolation methods to know about are the control groups (cgroups) built into the Linux kernel, and Docker.

Around 2007, support for control groups (referred to as *cgroups* throughout this text) was made available in the Linux kernel, beginning with version 2.6.24. This allows the execution of processes in a way that's *sandboxed* from other processes. In the context of Mesos, cgroups provide resource constraints for running processes, ensuring that they don't interfere with other processes running on the system. When using cgroups, any packages or libraries that the tasks might depend on (a specific version of Python, a working C++ compiler, and so on) must be already present on the host operating system. If your workloads, packages, and required tools and libraries are fairly standardized or don't readily conflict with each other, this might not be a problem. But consider figure 1.4, which demonstrates how using Docker can overcome these sorts of problems and allow you to run applications and workloads in a more isolated manner.

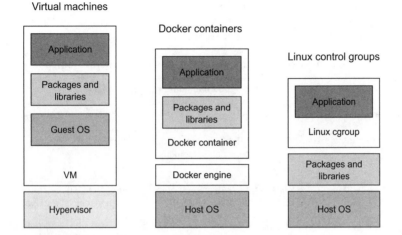

Figure 1.4 Comparing virtual machines, Docker containers, and Linux cgroups

Using low-level primitives in the Linux kernel, including cgroups and namespaces, Docker provides a means to build and deploy containers almost as if they were virtual machines. The application and all of its dependencies are packaged within the container and deployed atop a host operating system. They take a concept from the freight industry—the standardized industrial shipping container—and apply this to application deployment. In recent years, this new unit of software delivery has grown in popularity as it's generally considered to be more lightweight than deploying an entire virtual machine.

You don't need to understand all the implementation details and intricacies of building and deploying containers to use Mesos, though. If you'd like more information, please consult the following online resources:

- Linux control groups: www.kernel.org/doc/documentation/cgroup-v1/cgroups.txt
- Docker: https://docs.docker.com

1.1.3 Knowing when (and why) to use Mesos

Running applications at scale isn't reserved for large enterprises anymore. Startups with only a handful of employees are creating apps that easily attract millions of users. Re-architecting applications and datacenters is a nontrivial task, but certain components that are in a typical stack are already great candidates to run on Mesos. By taking some of these technologies and moving them (and their workloads) to a Mesos cluster, you can scale them more easily and run your datacenter more efficiently.

NOTE This book covers Mesos version 0.22.2, which provides an environment for running stateless and distributed applications. Beginning in version 0.23,

Mesos will begin work to support persistent resources, thus enabling support for stateful frameworks. For more information on this effort, see https://issues.apache.org/jira/browse/MESOS-1554.

For example, consider the stateless, distributed, and stateful technologies in table 1.1.

Table 1.1 **Technologies that are—and aren't—good candidates to run on Mesos**

Service type	Examples	Should you use Mesos?
Stateless—no need to persist data to disk	Web apps (Ruby on Rails, Play, Django), Memcached, Jenkins CI build slaves	Yes
Distributed out of the box	Cassandra, Elasticsearch, Hadoop Distributed File System (HDFS)	Yes, provided the correct level of redundancy is in place
Stateful—needs to persist data to disk	MySQL, PostgreSQL, Jenkins CI masters	No (version 0.22); potentially (version 0.23+)

The real value of Mesos is realized when running stateless services and applications—applications that will handle incoming loads but that could go offline at any time without negatively impacting the service as a whole, or services that run a job and report the result to another system. As noted previously, examples of some of these applications include Ruby on Rails and Jenkins CI build slaves.

Progress has been made running distributed databases (such as Cassandra and Elasticsearch) and distributed filesystems (such as Hadoop Distributed File System, or HDFS) as Mesos frameworks. But this is feasible only if the correct level of redundancy is in place. Although certain distributed databases and filesystems have data replication and fault tolerance built in, your data might not survive if the entire Mesos cluster fails (because of natural disasters, redundant power/cooling systems failures, or human error). In the real world, you should weigh the risks and benefits of deploying services that persist data on a Mesos cluster.

As I mentioned earlier, Mesos excels at running stateless, distributed services. Stateful applications that need to persist data to disk aren't good candidates for running on Mesos as of this writing. Although possible, it's not yet advisable to run certain databases such as MySQL and PostgreSQL atop a Mesos cluster. When you do need to persist data, it's preferable to do so by deploying a traditional database cluster outside the Mesos cluster.

1.2   *Why we need to rethink the datacenter*

Deploying applications within a datacenter has traditionally involved one or more physical (or virtual) servers. The introduction and mainstream adoption of virtualization has allowed us to run multiple virtual machines on a single physical server and make better use of physical resources. But running applications this way also means you're usually running a full operating system on each of those virtual machines, which consumes resources and brings along its own maintenance overhead.

This section presents two primary reasons that you should rethink how datacenters are managed: the administrative overhead of statically partitioning resources, and the need to focus more on applications instead of infrastructure.

1.2.1 Partitioning of resources

When you consider the traditional virtual machine–based model of deploying applications and statically partitioning clusters, you quickly find this deployment model inefficient and cumbersome to maintain. By maximizing the use of each server in a datacenter, operations teams maximize their return on investment and can keep the total cost of ownership as reasonable as possible.

In computing circles, teams generally refer to a *cluster* as a group of servers that work together as a single system to provide a service. Traditionally, the deployment of these services has been largely node-centric: you dedicate a certain number of machines to provide a given service. But as the infrastructure footprint expands and service offerings increase, it's difficult to continue statically partitioning these services.

But now consider the demand for these services doubling. To continue scaling, a systems administrator needs to provision new machines and join them to the individual clusters. Perhaps the operations team, anticipating the need for additional capacity, scales each of those clusters to three times its current size. Although you've managed to scale each of those services, you now have machines in your datacenter sitting idle, waiting to be used. As such, if a single machine in any of those clusters fails, it quickly needs to be brought back online for the service to continue operating at full capacity, as shown in figure 1.5.

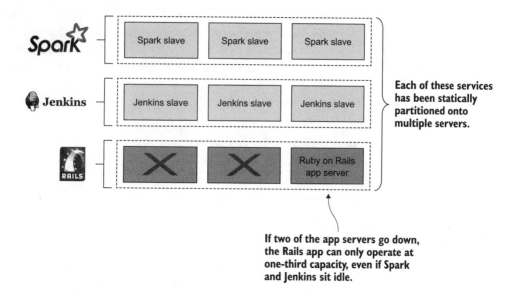

Figure 1.5　Three applications statically partitioned in a datacenter

Now consider solving the aforementioned scaling scenario by using Mesos, as shown in figure 1.6. You can see that you'd use these same machines in the datacenter to focus on running applications instead of virtual machines. The applications could run on any machine with available resources. If you need to scale, you add servers to the *Mesos* cluster, instead of adding machines to multiple clusters. If a single Mesos node goes offline, no particular impact occurs to any one service.

These services are run on Mesos, which dynamically schedules them within the cluster based on available capacity.

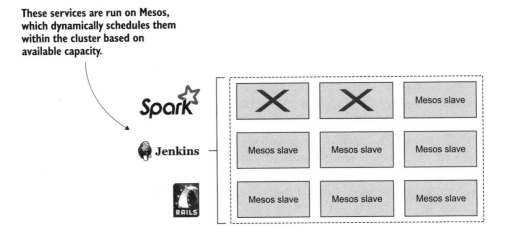

Figure 1.6   Three applications running on a Mesos cluster

Consider these small differences across hundreds or thousands of servers. Instead of trying to guess how many servers you need for each service and provision them into several static clusters, you're able to allow these services to dynamically request the compute, memory, and storage resources they need to run. To continue scaling, you add new machines to your Mesos cluster, and the applications running on the cluster scale to the new infrastructure. Operating a single, large computing cluster in this manner has several advantages:

- You can easily provision additional cluster capacity.
- You can be less concerned about where services are running.
- You can scale from several nodes to thousands.
- The loss of several servers doesn't severely degrade any one service.

1.2.2 *Deploying applications*

As we discussed previously, one of the major differences—and benefits—of deploying applications on a Mesos cluster is multitenancy. Not unlike a virtualization hypervisor running multiple virtual machines on a physical server, Mesos allows multiple applications to run on a single server in isolated environments, using either Linux *cgroups* or

Docker *containers*. Instead of having multiple environments (one each for development, staging, and production), the entire datacenter becomes a platform on which to deploy applications.

Where Mesos is commonly referred to—and acts as—a distributed *kernel*, other Mesos frameworks help users run long-running and scheduled tasks, similar to the init and Cron systems, respectively. You'll learn more about these frameworks (Marathon, Chronos, and Aurora) and how to deploy applications on them later in this book.

Consider the power of what I've described so far: Mesos provides fault tolerance out of the box. Instead of a systems administrator getting paged when a single server goes offline, the cluster will automatically start the failed job elsewhere. The sysadmin needs to be concerned only if a certain percentage of machines goes offline in the datacenter, as that might signal a larger problem. As such, with the correct placement and redundancy in place, scheduled maintenance can occur at any time.

1.3 *The Mesos distributed architecture*

To provide services at scale, Mesos provides a distributed, fault-tolerant architecture that enables fine-grained resource scheduling. This architecture comprises three components: *masters, slaves,* and the applications (commonly referred to as *frameworks*) that run on them. Mesos relies on Apache ZooKeeper, a distributed database used specifically for coordinating leader election within the cluster, and for leader detection by other Mesos masters, slaves, and frameworks.

In figure 1.7, you can see how each of these architecture components works together to provide a stable platform on which to deploy applications. I'll break it down for you in the sections that follow the diagram.

1.3.1 *Masters*

One or more Mesos masters are responsible for managing the Mesos slave daemons running on each machine in the cluster. Using ZooKeeper, they coordinate which node will be the *leading master*, and which masters will be on standby, ready to take over if the leading master goes offline.

The leading master is responsible for deciding which resources to offer to a particular framework using a pluggable *allocation module,* or scheduling algorithm, to distribute *resource offers* to the various schedulers. The scheduler can then either accept or reject the offer based on whether it has any work to be performed at that time.

A Mesos cluster requires a minimum of one master, and three or more are recommended for production deployments to ensure that the services are highly available. You can run ZooKeeper on the same machines as the Mesos masters themselves, or use a standalone ZooKeeper cluster. Chapter 3 goes into more detail about the sizing and deploying of Mesos masters.

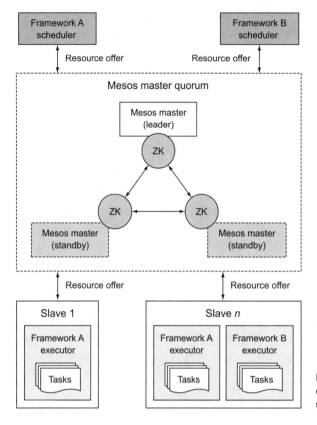

Figure 1.7   The Mesos architecture consists of one or more masters, slaves, and frameworks.

1.3.2   Slaves

The machines in a cluster responsible for executing a framework's tasks are referred to as Mesos *slaves*. They query ZooKeeper to determine the leading Mesos master and advertise their available CPU, memory, and storage resources to the leading master in the form of a resource offer. When a scheduler accepts a resource offer from the Mesos master, it then launches one or more *executors* on the slave, which are responsible for running the framework's tasks.

Mesos slaves can also be configured with certain attributes and resources, which allow them to be customized for a given environment. *Attributes* refer to key/value pairs that might contain information about the node's location in a datacenter, and *resources* allow a particular slave's advertised CPU, memory, and disk to be overridden with user-provided values, instead of Mesos automatically detecting the available resources on the slave. Consider the following example attributes and resources:

```
--attributes='datacenter:pdx1;rack:1-1;os:rhel7'
--resources='cpu:24;mem:24576;disk:409600'
```

I've configured this particular Mesos slave to advertise its datacenter; location within the datacenter; operating system; and user-provided CPU, memory, and disk resources. This information is especially useful when trying to ensure that applications stay online during scheduled maintenance. Using this information, a datacenter operator could take an entire rack (or an entire row!) of machines offline for scheduled maintenance without impacting users. Chapter 4 covers this (and more) in the Mesos slave configuration section.

1.3.3 Frameworks

As you learned earlier, a *framework* is the term given to any Mesos application that's responsible for scheduling and executing tasks on a cluster. A framework is made up of two components: a scheduler and an executor.

> **TIP** A list of frameworks known to exist at the time of writing is included in appendix B.

SCHEDULER

A *scheduler* is typically a long-running service responsible for connecting to a Mesos master and accepting or rejecting resource offers. Mesos delegates the responsibility of scheduling to the framework, instead of attempting to schedule all the work for a cluster itself. The scheduler can then accept or reject a resource offer based on whether it has any tasks to run at the time of the offer. The scheduler detects the leading master by communicating with the ZooKeeper cluster, and then registers itself to that master accordingly.

EXECUTOR

An *executor* is a process launched on a Mesos slave that runs a framework's tasks on a slave. As of this writing, the built-in Mesos executors allow frameworks to execute shell scripts or run Docker containers. New executors can be written using Mesos's various language bindings and bundled with the framework, to be fetched by the Mesos slave when a task requires it.

As you've learned, Mesos provides a distributed, highly available architecture. Masters schedule work to be performed on the cluster, and slaves advertise available resources to the schedulers, which in turn execute tasks on the cluster.

1.4 Summary

In this chapter, you've been introduced to the Apache Mesos project, its architecture, and how it attempts to solve scaling problems and make clustering simple. You've also learned how Mesos deployments compare and contrast with the traditional datacenter, and how an application-centric approach can lead to using resources more efficiently. We've discussed when (and when not) to use Mesos for a given workload, and where you can get help and find more information, should you need it. Here are a few things to remember:

- Mesos abstracts CPU, memory, and disk resources away from underlying systems and presents multiple machines as a single entity.
- Mesos slaves advertise their available CPUs, memory, and disk in the form of resource offers.
- A Mesos framework comprises two primary components: a scheduler and an executor.
- Containers are a lightweight method to provide resource isolation to individual processes.

In the next chapter, I'll walk you through a real-world example of how Mesos allows for more efficient resource use, and how you might run applications in your own data-center by building on projects in the Mesos ecosystem.

Managing datacenter resources with Mesos

This chapter covers

- Introducing Mesos with a real-world example
- Comparing standalone and general-purpose clusters
- Launching a Spark job on a Mesos cluster
- Exploring a framework's interaction with Mesos

The previous chapter introduced the Apache Mesos project, how it works, and how it compares to the architecture of a traditional datacenter. This chapter explores the benefits of Mesos by applying a real-world scenario: demonstrating multiple applications using Mesos cluster resources. The chapter demonstrates Apache Spark, a popular data-processing framework.

If you're not familiar with Spark, don't worry: the following sections use Spark as a demonstration of how Mesos distributes workloads and shares resources among multiple applications. I use Spark as an example to teach you about resource sharing and workload scheduling on a general-purpose Mesos cluster, and how Mesos compares to statically partitioned clusters within a datacenter. You'll also get a brief introduction to the Mesos and Spark web interfaces, and, who knows, maybe you'll even learn a thing or two about Spark in the process. Let's get started.

2.1   *A brief introduction to Spark*

To quote the project's website, "Apache Spark is a fast and general engine for large-scale data processing." It lives in the "big data" space along with other popular projects, such as Hadoop, and is often used for data science and analytics. In many cases, Spark performs tasks faster and more efficiently than Hadoop's MapReduce, both in memory and on disk.

Spark also provides APIs for several popular programming languages, including Python, Scala, and Java, and supports streaming workloads, interactive queries, and machine-learning libraries, in addition to MapReduce-like batch processing.

A brief history of Spark

In 2009, Matei Zaharia began development on Spark in the AMPLab at the University of California, Berkeley, the same organization that supported the development of Mesos. In fact, Matei is also one of the co-creators of Mesos.

After being open sourced in 2010, Spark was donated to the Apache Software Foundation and entered the Apache Incubator in 2013. It graduated to become a top-level project in 2014.

Databricks, a company co-founded by Matei in 2013, seeks to commercialize on Spark's successes and help clients with big data problems. Databricks remains a large contributor to the open source Spark project.

At the most basic level, Spark requires a cluster manager for distributing work, and access to a Hadoop-compatible data source. Out of the box, Spark includes support for several cluster managers:

- Spark standalone
- Mesos
- Hadoop YARN
- Pseudo-distributed (running locally on your laptop or workstation)

Although it's possible to run Spark locally and use the CPU cores on your laptop or workstation, that's useful only for development purposes: the number of CPU cores limits the number of executors. When you set up a production Spark cluster, you have two options: deploy a standalone, statically partitioned Spark cluster on a predetermined number of servers, or use a cluster manager such as Mesos or YARN to run the Spark job's tasks for you.

To best illustrate what a general-purpose cluster manager such as Mesos can offer, I'll compare and contrast Spark standalone with Mesos in the next few sections.

2.1.1 Spark on a standalone cluster

In figure 2.1, you see that a Spark driver program connects to a cluster manager—the Spark master—that in turn distributes tasks to various worker nodes.

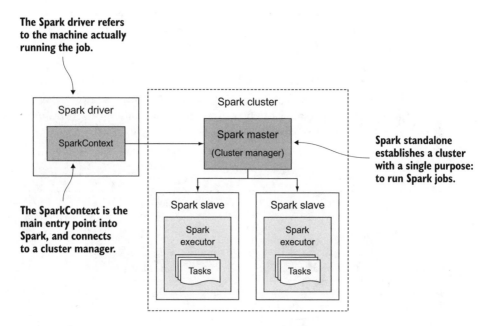

Figure 2.1   Components and architecture for a standalone Spark cluster

In the graphic, the *Spark Driver* refers to the machine running the Spark job, and the *SparkContext* is the main entry point to Spark. The SparkContext is responsible for connecting to a cluster manager and running tasks on the cluster. It's also responsible for creating Spark's distributed data sets. As you can also see, the two worker nodes in the Spark cluster are single-purpose: they are machines dedicated to running Spark tasks, and nothing else.

As you learned in the previous chapter, Mesos provides an excellent means for running multiple applications on a single cluster, and launching multiple tasks on a single worker node. Instead of setting up one or more statically partitioned Spark clusters, you can use Mesos to share cluster resources across multiple applications. Let's see what it looks like to run Spark on Mesos.

2.1.2 Spark on Mesos

Although setting up Spark to use a standalone cluster isn't a problem, consider the needs of multiple teams needing their own Spark clusters, or consider the bigger picture: multiple, statically partitioned clusters in a single datacenter.

If you're deploying these static clusters on physical hardware, you're clearly dedicating a certain amount of capital to that workload—and only that workload—without the possibility of sharing resources. Likewise, if you set up statically partitioned clusters on an Infrastructure as a Service (IaaS) provider like Amazon Web Services (AWS), you might be wasting money due to cloud instances sitting idle. Regardless of whether your workloads are running on premises or in the cloud, fine-grained resource sharing can help increase a system's utilization, and therefore improve datacenter efficiency.

To illustrate this point, let's take a look at figure 2.2. You have two standalone clusters serving two applications: Spark (the data-processing example used up to this point) and Jenkins, a popular, open source continuous integration framework. The use of Jenkins itself isn't particularly important for this example; what's important is that it's *some other* application that needs to run on multiple servers.

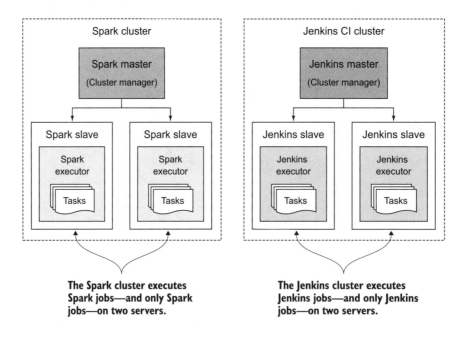

Figure 2.2 Visualizing two statically partitioned, or siloed, clusters

As figure 2.2 illustrates, you now have two statically partitioned clusters: one for Spark and one for Jenkins. Each cluster includes its own cluster manager (Spark master and Jenkins master) and two worker nodes on which to launch tasks or builds. You can also clearly see the static partitions (or silos, if you will) that these two services fall into, and that isn't any way to share compute resources between the two clusters. Chances are that neither of these services is using their computing resources 100% of the time. If the Spark cluster was 50% underpowered, and the Jenkins cluster 50% overpowered, Spark—and the data scientists using the Spark cluster—would benefit by being able to use the resources of three machines instead of just two.

Now let's consider running each of these systems atop a general-purpose cluster manager like Mesos that allows for this sort of fine-grained resource sharing. In figure 2.3, you're able to share compute resources and run multiple workloads on a single Mesos slave by allowing Mesos to isolate each framework's executors using Linux control groups (cgroups). At scale, this will lead to better resource utilization across the many machines within a modern datacenter.

Now that you've taken the time to understand how Spark can use Mesos for its cluster manager, and why adopting a general-purpose cluster manager like Mesos can lead to increased efficiency by sharing compute resources, let's take a look at what it's like to run a Spark job on a Mesos cluster. This will give you a better idea of how Mesos runs tasks before we get into installation and configuration of the cluster in chapter 3.

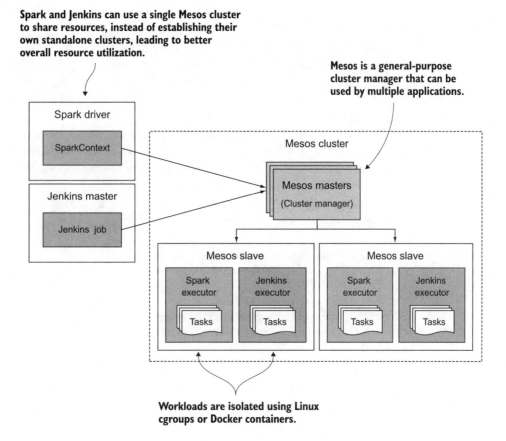

Figure 2.3   Mesos managing cluster resources for two applications

2.2 *Running a Spark job on Mesos*

The standalone Spark cluster discussed earlier in this chapter follows an architecture just as you might expect with any other distributed system: a master schedules work on one or more worker nodes. Figure 2.3 demonstrated how you could use Mesos to avoid statically partitioning your datacenter into multiple clusters, and instead declare the compute resources your workload requires of a single, general-purpose cluster. Now let's take a look at Mesos in action by demonstrating how it distributes work for a framework like Spark.

> **NOTE**   This section is about running Spark in the context of Mesos, not necessarily a primer on Spark itself. Although I show you how to run the example job on a Mesos cluster, you shouldn't expect to learn about using Spark for real-world data-processing jobs in this text. If you're interested in learning more about Spark, please check out the Spark project page at http://spark.apache.org and *Spark in Action* by Petar Zečević and Marko Bonaći (Manning, 2016).

2.2.1 *Finding prime numbers in a set*

To demonstrate how Spark connects to a Mesos cluster, accepts resource offers, launches executors, and executes tasks, I'll demonstrate a simple job in Spark. The job will create a data set of integers between 1 and 100,000,000, and then use Spark to determine which integers in the set are prime numbers (numbers that are not equal to 1 and are divisible only by 1 and themselves).

Instead of setting up a standalone Spark cluster for this job, Spark will use Mesos as a cluster manager for scheduling and distributing the individual tasks to available compute resources in the cluster. But before you get into running Spark on a Mesos cluster, let's discuss the order of events that takes place when a framework interacts with a Mesos cluster. Figure 2.4 maps out Spark registering as a Mesos framework, accepting resource offers from the Mesos master, and finally, launching tasks on a Mesos slave.

Several things are happening in this figure, and you'll see a breakdown of what's happening a little later in the chapter. For now, it's important to understand the following:

1 The SparkContext connects to ZooKeeper to determine the leading Mesos master.
2 The SparkContext registers with the leading Mesos master as a new framework.
3 The SparkContext receives resource offers from the leading Mesos master, with which it can launch tasks to perform its data-processing workloads.

Having learned the events—and the order they occur—from figure 2.4, let's take the time now to launch the Spark job and observe real output from the cluster. After you have a Mesos cluster up and running (which you'll learn about in the next chapter), feel free to install Spark and run the example.

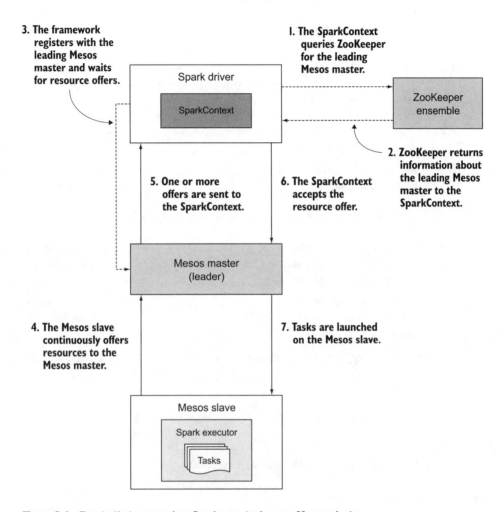

Figure 2.4   Events that occur when Spark runs tasks on a Mesos cluster

TIP Installation instructions for Spark on Mesos are available on the Spark website, http://spark.apache.org/docs/latest/running-on-mesos.html.

2.2.2 Getting and packaging up the code

I've included the example code for this Spark job with the book's supplementary materials, available on GitHub and on manning.com. The easiest way to get the example code is to clone the repository by using Git:

```
$ git clone https://github.com/rji/mesos-in-action-code-samples
$ cd mesos-in-action-code-samples/chapter02/spark-primes-example
```

Next, you need to package the job and its dependencies into a single Java Archive (JAR) file that can be used with the `spark-submit` command-line tool. Because this particular example is written in the Scala programming language, you'll need to ensure that a recent Java Development Kit (JDK) and Scala are both present on the system you're using to submit the job. I'll refer to this as the *gateway* machine.

After those prerequisites are met, package up the example by using sbt, a build tool for Scala that's similar to Maven or Ant in the Java community. If sbt isn't already installed on your system, you can find installation instructions for Linux, Mac OS X, and Windows at www.scala-sbt.org/release/tutorial.

Proceed to package the example by running the following command:

```
$ sbt package
```

After packaging has completed, you're ready to submit the job to a Mesos cluster. Although I won't cover the Mesos installation and configuration process until the next chapter, I thought it might be beneficial for you to understand how the cluster works before we dive in to deploying it.

2.2.3   Submitting the job

Having already packaged the example code into a simple JAR file, let's go ahead and submit the job. The following example assumes that Spark is installed at /opt/spark:

```
/opt/spark/bin/spark-submit --class com.manning.mesosinaction.PrimesExample
➥  target/scala-2.10/spark-primes-example_2.10-0.1.0-SNAPSHOT.jar
➥  100000000
```

This job should only take a few minutes to complete.

2.2.4   Observing the output

After submitting the job by using the `spark-submit` command, you observe a decent amount of output on your console; by default, Spark is logging to the console with `INFO`-level verbosity. The following listing includes some of the more important log messages, and I'll explain what they mean in the context of Mesos.

Listing 2.1   Spark job output when running on a Mesos cluster

```
15/04/12 22:35:56 INFO Utils: Successfully started service 'sparkDriver'
    on port 45957.

15/04/12 22:35:56 INFO Utils: Successfully started service
    'HTTP file server' on port 49444.

15/04/12 22:35:56 INFO SparkUI: Started SparkUI at
    http://10.132.171.224:4040
```

Spark queries ZooKeeper for the leading Mesos master.

```
I0412 22:35:57.401646   8991 sched.cpp:157] Version: 0.22.2

2015-04-12 22:35:57,415:8901(0x7f8ed93eb700):ZOO_INFO@check_events@1703:
    initiated connection to server [10.132.171.224:2181]

I0412 22:35:57.418431   8993 detector.cpp:452] A new leading master
    (UPID=master@10.132.171.224:5050) is detected

I0412 22:35:57.418504   8993 sched.cpp:254] New master detected at
    master@10.132.171.224:5050
```

Our SparkContext registers itself as a Mesos framework.

```
I0412 22:35:57.420454   8993 sched.cpp:448] Framework registered with
    20150412-214000-3769336842-5050-2832-0005

15/04/12 22:35:57 INFO MesosSchedulerBackend: Registered as framework ID
    20150412-214000-3769336842-5050-2832-0005
```

```
15/04/12 22:35:57 INFO SparkContext: Starting job: collect at
    PrimesExample.scala:22

15/04/12 22:39:34 INFO SparkContext: Job finished: collect at
    PrimesExample.scala:22, took 217.099354417 s
```

The Spark driver executes tasks on the Mesos cluster.

```
2 3 5 7 11 13 17 19 23 29 31 37 41 43 47 53 59 61 67 71 73 79

99999839 99999847 99999931 99999941 99999959 99999971 99999989
```

Output omitted for brevity

```
15/04/12 22:40:10 INFO SparkUI: Stopped Spark web UI at http://
    10.132.171.224:4040

15/04/12 22:40:10 INFO DAGScheduler: Stopping DAGScheduler
```

The Spark-Context shuts down its scheduler.

The Spark framework is unregistered from the Mesos master.

```
I0412 22:40:10.902202   8931 sched.cpp:1589] Asked to stop the driver

I0412 22:40:10.902323   8997 sched.cpp:831] Stopping framework
    '20150412-214000-3769336842-5050-2832-0005'

15/04/12 22:40:10 INFO MesosSchedulerBackend: driver.run() returned
    with code DRIVER_STOPPED

15/04/12 22:40:11 INFO SparkContext: Successfully stopped SparkContext
```

Although a lot more activity exists in the Spark logs, and you probably don't need INFO-level verbosity on a regular basis, the lines selected for this listing serve as a good example to understand how Spark is using Mesos to handle its workload, or at least the order of events when launching a Spark workload on Mesos, just as we visualized previously in figure 2.4.

Now that you understand this order of events for a real-world workload, let's take a look at more ways you can observe the output and status of the frameworks and tasks running on a Mesos cluster.

2.3   *Exploring further*

Having just submitted and run a Spark job on a Mesos cluster—and observed the output from the job on the console—perhaps it's a good time to start introducing you to the various happenings under the hood. In this section, you'll take a quick look at the Mesos and Spark web interfaces so you can observe the work being performed on your cluster in real time. Although you won't install and configure Mesos until the next chapter, the next few sections serve as a starting point for topics that you'll learn in part 2 of this book.

2.3.1   *Mesos UI*

The Mesos masters provide a web interface for viewing the status of the cluster and the work being performed. This web interface provides information on the cluster, including the following:

- Overview of all tasks and their current status
- Registered frameworks and associated tasks
- Mesos slaves, their resources, and the tasks they're currently executing
- Outstanding resource offers (offers that haven't yet been accepted or rejected)

In figure 2.5, you can see that the Spark Primes Example framework is registered to the cluster, is currently consuming 6 CPUs and 2.6 GB memory, and is running several tasks. For now, don't worry about every feature in the web interface; you're concerned only with observing how the cluster responds to a single Spark job running on it, in an attempt to familiarize you with the features available in Mesos. Chapter 5 revisits the web interface in greater depth.

Clicking the Sandbox link for any of those tasks allows you to drill down into the files and log output present in the Mesos *sandbox*, or working directory, for individual tasks. In figure 2.6, the sandbox contains your Spark job's JAR file and files that have captured the console output from stdout and stderr.

2.3.2   *Spark UI*

In addition to the web interface provided by Mesos, Spark launches its own web interface for monitoring the progress of your Spark jobs. You saw evidence of this in the Spark job's output in listing 2.1. Although accessing this interface isn't necessary for the proper functioning of the Mesos cluster, it does provide a nicer, cluster manager–agnostic view of the progress of a particular Spark job.

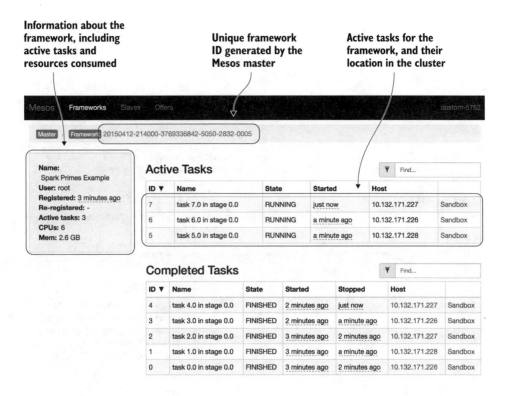

Figure 2.5   The Spark Primes Example framework is consuming cluster resources and running tasks.

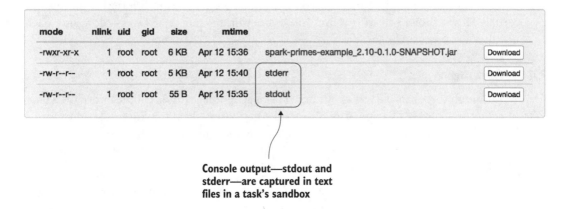

Figure 2.6   Files within a Mesos sandbox for a single Spark task

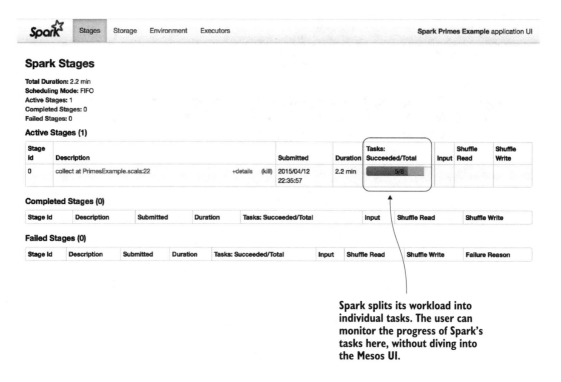

Figure 2.7   The Spark web interface shows the progress of the Spark Primes Example job

In figure 2.7, you can see that the job's only stage, "collect at PrimesExample.scala:22," is currently running on the cluster and has completed 5/8 of its tasks.

Regardless of whether this job was running on Mesos or on another cluster manager, the tasks would be distributed in a similar fashion. The difference, however, is that Mesos allows you to run multiple frameworks—and their tasks—alongside each other in an isolated manner.

2.4   Summary

Although this example was about how Mesos schedules and distributes work on a cluster in the context of a Spark job, hopefully it was beneficial for you to see an example Mesos workload—and Mesos in action—all in a single chapter. By doing so, you now know what you can expect after deploying Mesos following the directions in part 2 of this book. To recap, you learned the following from this chapter:

- Distributed frameworks such as Apache Spark and Jenkins CI can use Mesos as their cluster manager, simultaneously.
- Mesos' fine-grained resource sharing can lead to higher resource utilization across the datacenter.

- A Spark job is composed of a number of individual tasks, or units of work, that are distributed on the Mesos cluster.
- The Mesos web interface provides a glimpse into the current state of the cluster.

In part 2 of this book, you'll revisit each of the concepts explained in chapters 1 and 2, including resource isolation and fault tolerance, and dive more into logging, debugging, slave resources, and slave attributes. If you'd like, you can download the Spark Primes Example from the book's supplementary materials (available on GitHub and on manning.com) and test it on your own Mesos cluster; the next chapter covers installation and configuration.

In the meantime, if you'd like more information on using Spark with Mesos as a cluster manager, or more information on Spark in general, check out the following links:

- https://spark.apache.org/docs/latest/
- https://spark.apache.org/docs/latest/spark-standalone.html
- https://spark.apache.org/docs/latest/running-on-mesos.html

Part 2

Core Mesos

In part 2, I provide the fundamental knowledge that you'll need to deploy a Mesos cluster in a production environment. You'll learn about the installation and configuration process of Mesos, ZooKeeper, and Docker, as well as the highly available architecture, monitoring, and access control of Mesos.

Setting up Mesos 3

This chapter covers

- Deployment considerations for development and production clusters
- Installing and configuring Mesos, ZooKeeper, and Docker
- Upgrading Mesos without downtime

Regardless of whether you're using a configuration management tool (such as Puppet, Chef, or Ansible), or using SSH or Fabric to execute commands and scripts on remote systems, it's important to understand how to deploy Mesos using publicly available packages, and how to compile it from source code for customizing your deployment or building your own packages.

This chapter walks you through the installation and configuration of the Mesos master and slaves, including Apache ZooKeeper for cluster coordination, and Docker for launching containers. You'll learn about the installation and configuration of Mesos and ZooKeeper for highly available production deployments as well as for installing everything on a single node for development purposes.

Configuration management with Puppet

A good configuration management strategy is key to any well-run datacenter. Many of the instructions included in this chapter—including the installation and configuration of Mesos, ZooKeeper, and Docker—can be performed using Puppet, an open source configuration management tool (and as of this writing, the most popular of the several configuration management tools in the configuration management space). Three Puppet modules in particular can help you automate and maintain the configuration of your Mesos cluster:

- https://forge.puppetlabs.com/deric/mesos
- https://forge.puppetlabs.com/deric/zookeeper
- https://forge.puppetlabs.com/garethr/docker

Because Puppet usage is best left to the official documentation or other books already available on the topic, this chapter doesn't cover it. You can find and download Puppet from most Linux distributions' package repositories or from puppetlabs.com.

Regardless of whether or not you're planning to use a configuration management tool for the deployment of your Mesos cluster, it's still a good idea to read through this chapter and understand how the various components depend on and interact with each other.

3.1   Deploying Mesos

When deploying any new technology or system, whether it's in development, staging, or production, it's always a good idea to understand as much as you can about it. This way, you're prepared when something inevitably goes awry. The next few sections teach you about the components that make up a Mesos cluster. You'll also learn a few things to take into consideration when deploying clusters in development and in production.

3.1.1   Mesos cluster components

Let's revisit the various components and how they communicate with each other. Regardless of whether or not you're attempting to deploy Mesos in a development environment or a production environment, a cluster deployment is made up of some (or all) of the following components:

- *Required—One or more Mesos masters.* (If the number of masters is greater than 1, this must be an odd number.)
- *Required—One or more Mesos slaves.* (Generally speaking, the more nodes in a cluster, the better.)
- *Optional—A ZooKeeper ensemble consisting of one or more machines.* Required only if deploying Mesos in a highly available configuration. (If the number of ZooKeeper nodes is greater than 1, this must be an odd number.)
- *Optional—Docker Engine running on each of the Mesos slaves.*

Depending on your intended purpose, you may need to consider additional information for development and production environments. The next couple of sections cover this topic.

3.1.2 *Considerations for a development environment*

When installing and configuring Mesos for development purposes, it's reasonable to deploy all of the components for a Mesos deployment on a single node, opting for a simpler deployment in lieu of a highly available one. For a development environment, you need to install, configure, and deploy the following components, in the following order:

1 A single instance of ZooKeeper. Note that this is optional, and needed only if your framework needs ZooKeeper for coordination or to maintain state (as needed by highly available frameworks).
2 The Mesos master service.
3 The Mesos slave service.
4 Docker Engine (optional).

When you reach the installation and configuration of Mesos later in this chapter, install all the components on a single machine. But it's worth noting that this use case is so common for development purposes that the team over at Mesosphere, Inc. has developed a project for just this purpose: Playa Mesos.

INTRODUCING PLAYA MESOS

A popular way of distributing reproducible development environments between systems or team members is to use Vagrant (www.vagrantup.com). Playa Mesos is one such development environment created and maintained by Mesosphere as an easy way to provision a Mesos cluster on a single VM, and experiment with developing frameworks, running applications (via Marathon), and running scheduled tasks (via Chronos). Out of the box, it also includes a single instance of ZooKeeper, and Docker Engine, both preinstalled and preconfigured.

> **TIP** The Playa Mesos project can be found on GitHub at https://github.com/mesosphere/playa-mesos.

Assuming you already have a working Vagrant setup (which requires virtualization software such as VirtualBox, VMware Fusion, or VMware Workstation), getting up and running in a development environment is easy:

```
$ git clone https://github.com/mesosphere/playa-mesos
$ cd playa-mesos
$ vagrant up --provision
```

The same general components and concepts apply to production environments as well, but some additional considerations need to be taken in order to deploy the various components in a highly available manner. Let's take a look at this now.

3.1.3   *Considerations for a production environment*

This section contains some best practices to consider for deploying the Mesos cluster. It's worth noting, however, that this isn't an extensive guide for running Mesos in production. This section is intended to help you make certain provisioning decisions at this stage of the book. Chapter 6 provides more details about running Mesos in a production environment, including logging, monitoring, and access control.

PRODUCTION DEPLOYMENT OVERVIEW

For a production environment, you'll want a minimum of three Mesos masters and three servers making up the ZooKeeper ensemble. For development purposes, you can get away with a single Mesos master running a single instance of ZooKeeper, but note that you won't have any redundancy in the system.

In figure 3.1, you can visualize the multiple Mesos masters using ZooKeeper for coordination, and the various Mesos slaves (in this case, also running Docker) communicating with the leading Mesos master.

Although ZooKeeper is illustrated as a standalone service running separate from the Mesos masters, you'll opt for a slightly simpler deployment overall and install ZooKeeper alongside Mesos on each of the Mesos master machines. Don't worry about memorizing this graphic; I'll repeat it as you make your way through the installation and configuration of the cluster.

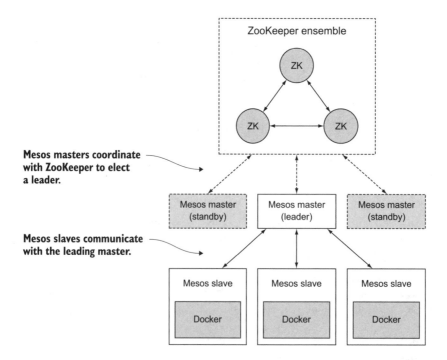

Figure 3.1   Components in a Mesos deployment

This almost goes without saying, but when deploying these services on dedicated hardware or using your virtualization or cloud provider of choice, be sure to account for redundancy at all hardware levels. If you're running in a physical datacenter, your Mesos masters and ZooKeeper servers should perhaps be placed in different racks, connected to different (or multiple) network switches, be connected to multiple power distribution units, and so forth. If you're running in a virtualized or cloud environment, ensure that the necessary policies are in place to keep the virtual machines running on different hypervisors or in different availability zones.

Considering that all of your cluster coordination will be happening through the Mesos masters and the ZooKeeper ensemble, you want to keep the single points of failure to a minimum. If you have multiple datacenters or a disaster recovery datacenter, you might even consider using them, assuming the network latency is low enough.

MESOS MASTERS

If you're planning to run a Mesos cluster spanned across multiple datacenters, it's a good idea to ensure that low network latency exists between each of the masters and datacenters. Otherwise, Mesos registry updates could fail if the leading master can't write to the standby masters' registries within the `registry_store_timeout` (default: five seconds). If you need to increase this time-out, you may consider increasing the `registry_fetch_timeout` (default: one minute) as well. Depending on your environment, you might want to consider running a separate Mesos cluster at each site and load-balancing across datacenters instead.

ZOOKEEPER ENSEMBLE

Considering that ZooKeeper is required for all coordination between Mesos masters, slaves, and frameworks, it goes without saying that it needs to be highly available for production deployments. A ZooKeeper cluster, known as an *ensemble*, needs to maintain a *quorum*, or a majority vote, within the cluster. The number of failures you're willing to tolerate depends on your environment and service-level agreements to your users, but to create an environment that tolerates F node failures, you should deploy $(2 \times F + 1)$ machines, as shown in table 3.1.

Table 3.1   Number of ZooKeeper nodes required for a quorum

ZooKeeper cluster size (number of nodes)	Quorum size	Number of machine failures tolerated
1	1	0
3	2	1
5	3	2
$2 \times F + 1$	$F + 1$	F

Because the ZooKeeper ensemble requires a majority vote to make cluster decisions, it usually makes sense to deploy ZooKeeper clusters with an odd number of nodes. Generally speaking, I recommend that you start with five ZooKeeper nodes for a production environment. This enables one of the nodes to be taken offline for maintenance and the cluster to still tolerate an unexpected failure.

> **WARNING** Before setting up a ZooKeeper ensemble in a production environment, please take the time to read the ZooKeeper Administrator's Guide at http://zookeeper.apache.org/doc/current/zookeeperAdmin.pdf.

Now, installing ZooKeeper on the same machines as the Mesos masters isn't a requirement, but it does make for simpler deployments and is generally an acceptable approach. If you're planning to deploy other software that also requires ZooKeeper, I recommend that you deploy a separate, standalone ZooKeeper ensemble for those applications and leave the Mesos ZooKeeper ensemble dedicated to serving the Mesos cluster. Later in this chapter, I'll have you install ZooKeeper on each of the Mesos masters to reduce complexity.

As I said previously, this isn't an exhaustive list of best practices, but rather some guidelines for planning the number and location of ZooKeeper nodes and Mesos masters for your deployment. Chapter 6 discusses additional production considerations for both Mesos and ZooKeeper, including logging, monitoring, and access control.

3.2   Installing Mesos and ZooKeeper

Mesos installations are supported on Linux and Mac OS X, and may work on other UNIX-like operating systems. You have two options for installing Mesos and ZooKeeper:

- Using your operating system's package manager
- Compiling the source code and installing the resulting binaries

In this section, you'll learn how to install Mesos on two of the most popular Linux distributions: Red Hat Enterprise Linux (RHEL) / CentOS 7, and Ubuntu 14.04 LTS (code name Trusty).

> **NOTE** Remember that with any on-premises or cloud deployment, you're still responsible for managing the installation, configuration, and health of services. Some cloud providers, such as Amazon Web Services (AWS), provide tools to create templates for provisioning infrastructure automatically. Because these tools are specific to the provider and not related to Mesos, this text doesn't cover them, instead opting to cover configuration of the system at the operating-system level. You should consult your provider's documentation for more information on how to use their various solutions to automate your Mesos cluster deployment.

3.2.1   *Installing from packages*

Mesosphere provides Mesos package repositories for several Linux distributions that are commonly found in production environments. As of this writing, they include the following operating systems and OS releases:

- RHEL / CentOS 6 and 7
- Ubuntu 12.04 through 14.04
- Debian 7 (code name Wheezy)

This example includes installation instructions for the latest release of RHEL/CentOS and the latest long-term support (LTS) release of Ubuntu. Documentation for setting up Mesosphere repositories on other supported operating systems can be found on its website at https://mesosphere.com/downloads.

RHEL / CentOS 7

First, you need to download the package that installs and configures your system for the Mesosphere repository. You can do this by running the following command:

```
$ sudo rpm -Uvh http://repos.mesosphere.io/el/7/noarch/RPMS/
➥ mesosphere-el-repo-7-1.noarch.rpm
```

After the repository has been installed, you need to install the Mesos package on the masters and slaves. On the masters, you'll also install Mesosphere's ZooKeeper packages. To do so, run the following command:

```
$ sudo yum -y install mesos-0.22.2-0.2.62.centos701406
➥ mesosphere-zookeeper
```

On the slaves, install Mesos by running this command:

```
$ sudo yum -y install mesos-0.22.2-0.2.62.centos701406
```

Installing these packages also installs any dependent packages required by Mesos and ZooKeeper. After these packages are installed, feel free to skip ahead to section 3.3.

UBUNTU 14.04 (TRUSTY)

To set up the package repositories on Ubuntu, you first need to fetch Mesosphere's GPG public key, which is used to sign the packages. You'll then add Mesosphere's repository to Apt's sources list, and refresh all of the package metadata on the system:

```
$ sudo apt-key adv --keyserver keyserver.ubuntu.com --recv E56151BF
$ echo "deb http://repos.mesosphere.io/ubuntu trusty main" |
➥ sudo tee /etc/apt/sources.list.d/mesosphere.list
$ sudo apt-get update
```

After the Mesosphere key is present and the repository is available, you can install the Mesos package on the masters and slaves. On the masters, you'll also install the Zoo-Keeper package. To do so, run the following command:

```
$ sudo apt-get install mesos=0.22.2-0.2.62.ubuntu1404 zookeeperd
```

Now, on the slaves, install Mesos by running this command:

```
$ sudo apt-get install mesos=0.22.2-0.2.62.ubuntu1404
```

Installing these packages also installs any dependent packages required by Mesos and ZooKeeper. After these packages are installed, feel free to skip ahead to section 3.3.

3.2.2   Compiling and installing from source

Although installing Mesos from the packages provided by Mesosphere is by far the quickest way to get up and running with Mesos, I thought it best to also demonstrate how to build Mesos from source. You might consider doing this for a few reasons:

- You need to modify the Mesos build configuration or enable additional functionality.
- You prefer to build your own packages, potentially with site-specific modifications.
- You prefer to obtain the code directly from the Apache Software Foundation.

You can configure, compile, and install Mesos in various ways. In the following example, you'll use the default configuration as specified by the Mesos configure script. It's worth noting that by default, compiling Mesos also compiles a bundled version of ZooKeeper.

If you'd like to compile ZooKeeper separately or use a different version, you can do so by configuring Mesos prior to compilation time. A complete list of the options you can pass to the configure script can be found with the Mesos project documentation at http://mesos.apache.org/documentation/latest/configuration/.

> **NOTE**   Although I've done my best to capture the prerequisite steps and walk you through the build process, these instructions are subject to change for future releases. For the most up-to-date instructions, see http://mesos.apache.org/gettingstarted/.

In short, compiling Mesos requires the following:

- A 64-bit Linux distribution
- GNU Compiler Collection (GCC) 4.4 or newer, or Clang 3.3 or newer

> **TIP**   Starting with Mesos 0.23, the minimum compiler version has been upgraded to GCC 4.8 and Clang 3.5 for all supported platforms. For more information, see https://issues.apache.org/jira/browse/MESOS-2604.

Because the number of Linux distributions is always growing, it isn't feasible for me (or the Mesos authors) to provide instructions on how to set up the environment to compile Mesos for all of them. For parity with the package installation instructions I covered in the previous section, the next two sections include instructions for compiling Mesos on RHEL / CentOS 7 and Ubuntu 14.04 LTS (Trusty).

RHEL / CentOS 7 Prerequisites

Fortunately, RHEL 7 includes GCC 4.8.3 as part of its base package offering. This enables you to compile Mesos version 0.22.2, and ensure that you're able to compile version 0.23 and beyond, without requiring you to upgrade the compiler.

All of the dependencies required to compile Mesos are available via RHEL's Yum package manager, except one: Boto, a Python module that provides an interface to the AWS API. You'll need to install this one optional package by using Python's easy_install utility, which is included with RHEL.

To install the dependencies required to compile Mesos on RHEL / CentOS 7, run the following commands:

```
$ sudo yum -y groupinstall "Development Tools"

$ sudo yum -y install subversion-devel java-1.8.0-openjdk-devel zlib-devel
➥ libcurl-devel openssl-devel cyrus-sasl-devel cyrus-sasl-md5 apr-devel
➥ apr-util-devel maven python-devel

$ sudo easy_install boto
```

After these development dependencies are installed, feel free to skip to the upcoming "Compiling" section.

Ubuntu 14.04 (Trusty) Prerequisites

Fortunately, Ubuntu 14.04 includes GCC 4.8.4 as part of its base package offering. This enables you to compile Mesos version 0.22.2, and ensure that you're able to compile version 0.23 and beyond, without requiring you to upgrade the compiler.

All of the dependencies required to compile Mesos are available via Ubuntu's Apt package manager, including Boto, the optional Python module that provides an interface to the AWS API.

To install the dependencies required to compile Mesos on Ubuntu 14.04, run the following commands:

```
$ sudo apt-get update

$ sudo apt-get -y install build-essential openjdk-7-jdk python-dev
➥ python-boto libcurl4-nss-dev libsasl2-dev maven libapr1-dev libsvn-dev
```

After these development dependencies are installed, proceed to the next section to compile Mesos and ZooKeeper.

COMPILING

After you have all the development tools needed to compile Mesos, you can download a Mesos release and begin the compilation process. As mentioned previously, you have many options to configure Mesos at compilation time. For this example, you'll accept most of the defaults, but you'll specify the option `--prefix="/usr/local/mesos"` to ensure that all Mesos-related files are kept in a single directory. Feel free to modify this to suit your preferences or environment.

Run the following commands to download, configure, and compile Mesos 0.22.2:

```
$ curl -L -O https://www.apache.org/dist/mesos/0.22.2/mesos-0.22.2.tar.gz
$ tar zxf mesos-0.22.2.tar.gz
$ cd mesos-0.22.2
$ mkdir build && cd $_
$ ../configure --prefix="/usr/local/mesos"
$ make
```

> **TIP** You can speed up compilation time, increasing the number of jobs that Make launches simultaneously, by using the `-j` argument. For example: on a machine with four CPU cores, you can use `make -j4`. Note that each job requires about 2 GB of memory.

Depending on the number of cores available on your system, compiling Mesos could take several minutes. After it has finished building, you might want to run the included test suite. This next step is optional, but it's a good idea if you intend to use any of the example frameworks included with the Mesos source code.

To run the test suite, run the following command:

```
$ make check
```

You'll observe output throughout the test suite, and at the end you should see a test summary resembling the following:

```
[==========] 539 tests from 86 test cases ran. (260794 ms total)
[  PASSED  ] 539 tests.
```

Now that you've compiled Mesos and ensured that the tests are passing on your system, you can go ahead and install Mesos.

INSTALLING MESOS

After Mesos has finished building, you can run the following command to install Mesos:

```
$ sudo make install
```

By specifying `--prefix="/usr/local/mesos"` when running the configure script earlier in the build process, Mesos will install itself into the /usr/local/mesos directory.

Let's take a look at the subdirectories that are now present in the installation directory, as well as their purposes and contents:

- bin/ contains command-line tools for interacting with a Mesos cluster. Some of these tools include mesos-local, mesos-execute, and mesos-ps.
- etc/mesos/ contains configuration files for the Mesos cluster.
- include/ contains the various C++ header files used for interfacing with Mesos.
- lib/ contains native Mesos libraries, such as libmesos.so.
- libexec/mesos/ contains Mesos helper binaries and scripts.
- sbin/ contains several scripts used to start and stop Mesos masters and slaves. Some of these include mesos-master, mesos-slave, and mesos-daemon.sh.
- share/mesos/webui/master/static/ contains the static code for the Mesos web interface.

It's worth noting that because you should be able to compile Mesos on any Linux distribution (provided you have the necessary development tools), it isn't feasible for the Mesos project maintainers to include service wrapper scripts for all Linux operating systems. But as mentioned previously, a set of scripts in the Mesos sbin/ directory enables you to start masters and slaves, both in the foreground and as daemons. You should be able to write a simple wrapper around the included scripts to start, stop, and restart the `mesos-master` and `mesos-slave` services using your operating system's service manager or your service manager of choice.

> **TIP** The mesos-init-wrapper script, which is included with the Mesos packages provided by Mesosphere, is open source and can be found in the following GitHub repository: https://github.com/mesosphere/mesos-deb-packaging/blob/master/mesos-init-wrapper.

INSTALLING ZOOKEEPER

When you compiled Mesos in the build/ directory, you also compiled a version of ZooKeeper that the Mesos maintainers bundle in the Mesos source tree. The compiled ZooKeeper release is located within the build/3rdparty directory, and is now ready to be installed.

Chances are you'll want to relocate ZooKeeper somewhere a little more permanent, so let's go ahead and copy it alongside the Mesos installation in /usr/local:

```
$ sudo cp -rp 3rdparty/zookeeper-3.4.5 /usr/local/
$ sudo chown -R root:root /usr/local/zookeeper-3.4.5
```

Located within the ZooKeeper distribution are several scripts in the bin/ directory that assist you with starting and stopping the ZooKeeper cluster. Specifically, you'll want to pay attention to zkServer.sh, as this script will allow you to start, stop, and restart your Zookeeper cluster.

As was mentioned previously when you were installing Mesos, it's not feasible for the ZooKeeper project maintainers to maintain service scripts for all of the operating systems ZooKeeper can run on. Some init scripts for RPM-based and Deb-based operating systems are located in the src/packages/ directory of the ZooKeeper distribution. But otherwise, you should be able to write a small wrapper script for your operating system's service manager, or your service manager of choice, using the zkServer.sh script.

Now that you've downloaded, compiled, and installed both Mesos and ZooKeeper, you're ready to learn about the various configuration options—and the methods for specifying those options—available for both Mesos and ZooKeeper.

3.3   *Configuring Mesos and ZooKeeper*

Now that you understand the components that make up a Mesos deployment and have installed Mesos and ZooKeeper, you need to configure everything so you can fire up the services and start using your Mesos cluster.

The ways you'll configure ZooKeeper and Mesos will differ slightly based on whether you chose to install from packages or compile from source in the preceding section. But not to worry—you'll learn about both as you work your way through this section.

3.3.1   *ZooKeeper configuration*

First and foremost, you'll begin by configuring ZooKeeper, which is required for Mesos cluster coordination and leader election. Figure 3.2 shows ZooKeeper's role in the cluster you're deploying.

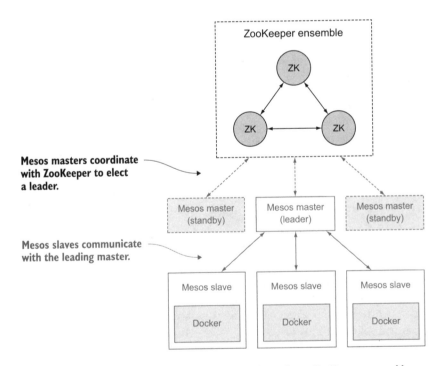

Figure 3.2   Mesos masters coordinate leader election using a ZooKeeper ensemble.

The location of the configuration file, zoo.cfg, varies depending on whether you installed ZooKeeper from packages or compiled it as part of Mesos:

- For package-based installations, the configuration file is located at /etc/zoo-keeper/conf/zoo.cfg.
- For source-based installations (assuming you placed the ZooKeeper distribution at /usr/local/zookeeper-3.4.5 as instructed), the configuration file is located at /usr/local/zookeeper-3.4.5/conf/zoo.cfg.

The following listing provides basic settings needed to get a ZooKeeper 3.4.*x* cluster up and running.

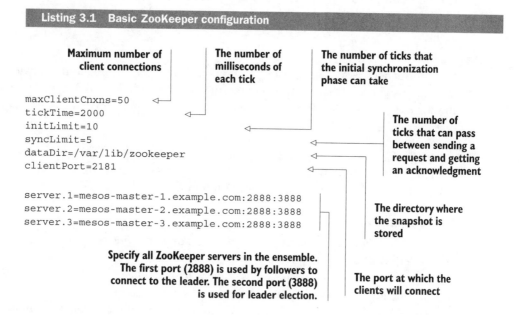

Listing 3.1 Basic ZooKeeper configuration

In addition to creating the zoo.cfg configuration file, you'll need to assign each node in the ZooKeeper ensemble a unique ID. You'll notice in this listing that the servers are numbered: `server.1`, `server.2`, and so on. On each of those machines, create the file myid within ZooKeeper's conf/ directory. The file's only contents should be an integer between 1 and 255, representing the unique ID for that particular ZooKeeper node.

NOTE The ID number configured in the myid file on a given ZooKeeper node must correspond with the ID number it's given in zoo.cfg.

STARTING THE SERVICES

Although I've covered only the bare-minimum ZooKeeper configuration required, it's enough to bring up the machines in the ensemble and allow them to serve clients. Let's go ahead and start the ZooKeeper service on each of the masters:

- For package-based installations—`service zookeeper start`
- For source-based installations—`/usr/local/zookeeper-3.4.5/bin/zkServer.sh start`

When the service is up and running, you can ensure that the ZooKeeper server is in a healthy state by using Netcat to send it a health-check command. You should be able to send ZooKeeper the `ruok` command, and it should respond with `imok`:

```
$ echo ruok | nc 127.0.0.1 2181
imok
```

If that last check worked, fantastic! ZooKeeper is up and running and ready to serve your Mesos cluster. Chapter 6 covers monitoring the ZooKeeper cluster a bit more. But for now, the ZooKeeper ensemble is up and running, so let's proceed to configure Mesos.

> **TIP**   For additional configuration options that might apply to your environment, please consult the ZooKeeper Administrator's Guide at http://zookeeper .apache.org/doc/current/zookeeperAdmin.pdf.

3.3.2   *Mesos configuration*

Now that the ZooKeeper ensemble is up and ready to provide services for your Mesos cluster, let's discuss how to go about configuring Mesos.

The configuration provided here is enough to get a cluster ready to handle distributed workloads, but it won't go into all the configuration options that Mesos provides. You should refer to http://mesos.apache.org/documentation/latest/configuration for the latest documentation and configuration options.

CONVENTIONS

Multiple conventions exist for configuring a Mesos deployment:

- *File-based*—When using Mesos packages provided by Mesosphere, configuration values can exist in files on disk, with each file named after the configuration option. Some examples of this include /etc/mesos/zk and /etc/mesos-slave/ attributes/rack.
- *Environment-based*—For both package-based and source-based installations, configuration values can exist as environment variables that are read when the `mesos-master` or `mesos-slave` services start. They can already be part of the environment, or in a shell script that's sourced before the services are started. For example: `MESOS_zk="zk://..."`

- *Command-line arguments*—Configuration values can also be passed in as arguments to the `mesos-master` and `mesos-slave` binaries and service scripts. For example: `mesos-master --zk=zk://...`

Chances are you'll be interacting with Mesos more as a service and less on the command line, so this section explains configuring the masters and slaves by using the file-based and environment-based methods. But it's worth noting that all the configuration options can be specified as command-line arguments, if you so desire.

To determine the locations of the configuration files for your installation method and operating system, take a look at table 3.2. This table assumes that for compiled installations, you installed Mesos to /usr/local/mesos.

Table 3.2   Mesos configuration file locations

Operating system	Installation method	Configuration method	Configuration locations
RHEL and CentOS 7	Packages (Mesosphere)	File	/etc/mesos/ /etc/mesos-master/ /etc/mesos-slave/
RHEL and CentOS 7	Packages (Mesosphere)	Environment	/etc/default/mesos /etc/default/mesos-master /etc/default/mesos-slave
Ubuntu 14.04	Packages (Mesosphere)	File	/etc/mesos/ /etc/mesos-master/ /etc/mesos-slave/
Ubuntu 14.04	Packages (Mesosphere)	Environment	/etc/default/mesos /etc/default/mesos-master /etc/default/mesos-slave
All	Source	Environment	/usr/local/mesos/etc/mesos/mesos-master-env.sh /usr/local/mesos/etc/mesos/mesos-slave-env.sh

Please refer to the paths in this table for the configuration method of your choosing. The following sections cover common options for Mesos master and slave configuration without necessarily referencing the configuration files (or their locations) directly.

MASTER CONFIGURATION

You must use several required configuration settings for the proper functioning of the Mesos masters: the ZooKeeper URL, the size of the Mesos master quorum, and the Mesos master's working directory. Figure 3.3 shows where you're at in the deployment process: configuring the Mesos masters.

The `--zk` option sets the ZooKeeper URL, which is used for leader election and coordination among the masters. This option is used in highly available deployments

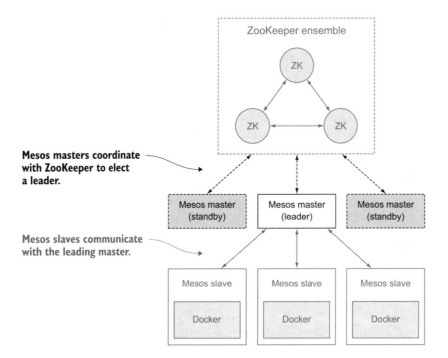

Mesos masters coordinate with ZooKeeper to elect a leader.

Mesos slaves communicate with the leading master.

Figure 3.3   Mesos masters use the previously configured ZooKeeper ensemble for leader election.

and isn't required if you're running Mesos in standalone mode. The ZooKeeper URL uses the following convention:

```
zk://mesos-master-1.example.com:2181,
    mesos-master-2.example.com:2181,
    mesos-master-3.example.com:2181/mesos
```

If you have authentication enabled on the ZooKeeper cluster, you can either specify a username and password in the URL itself, or reference a file on disk that contains the ZooKeeper URL with your authentication details:

```
zk://username:password@host1:2181,host2:2181,host3:2181/mesos
file:///path/to/zk_url
```

If you set up the ZooKeeper cluster by following the instructions in this chapter, don't worry about authentication for now. Chapter 6 covers securing your Mesos and Zoo-Keeper installations.

The --quorum option establishes the majority of the Mesos masters in the cluster, and is used for the Mesos replicated registry. Much like the ZooKeeper quorum, it should be set according to table 3.3, where N is the value of the quorum option.

Table 3.3   Number of Mesos masters required for a quorum

Number of Mesos masters	Mesos master quorum	Number of machine failures tolerated
1	1	0
3	2	1
5	3	2
$2 \times N - 1$	N	$N - 1$

WARNING   When configuring the `quorum` option, it's important to ensure that the number of Mesos masters in the cluster matches table 3.3. Any additional masters could violate the quorum and corrupt the replicated log. Chapter 6 provides additional information on how to safely increase and decrease the Mesos master quorum size.

In the context of the Mesos masters, the `--work_dir` option specifies the location on disk that Mesos will use for its own replicated log. There's no default, so this must be specified. Usually a path such as /var/lib/mesos is a good option.

Although it's not required, it's a great idea to set the `--log_dir` option as well. This ensures that Mesos will log events to disk, so that you can more easily debug your Mesos cluster going forward. The packages provided by Mesosphere already set `log_dir` to /var/log/mesos.

TIP   I recommend setting two additional configuration options: `--hostname` and `--ip`. Setting these options ensures that the hostname used by the Mesos service, and the IP address for the Mesos service to communicate on, are configured properly and not autodiscovered. Setting values for these two options becomes even more important on machines with more than one network interface.

Based on the preceding examples, here's what the mesos-master-env.sh script might look like on a source-based installation of Mesos:

```
export MESOS_zk=zk://mesos-master-1.example.com:2181,
➥ mesos-master-2.example.com:2181,mesos-master-3.example.com:2181/mesos
export MESOS_quorum=2
export MESOS_work_dir=/var/lib/mesos
export MESOS_log_dir=/var/log/mesos
```

After you've applied a basic configuration, all that's left to do is to start the mesos-master service by running the following command:

```
$ sudo service mesos-master start
```

It's also a good idea to disable the `mesos-slave` service on the masters:

- On RHEL / CentOS 7—`sudo systemctl disable mesos-slave.service`
- On Ubuntu 14.04—`echo "manual" | sudo tee /etc/init/mesos-slave.override`

You should now be able to open a web browser and connect to one of the Mesos masters by visiting http://mesos-master-1.example.com:5050, replacing the hostname with one of your own Mesos masters' hostnames or IP addresses. If you connect to a Mesos master that isn't the current leading master, you'll be redirected to the leader automatically.

SLAVE CONFIGURATION

You need to set several configuration options for the proper functioning of a Mesos slave, specifically the ZooKeeper URL and the slave's working directory. Figure 3.4 shows where you're at in the deployment process: configuring the Mesos slaves.

The `--master` option sets the ZooKeeper URL, which is used by the Mesos slave to detect the leading Mesos master and connect to the cluster. The ZooKeeper URL uses the following convention:

```
zk://mesos-master-1.example.com:2181,
    mesos-master-2.example.com:2181,
    mesos-master-3.example.com:2181/mesos
```

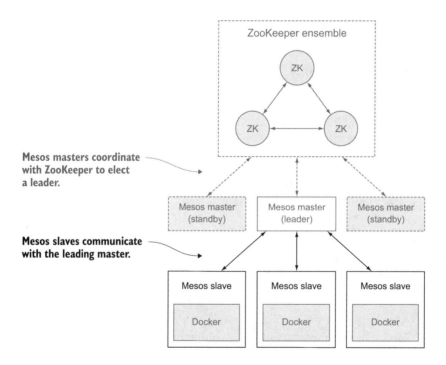

Figure 3.4   Mesos slaves use ZooKeeper to detect—and register with—the leading Mesos master.

When you have authentication enabled on the ZooKeeper cluster, you can either specify a username and password in the URL itself, or reference a file on disk that contains the ZooKeeper URL with your authentication details:

```
zk://username:password@host1:2181,host2:2181,host3:2181/mesos
file:///path/to/zk_url
```

> **NOTE** If you're using the Mesos packages provided by Mesosphere, you should set the ZooKeeper URL for the Mesos slave daemon in the file /etc/mesos/zk, not in /etc/mesos-slave/master.

In the context of the Mesos slaves, the `--work_dir` option specifies the location on disk that Mesos frameworks will use for their working directories and sandboxes. There's no default, so this must be specified. Usually a path such as /var/lib/mesos is a good option. It's also a good idea to ensure that the partition that this directory resides on isn't mounted with the `noexec` option, as /tmp often is.

Although it's not required, it's a great idea to set the `--log_dir` option as well. This ensures that Mesos will log events to disk so that you can more easily debug your Mesos cluster going forward. The packages provided by Mesosphere already set `--log_dir` to /var/log/mesos.

Based on the preceding examples, here's what the mesos-slave-env.sh script might look like on a source-based installation of Mesos:

```
export MESOS_master=zk://mesos-master-1.example.com:2181,
➥  mesos-master-2.example.com:2181,mesos-master-3.example.com:2181/mesos
export MESOS_work_dir=/var/lib/mesos
export MESOS_log_dir=/var/log/mesos
```

After you've applied a basic configuration, all that's left to do is to start the `mesos-slave` service by running the following command:

```
$ sudo service mesos-slave start
```

It's also a good idea to disable the `mesos-master` service on the slaves:

- On RHEL 7—`sudo systemctl disable mesos-master.service`
- On Ubuntu—`echo "manual" | sudo tee /etc/init/mesos-master.override`

If you navigate to the web interface for the Mesos master, you should now notice that the newly configured slave has appeared and is advertising its resources to the cluster.

As mentioned earlier, this is the bare-minimum configuration required to get a Mesos cluster up and running. For an extensive list of configuration options for both the masters and slaves, please consult the official Mesos documentation at http://mesos.apache.org/documentation/latest/configuration. Chapter 4 discusses additional configuration options, such as slave attributes and resources.

3.4   *Installing and configuring Docker*

Because multiple applications' workloads can run simultaneously on any given Mesos slave, each executor runs inside a container. In addition to the Mesos native containerizer (which uses Linux control groups), you also have the option of launching containers by using Docker. This section explains a bit more about deploying Docker, including installation and some of the commonly used configuration options.

Figure 3.5 shows where you're at in the deployment process: installing and configuring Docker on the Mesos slaves.

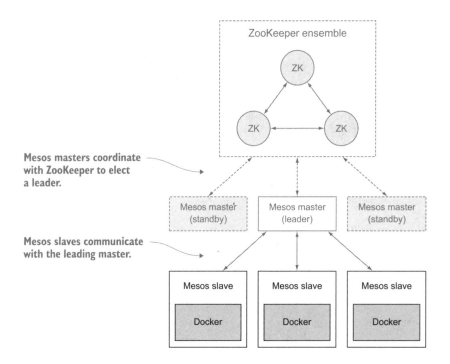

Figure 3.5   Mesos slaves can launch Docker containers, in addition to using Linux control groups.

If you aren't interested in launching Docker containers on your Mesos cluster just yet, no worries; you can always come back to this section. But it's worth knowing that later chapters in this book include examples that involve launching Docker containers on a Mesos cluster.

3.4.1   *Installation*

As I mentioned in chapter 1, custom executors must be available on each Mesos slave. Although Docker is a Mesos containerizer, it is no exception: the Docker daemon must be installed, configured, and running on each Mesos slave before you can launch Docker containers on the cluster.

RHEL / CentOS 7

Red Hat includes Docker packages in the "extras" channel (repository), so you don't need to install any additional repositories in order to install the package. You can use the Yum package manager to install it:

```
$ sudo yum -y install docker
```

As of Docker 1.5.0, the service doesn't automatically start on RHEL 7. To start services, run the following command:

```
$ sudo service docker start
```

> ### If the Docker service fails to start on RHEL / CentOS 7
>
> The Docker daemon might fail to start if you haven't installed the latest software updates. Specifically, if the package `device-mapper-event-libs` is older than version 1.02.90, you'll see the following cryptic error message:
>
> ```
> /usr/bin/docker: relocation error: /usr/bin/docker:
> symbol dm_task_get_info_with_deferred_remove,
> version Base not defined in file libdevmapper.so.1.02
> with link time reference
> ```
>
> To resolve this issue, install the latest patches for RHEL by running `yum update`, or upgrade this particular package with `yum update device-mapper-event-libs`.

Ubuntu 14.04 (Trusty)

The Apt repository for Docker is available only by using HTTPS. If your system doesn't already have the `apt-transport-https` package installed, you'll need to install it first:

```
$ sudo apt-get update
$ sudo apt-get install apt-transport-https
```

Next, fetch Docker's package-signing key, and add the Docker repository to Apt's sources list:

```
$ sudo apt-key adv --keyserver keyserver.ubuntu.com --recv A88D21E9

$ echo "deb https://get.docker.com/ubuntu docker main" |
➡ sudo tee /etc/apt/sources.list.d/docker.list

$ sudo apt-get update
```

Finally, install the package for Docker Engine:

```
$ sudo apt-get -y install docker-engine
```

As of Docker 1.6.0, the Docker service will automatically be started after the package is installed. You can verify this by running the following command:

```
$ sudo service docker status
```

3.4.2 *Configuration*

If you need to make any configuration changes to the Docker daemon, such as configuring a proxy or specifying certain DNS servers, now is a good time. Because Docker works well using the default configuration, this section doesn't go into Docker's configuration in too much detail. But I will cover some of the more common configuration settings for both RHEL / CentOS 7 and Ubuntu 14.04.

> **TIP** You can find a complete list of Docker's configuration settings on its website at https://docs.docker.com/engine/reference/commandline/daemon/.

If your environment doesn't require the use of an HTTP proxy and you have a properly working DNS deployment, feel free to skip ahead to the next section.

RHEL / CENTOS 7

On RHEL / CentOS 7, Docker's configuration file is located at /etc/sysconfig/docker. The following code snippet demonstrates using an HTTP proxy for connecting to Docker Hub, enabling SELinux support in Docker itself, and specifying external DNS servers:

```
                                                            Specify the path to
                                                            an HTTP proxy.
http_proxy="http://127.0.0.1:3128/"                       ◄┘
OPTIONS="--selinux-enabled --dns 8.8.8.8 --dns 8.8.4.4"   ◄─┐ Pass additional
                                                            options to the
                                                            Docker daemon.
```

If you made any changes to the configuration file, be sure to restart the Docker service:

```
$ sudo service docker restart
```

UBUNTU 14.04 (TRUSTY)

On Ubuntu 14.04, Docker's configuration file is located at /etc/default/docker. The following code snippet demonstrates using an HTTP proxy for connecting to Docker Hub, enabling SELinux support in Docker itself, and specifying external DNS servers:

```
                                                            Use DOCKER_OPTS to
                                                            modify the options passed
                                                            to the Docker daemon.
DOCKER_OPTS="--dns 8.8.8.8 --dns 8.8.4.4"                 ◄┘
export http_proxy="http://127.0.0.1:3128/"               ◄─┐
                                                            Specify the path
                                                            to an HTTP proxy.
```

If you made any changes to the configuration file, be sure to restart the Docker service:

```
$ sudo service docker restart
```

Now that you have the Docker service running and any environment-specific configurations applied, let's look at the small configuration changes you need to make to Mesos in order for it to launch Docker containers.

3.4.3 Configuring Mesos slaves for Docker

With Docker up and operational, you'll need to modify the list of containerizers available to the Mesos slave and increase the executor registration time-out. By increasing the executor registration time-out, Docker is given more time to fetch images from Docker Hub (or from your private Docker Registry) before Mesos thinks something failed. Here, you'll set this value to 5mins. Assuming you're using the file-based configuration that the Mesosphere packages allow for, the configuration will look something like the following:

```
$ echo "docker,mesos" | sudo tee /etc/mesos-slave/containerizers
$ echo "5mins" | sudo tee /etc/mesos-slave/executor_registration_timeout
```

Now restart the mesos-slave service to apply the changes:

```
$ sudo service mesos-slave restart
```

> **NOTE** Unlike the default mesos containerizer, the docker containerizer in Mesos doesn't enforce a disk quota (as of Mesos 0.22.2). For more information, see https://issues.apache.org/jira/browse/MESOS-2502.

3.5 Upgrading Mesos

In contrast to distributed systems that set up statically partitioned clusters or that use only a single master, the fault-tolerant architecture of Mesos allows upgrades to occur on both the masters and the slaves without any cluster downtime. The Mesos API even provides a means to notify frameworks that a failure or leader election occurred, allowing them to take appropriate action if needed. This section explains the process for upgrading both Mesos masters and slaves.

> **NOTE** Prior to Mesos reaching version 1.0, the Mesos maintainers support only $N + 1$ upgrades. If you're running Mesos 0.22 and wish to upgrade to 0.24, you'll need to upgrade to 0.23 first. When performing upgrades, it's always a good idea to consult the latest release notes and upgrade documentation on the Mesos project page. This documentation is located at http://mesos.apache.org/documentation/latest/upgrades.

As with any piece of software, eventually a time comes when we must upgrade it. Whether it's for new features or to patch security vulnerabilities, software upgrades are usually associated with scheduled downtime. In contrast, Mesos can be upgraded without taking the cluster offline.

This section discusses the procedure for upgrading both the Mesos masters and the slaves, which is largely the same as the Mesos installation you performed previously, with a few additional considerations. Chapter 4 explains how Mesos makes this possible.

3.5.1   Upgrading Mesos masters

As the number of Mesos masters will be much smaller than the number of Mesos slaves, it's a good idea to use some sort of configuration management or orchestration tool to ensure that the entire master quorum isn't upgraded at the same time. Using a configuration management tool such as Puppet or Chef, you can ensure that each individual master is upgraded only on a set schedule. Using an orchestration tool such as Ansible or Fabric, you can ensure that upgrades are serially executed across multiple masters.

To upgrade the Mesos masters, you need to take the following steps:

1 Upgrade the Mesos binaries and restart the master daemon.
2 Upgrade the schedulers to use the new Mesos native library, JAR, or egg.
3 Restart the schedulers.

3.5.2   Upgrading Mesos slaves

Using features known as *slave recovery* and *checkpointing*, Mesos allows for slaves to upgrade themselves without interrupting running tasks. When the `mesos-slave` service is stopped and the Mesos binaries are upgraded, the executors—and their tasks—will continue running. If they finish before the Mesos slave daemon comes back online, they'll wait the `recovery_timeout`, a configurable slave option that defaults to 15 minutes. But if this threshold is exceeded, any executors waiting to connect to the Mesos slave process will self-terminate.

> **TIP**   Chapter 4 covers slave recovery and checkpointing in more detail.

When performing rolling upgrades on your Mesos infrastructure, it's good to have some sort of configuration management or orchestration tooling in place. This will ensure that only a percentage of the cluster is upgrading at any given time in case it becomes necessary to stop the upgrade, or if the upgrade coincides with other scheduled maintenance (for example, applying security patches). To upgrade the Mesos slaves, you need to take the following steps:

1 Upgrade the Mesos binaries and restart the slave daemon.
2 Upgrade the executors to use the new Mesos native library, JAR, or egg (if needed).

3.6 *Summary*

Following the examples provided in this chapter, you should have a properly functioning, highly available Mesos and ZooKeeper cluster that's ready to execute tasks and launch Docker containers. Here are a few things to remember:

- The Mesos masters use Apache ZooKeeper for leader election and coordination. Mesos slaves and schedulers also use ZooKeeper to detect the leading Mesos master.
- For highly available deployments, you should deploy at least three machines running ZooKeeper and three machines to serve as Mesos masters. For a simplified deployment, you can run the ZooKeeper services on the same machines as the Mesos masters, but you might want to separate them if you plan on using other software that depends on ZooKeeper.
- You should install and configure ZooKeeper, followed by Mesos masters, followed by Mesos slaves.
- Docker is a popular option for running distributed applications within a datacenter. Although Mesos has native Docker support out of the box, it still needs to be installed separately. Mesos requires slight configuration to enable Docker support.
- Both the Mesos masters and slaves can be upgraded without incurring any cluster downtime.
- Puppet, an open source configuration management tool, can automate the installation and configuration of your Mesos, ZooKeeper, and Docker infrastructure. The Puppet Forge contains modules to manage each of the components in a Mesos deployment.

The next chapter presents more Mesos fundamentals, including how Mesos implements resource isolation, slave resources, and fault tolerance.

Mesos fundamentals

This chapter covers

- Resource scheduling, allocation, and reservations
- Customizing slave resources, attributes, and roles
- Using containers to isolate and monitor resources
- Fault-tolerance and high availability

Now that you've learned about the Mesos architecture and how it provides a means to run multiple applications on a single, general-purpose cluster, let's dive into how Mesos works. This chapter covers how a Mesos master handles resource scheduling and allocation, how a workload's resources can be isolated and monitored, and how Mesos provides a fault-tolerant and highly available environment on which to build and run distributed applications.

4.1 Scheduling and allocating datacenter resources

By now, you've learned that Mesos offers available cluster resources to framework schedulers in the form of resource offers. By default, these resources include available CPUs, memory, storage, and network ports. In this section, you'll learn how Mesos schedules resources, and how its allocation module offers those resources to various frameworks. This section also covers how to fine-tune this decision making to fit the needs of your environment.

4.1.1 Understanding resource scheduling

Mesos implements a two-tier scheduling system: as Mesos slaves offer their available resources to the master, which in turn offers resources to schedulers, the schedulers can then accept the whole offer, part of the offer, or decline it completely. Let's take a look at figure 4.1. This graphic demonstrates how a single resource offer from a Mesos slave can be advertised to multiple framework schedulers.

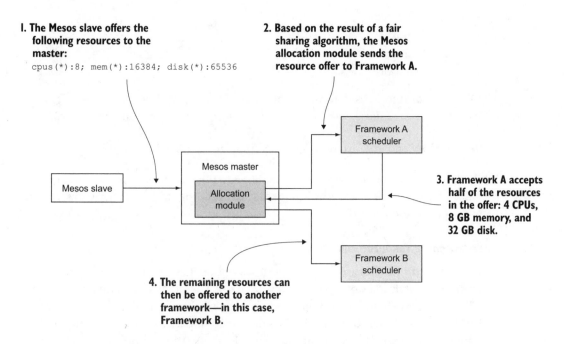

I. The Mesos slave offers the following resources to the master:
`cpus(*):8; mem(*):16384; disk(*):65536`

2. Based on the result of a fair sharing algorithm, the Mesos allocation module sends the resource offer to Framework A.

Mesos master

Allocation module

Mesos slave

Framework A scheduler

3. Framework A accepts half of the resources in the offer: 4 CPUs, 8 GB memory, and 32 GB disk.

Framework B scheduler

4. The remaining resources can then be offered to another framework—in this case, Framework B.

Figure 4.1   Other frameworks can use unallocated resources from a resource offer.

Before we continue, let's break down the events in the figure:

1   A Mesos slave advertises to the leading Mesos master that it has 8 CPUs, 16 GB of memory, and 64 GB of disk space available. The asterisk (*) denotes that these resources belong to the *default role*, a concept covered in the next section.

2   The Mesos allocation module decides that the master should advertise the entire resource offer to Framework A's scheduler.

3 Framework A's scheduler accepts only half of the resources offered to it, leaving 4 CPUs, 8 GB memory, and 32 GB disk available for other applications.

4 The Mesos allocation module decides that the master should advertise all the remaining (unallocated) resources in the offer to Framework B's scheduler.

This process repeats itself every few seconds as slaves have available resources and as tasks complete and resources are freed.

Because most applications require some amount of CPUs, memory, storage, and network, Mesos predefines some of these resources for you. Let's take a look at the default resources that Mesos offers to frameworks.

DEFAULT RESOURCES

Resource offers from Mesos slaves contain the following resources by default:

- cpus—CPU cores
- mem—Memory
- disk—Storage
- ports—Network ports

The free system resources determine the values for each of these resources when the mesos-slave service starts, less some system resources for operational overhead.

TIP Memory and disk are both specified in terms of megabytes (MB).

While slaves continually advertise these resources to the master, another part of Mesos— the allocation module—is responsible for determining which frameworks should receive a given resource offer.

4.1.2 *Understanding resource allocation*

As I mentioned in the last section, the Mesos master has an allocation module that determines which frameworks to offer resources to. The pluggable nature of this module allows systems engineers to implement their own sharing policies and algorithms to suit the needs of their organization. As described in part 1 of this book, the built-in allocation module uses the Dominant Resource Fairness (DRF) algorithm, which should suit the needs of most Mesos users.

TIP For more information about the default allocation module and allocation algorithm, see http://mesos.apache.org/documentation/latest/allocation-module/.

Out of the box, Mesos provides several means to fine-tune resource scheduling without replacing or reimplementing the default allocation module. These come in the forms of *roles*, *weights*, and *resource reservations*. In figure 4.2, you can see that Mesos slave resources can be reserved to a particular role, and are then offered only to frameworks that are also registered with that role.

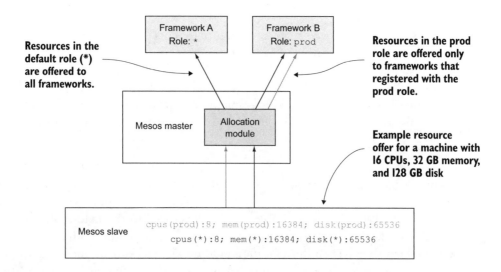

Figure 4.2   Mesos slave resources can be reserved for frameworks in a given role.

By combining roles, weights, and resource reservations, you can provide guarantees about the cluster resources that are available to specific applications, and control how often those applications receive resource offers. The next few sections explore these concepts a bit further.

ROLES

The concept of *roles* on a Mesos cluster allows you to organize frameworks and resources into arbitrary groups. To use roles on a given Mesos cluster, you first need to configure the masters with a static list of all of the acceptable roles that will exist across the cluster. By setting a value for the --roles configuration option, the following example allows frameworks to register with three common roles in a given datacenter—development, staging, and production:

```
--roles="dev,stage,prod"
```

Frameworks can then specify one of these roles when they register with the Mesos master. This allows multiple teams—or multiple environments—to share a large Mesos cluster, instead of creating several smaller clusters. The master then dynamically calculates each role's dominant resource when making decisions about which framework to offer resources to. You can also use roles to ensure that a specific type of workload runs on only a subset of machines; for example, a load balancer or reverse proxy running on a dedicated edge node.

In addition to frameworks specifying a role, Mesos slaves can also specify which resources should belong to a given role; this is known as a *resource reservation*, which you'll learn about a little bit later in this chapter.

WEIGHTS

In addition to roles, the cluster can configure weights per role as a means to give priority to one role over another. When making decisions about which framework to offer resources to first, Mesos offers it to whichever framework is furthest below its weighted fair share.

Using the same roles—dev, stage, and prod—that you used in the last section, you can configure the master to prioritize the prod role above that of dev and stage:

```
--weights="dev=10,stage=20,prod=30"
```

To understand this in practice, consider the weight you've given to the prod role. Frameworks in this role will be offered three times as many resources as frameworks in the dev role. When a new resource offer is advertised to the master, the allocation module checks the roles on the cluster to determine which one is furthest below its weighted fair share. Then the allocation module will check the frameworks within the role and offer resources to the framework that is furthest below its fair share.

RESOURCE RESERVATIONS

Despite weights being a good way to ensure that certain roles get more resource offers than other roles, Mesos also provides a means to create resource reservations. Reservations guarantee that certain roles will always receive a certain amount of the slave's resources, but at a price: doing so could lead to overall decreased cluster utilization.

Imagine for a moment that you have a single machine with 16 CPUs, 32 GB memory, and a 128 GB disk. You'd like to ensure that half of the resources on the machine (8 CPUs, 16 GB memory, and 64 GB disk) are always available for frameworks registered with the prod role. The reservation can be created with the following configuration on the Mesos slave:

```
--resources="cpus(prod):8; mem(prod):16384; disk(prod):65536"
```

Any remaining resources (8 CPUs, 16 GB memory, and 64 GB disk, less any resources allocated to handle system overhead) will then be assigned to the default role (*) and offered to frameworks that didn't specify a specific role when they registered to the master.

> **TIP** The default role name in Mesos is an asterisk (*) by default. This can be customized using the Mesos slave's --default_role configuration option.

Up to this point, I've discussed how you can customize the default, predefined resources that all Mesos slaves offer. But Mesos allows you to configure each individual slave's resources as well, which could include hardcoding the number of CPUs or amount of memory a slave offers, or adding a new resource altogether.

4.1.3 *Customizing Mesos slave resources and attributes*

In the preceding section, you learned that resources could be assigned to specific roles on the slave, creating resource reservations. But what about creating custom resources or overriding the default values? Like many things in Mesos, the resources advertised in the resource offer are customizable. This is useful if you need to introduce a new resource (such as `ephemeral_ports`, which is introduced later in this chapter) or you wish to hardcode the number of CPUs or memory, to allow other services running on the slave a bit of breathing room.

By default, Mesos advertises the `cpus`, `mem`, `disk`, and `ports` resources in the resource offer. Let's take a look at what it takes to customize the resources on a slave.

CUSTOMIZING SLAVE RESOURCES

Mesos provides three different types of resources: scalars, ranges, and sets. Here are a few examples of these types:

- Scalar—The resource `cpus` with the value `8`; the resource `mem` with the value `16384`
- Range—The resource `ports` with values `10000` through `20000`
- Set—The resource `disks` with the values `ssd1`, `ssd2`, and `ssd3`

NOTE A Mesos slave that doesn't contain any `cpus` or `mem` resources will never have its resource offers sent to frameworks!

Because I touched on customizing slave resources previously when talking about resource reservations, I won't go into too much detail here. You can use the `--resources` configuration option to configure the resources on the slave, for the default role and/or custom roles:

```
--resources="cpu(*):4; mem(*):8192; disk(*):32768; ports(*):[40000-50000];
➥ cpu(prod):8; mem(prod):16384; disk(prod):65536"
```

CUSTOMIZING SLAVE ATTRIBUTES

In addition to customizing the consumable slave resources, you can specify slave attributes. These optional attributes are arbitrary key/value pairs that can be used to provide the master and frameworks with some data about the machine. As of this writing, all attributes' values are considered to be text strings.

The following example uses the `--attributes` configuration option to set the machine's datacenter, rack, operating system, and available Python versions:

```
--attributes="datacenter:pdx1; rack:1-1; os:rhel7; pythons:python2,python3"
```

Now, in every resource offer the Mesos slave sends to the master (and the master sends to the framework), you'll also see these attributes. This could allow you to make more intelligent decisions about scheduling work in heterogeneous environments.

> **TIP**   For more information on Mesos slave resources and attributes, see http://mesos.apache.org/documentation/latest/attributes-resources.

4.2   *Isolating resources with containers*

Containers are a fantastic way to squeeze efficiency out of your infrastructure. Being much more lightweight than a virtual machine, containers allow you to run applications and code in an environment isolated from other workloads. One of Mesos's fundamental ideas is that isolating processes using containers is the most efficient way to utilize computing resources.

Out of the box, Mesos implements support for Linux control groups and Docker, two of the most popular container technologies as of this writing. By running executors and tasks within a container, Mesos slaves allow for multiple frameworks' executors to run side by side without impacting other workloads. This is analogous to how virtualization hypervisors can run multiple virtual machines per physical host, except that containers are much more lightweight than booting an entire operating system.

One of the fundamental components of Mesos is known as the containerizer. As of this writing, Mesos includes two containerizers, configurable with the `--containerizers` configuration option on the Mesos slave: these are `mesos` and `docker`. The `mesos` containerizer is responsible for isolating workloads by using cgroups, or monitoring resource consumption, whereas `docker` invokes the Docker container runtime, allowing you to launch premade images on your Mesos cluster.

> **TIP**   Mesos also provides an External Containerizer API that allows you to implement another container specification. Chances are you won't need to write your own containerizer (and this text doesn't cover Mesos internals), so I haven't included it in this chapter. But if you're interested in learning more about the External Containerizer API, or enhancing Mesos with a new container specification, please see http://mesos.apache.org/documentation/latest/external-containerizer.

In addition to containerizers, Mesos provides multiple means of resource isolation. Some, such as the defaults `posix/cpu` and `posix/mem`, provide resource monitoring. Others, such as `cgroups/cpu` and `cgroups/mem`, provide real resource isolation and quota enforcement on Linux by using the cgroups feature of the Linux kernel. In the next few sections, I'll provide a look into the various resource-isolation methods available to Mesos.

4.2.1   *Isolating and monitoring CPU, memory, and disk*

To ensure that one workload on a Mesos slave doesn't impact another workload running on the same slave, Mesos provides multiple means of resource isolation. As mentioned earlier, Mesos has support for Linux control groups, Docker, and basic POSIX resource monitoring (but not isolation) for POSIX-compatible operating systems.

Let's look at how to isolate and monitor resource use for CPU, memory, and disk. Isolation methods for the containerizer are configured on the slave by providing a comma-separated list to the `--isolation` configuration option.

RESOURCE ISOLATION ON LINUX

The following resource-isolation methods are available on Linux:

- `cgroups/cpu` and `cgroups/mem`—Isolates CPU and memory by using a feature of the Linux kernel known as *control groups*.
- `filesystem/shared`—Maps a directory inside a container to a location on disk, ensuring that the container has a private working directory that's either read-write or read-only. Can be specified by the framework, or used in conjunction with the `--default_container_info`. The following example maps the `/tmp` directory in the container to the private directory relative to the sandbox's working directory:

```
{
  "type": "MESOS",
  "volumes": [
    {
      "host_path": "private",
      "container_path": "/tmp",
      "mode": "RW"
    }
  ]
}
```

- `namespaces/pid`—Enables process ID (PID) namespaces, ensuring that a container can't see processes belonging to other containers.
- `posix/disk`—A storage isolator for Linux that monitors a container's disk usage. When combined with the `--enforce_container_disk_quota` slave configuration option, it can also be used to ensure that a single container doesn't go above its allocated storage.
- `posix/cpu` and `posix/mem`—These are the default isolators for Mesos, and provide CPU and memory resource monitoring only; see the next section for more information on these isolators.

NOTE When using the `filesystem/shared` isolator, the mount point within the container can't mask part of the filesystem. For example, if the Mesos slave's `work_dir` is `/tmp/mesos`, the `container_path` can't be `/tmp`.

When querying a slave's `/monitor/statistics.json` HTTP API endpoint, you can obtain per container metrics such as the following:

- `cpus_system_time_secs`
- `cpus_user_time_secs`
- `mem_anon_bytes`

- `mem_file_bytes`
- `mem_mapped_file_bytes`
- `mem_rss_bytes`

Using cURL, you could query the leading Mesos master for its statistics by running the following command:

```
$ curl -s http://mesos-leader:5050/monitor/statistics.json |
➥ python -m json.tool
```

TIP   Chapter 6 covers the various ways to monitor your Mesos cluster.

Although Linux provides the most resource-isolation methods for Mesos (at least as of this writing), it's possible to monitor resources on other POSIX operating systems, such as Mac OS X.

RESOURCE MONITORING ON OTHER POSIX SYSTEMS

The following resource-isolation methods are available for other POSIX systems where Mesos might not support resource isolation, but it does support resource monitoring. As of Mesos 0.22.2, POSIX-compatible but non-Linux operating systems are limited to the following isolators:

- `posix/cpu` and `posix/mem`—Provide CPU and memory-resource monitoring only; no isolation or enforcement.

Currently, each of these isolators provides only per-executor (per-process) CPU and memory-resource monitoring, similar to the output from running the `ps` command. Because Mesos subtracts any allocated resources from a slave's resource offers, this might not be too problematic if your non-Linux cluster isn't operating near 100% utilization. But if a task goes over its allocated memory (due to a memory leak, misconfigured heap size, and so forth), the lack of resource isolation here has the ability to impact other tasks running on a given slave. Compare these resource-monitoring methods to Linux's cgroups that would invoke the out-of-memory (OOM) killer and stop the offending task.

4.2.2   *Network monitoring and rate limiting*

If you're interested in monitoring network traffic and rate-limiting egress traffic on a per-container basis, Mesos provides an optional network isolator that you may find useful. As of this writing, it provides statistics through a JSON API on the Mesos slave. The network monitoring is transparent to the container, and all containers will continue to share the public IP address of the Mesos slave.

Network monitoring and rate limiting is a relatively new feature, introduced in Mesos 0.20, and uses features present in modern Linux kernels. The next few sections will show you how to compile Mesos with network isolator support and how to monitor network traffic for the tasks running on a given Mesos slave.

COMPILING MESOS WITH NETWORK ISOLATOR SUPPORT

By default, Mesos is not built with the network isolator, and as of this writing it's not enabled in the packages provided by Mesosphere. To enable this, you'll need to configure and build Mesos by using the `--with-network-isolator` argument. As of Mesos 0.22.2, the network isolator works only with the Linux kernel, version 3.15 and later, and requires some prerequisites and additional setup.

An important note on Linux kernel versions and patches

For Mesos's per-container network monitoring to work, several key patches must be applied to the Linux kernel you're planning to use on the Mesos slave.

As of this writing, the current release of RHEL/CentOS is 7.1, which contains kernel 3.10. The required kernel patches haven't been backported by Red Hat. Unfortunately, there's no straightforward means of upgrading the kernel, short of compiling it yourself, which is outside the scope of this book and isn't supported by Red Hat. On CentOS, you may find ELRepo helpful: http://elrepo.org/tiki/tiki-index.php.

On Ubuntu 14.04.3 LTS, the kernel version is already 3.19. If you're running an older LTS release (like 14.04.2), you can upgrade the kernel by using the package manager. Run the following command, and restart the machine to load the new kernel:

```
$ sudo apt-get -y install linux-image-generic-lts-utopic
```

If you're not using one of these operating systems or releases, be sure to install kernel 3.15 or later, which contains the necessary networking patches. If you need to use a kernel older than 3.15, the following patches need to be manually applied, and the kernel recompiled. The patches (in the Git SHAs referenced next) can all be found on git.kernel.org:

- 6a662719c9868b3d6c7d26b3a085f0cd3cc15e64
- 0d5edc68739f1c1e0519acbea1d3f0c1882a15d7
- e374c618b1465f0292047a9f4c244bd71ab5f1f0
- 25f929fbff0d1bcebf2e92656d33025cd330cbf8

In addition to using a modern Linux kernel, you need a recent version of the Netlink Protocol Library Suite, also known as *libnl*. To use the network isolator, Mesos requires libnl version 3.2.25 or later.

Compiling the Netlink Protocol Library Suite

As of this writing, the latest packaged version of the Netlink Protocol Library Suite (libnl) is version 3.2.21, on both RHEL 7 and Ubuntu 14.04 LTS. To build Mesos with the network isolator, you need to download and compile libnl3 from www.infradead.org/~tgr/libnl.

(continued)

Building libnl3 requires Bison and Flex, both of which can be installed on RHEL / CentOS 7 and Ubuntu 14.04 using the system's package manager. After these prerequisites are installed, run the following commands:

```
$ curl -LO http://www.infradead.org/~tgr/libnl/files/libnl-3.2.25.tar.gz
$ tar zxf libnl-3.2.25.tar.gz
$ cd libnl-3.2.25
$ ./configure
$ make
$ sudo make install
$ sudo ldconfig
```

By default, libnl3 is configured with /usr/local for its prefix, meaning its header files will be installed to /usr/local/include/libnl3/netlink. You should now be able to proceed with compiling Mesos with the network isolator.

After following the prerequisite build instructions in chapter 3 to set up the tools required to compile Mesos, run the following commands to compile Mesos with the network isolator. If you already built Mesos once already, be sure to run make clean before recompiling.

NOTE Because of a bug present in the configure script in Mesos 0.22.2, you need to override the LIBNL_CFLAGS variable in the Makefile. By default, libnl3 installs its header files to /usr/local/include/libnl3. I've included the work-around in the following code. For more information, see https://issues .apache.org/jira/browse/MESOS-1856.

```
$ ../configure --prefix=/usr/local/mesos --with-network-isolator
$ make LIBNL_CFLAGS="-I/usr/local/include/libnl3"
```

After Mesos has finished compiling, proceed with the remaining installation and configuration instructions as first mentioned in chapter 3.

CONFIGURING THE HOST

When per-container network monitoring is enabled, each container on the Mesos slave uses network namespaces in the Linux kernel, and each container has a separate network stack. The first thing you need to do to prepare your host for container network monitoring is to limit the range of ephemeral ports that the operating system will allocate to processes, thereby reserving ephemeral ports for your running containers.

NOTE The instructions provided in this section are an example. Based on the software you deploy and the network ports in use, your environment may warrant a different network configuration. You may also be interested in reading the Mesos project's documentation regarding network monitoring, located at http://mesos.apache.org/documentation/latest/network-monitoring. If you're interested in learning how network namespaces work in the Linux kernel, the following LWN article is also a good source of information: http://lwn.net/Articles/580893.

To modify the host's ephemeral port range, append the following line to /etc/sysctl.conf and reboot the machine:

```
net.ipv4.ip_local_port_range = 57345 61000
```

Although you could also run sysctl -p to apply the new configuration, rebooting the machine at this point will ensure that any services using an ephemeral port in the old port range will be assigned a port in the new range, avoiding any potential port collisions. If the change was successful, you should see output similar to the following:

```
$ cat /proc/sys/net/ipv4/ip_local_port_range
57345 61000
```

CONFIGURING THE MESOS SLAVE

You then need to configure Mesos to enable network monitoring and offer the ephemeral_ports resource—the range of ports reserved for containers. Specifically, this includes the following:

1 Append network/port_mapping to the list of resource isolators.
2 Modify the slave's resources to offer a range of ephemeral network ports for containers to use.
3 Configure the number of ephemeral ports per container for normal network traffic.

The configuration for these points will likely resemble the following:

```
--isolation="cgroups/cpu,cgroups/mem,network/port_mapping"
--resources="ports:[31000-32000];ephemeral_ports:[32768-57344]"
--ephemeral_ports_per_container=1024
```

> **NOTE** Be sure that the ephemeral_ports resource doesn't overlap with the ephemeral port range provided to the host operating system!

If you'd also like to rate-limit each container's egress (outbound) traffic, you may do so by configuring the Mesos slave with the --egress_rate_limit_per_container option, which expects a value in bytes.

> **TIP** The value passed to the egress_rate_limit_per_container option is specified as a Bytes *object* in the Mesos code base. Therefore, the following values are all valid: 10B, 10KB, 10MB, 10GB, 10TB.

The following slave configuration example limits per-container outbound network traffic to about 100 Mbps:

```
--egress_rate_limit_per_container=12500KB
```

GETTING CONTAINER NETWORK METRICS

After the `mesos-slave` daemon is up and running with the `network/port_mapping` isolator, you'll be able to get the following network metrics for running containers (in addition to the metrics that Mesos provides by default):

- `net_tx_bytes` and `net_rx_bytes`
- `net_tx_dropped` and `net_rx_dropped`
- `net_tx_errors` and `net_rx_errors`
- `net_tx_packets` and `net_rx_packets`

These statistics are available as part of the Mesos slave's `/monitor/statistics.json` HTTP API. It can be queried like this:

```
$ curl -s http://slave1:5051/monitor/statistics.json | python -m json.tool
```

Now that you've seen how Mesos schedules and allocates resources and uses containers to isolate workloads running on a single machine, let's explore how it does all of this in a fault-tolerant and highly available manner.

4.3   *Understanding fault tolerance and high availability*

By design, Mesos provides a fault-tolerant environment for running applications. The Mesos services—the master daemon and the slave daemon—operate in a distributed and highly available manner, ensuring that no one component can cause an outage of the entire cluster. Let's take a look at figure 4.3, which explores the fault-tolerant and highly available properties of various Mesos cluster components.

> **Fault tolerance vs. high availability**
>
> The terms *fault tolerance* and *high availability* are closely related, and are often used interchangeably. But they're two separate ideas. Before continuing, let's take a moment to come to an understanding on how they're used throughout this section:
>
> *Fault tolerance (FT)*—The ability for a system to gracefully handle (and recover from) a failure in one or more of its components.
>
> *High availability (HA)*—The ability for a system to be operational for long periods of time; aims for availability (uptime) to be as close to 100% as possible.

This section presents how various Mesos components—frameworks, masters, and slaves—handle and recover from failure.

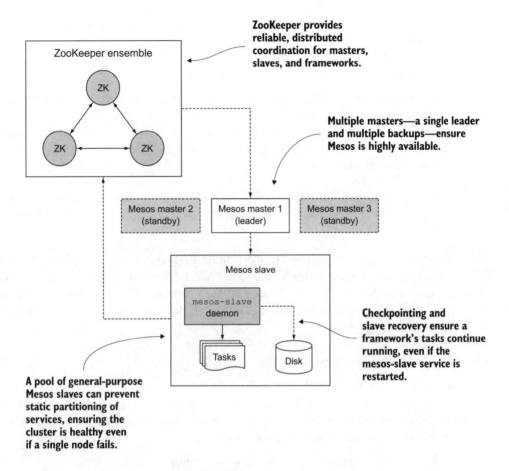

Figure 4.3   The fault-tolerant and highly available properties of various Mesos cluster components

4.3.1   Fault tolerance

To gracefully handle failures, Mesos implements two features (both enabled by default) known as *checkpointing* and *slave recovery*. Checkpointing, a feature enabled in both the framework and on the slave, allows certain information about the state of the cluster to be persisted periodically to disk. The checkpointed data includes information on the tasks, executors, and status updates. Slave recovery allows the mesos-slave daemon to read the state from disk and reconnect to running executors and tasks should the Mesos slave daemon fail or be restarted.

> **WARNING**   As of Mesos 0.22.2, slave recovery will fail if the configured resources are changed and the mesos-slave service is restarted, even if the new resources are a superset of the original resources (for example, increasing

the cpus resource from 8 to 16). For more information, see https://issues
.apache.org/jira/browse/MESOS-1739.

4.3.2 *High availability*

To ensure that Mesos is highly available to applications that use it as a cluster manager,
the Mesos masters use a single leader and multiple standby masters, ready to take over
in the event that the leading master fails. The masters use a ZooKeeper ensemble to
coordinate leadership among multiple nodes, and Mesos slaves and frameworks query
ZooKeeper to determine the leading master.

> **TIP** Remember that the number of Mesos master machine failures toler-
> ated for the cluster is based on the size of the master quorum, as discussed
> in chapter 3.

Through checkpointing, slave recovery, multiple masters, and coordination through
ZooKeeper, the Mesos cluster is able to tolerate failures without impacting the overall
health of the cluster. Because of this graceful handling of failures, Mesos is able to be
upgraded without downtime as well. Let's take a look now at how the cluster handles
failures and upgrades.

4.3.3 *Handling failures and upgrades*

A number of events typically cause downtime and outages for infrastructure, including network partitions, machine failures, power outages, and so on. For the purposes
of this section, you'll explore fault tolerance and high availability in Mesos within the
context of three potential failure scenarios:

- Machine failure—The underlying physical or virtual host fails.
- Service (process) failure—The mesos-master or mesos-slave daemon fails.
- Upgrades—The mesos-master or mesos-slave daemon is upgraded and
  restarted.

Fortunately, Mesos and Mesos frameworks are capable of handling each of these failure modes. Table 4.1 presents the various Mesos components that are involved in a
given failure scenario, and whether failover is possible for each of them.

Table 4.1 How Mesos frameworks, masters, and slaves handle typical failure scenarios. Yes/No denotes
whether failover is possible for the given component and failure scenario.

Failure scenario	Framework failover	Master failover	Slave failover
Machine failure	Yes	Yes	No
Service failure	Yes	Yes	Yes
Upgrade	Yes	Yes	Yes

NOTE   Before performing an upgrade, be sure to consult the latest upgrade documentation, located at http://mesos.apache.org/documentation/latest/upgrades.

FRAMEWORK FAILOVER

Because *frameworks* is just the Mesos term for distributed applications that use Mesos as a cluster manager, framework failover would occur similarly to any other HA setup: a single instance of the framework's scheduler is elected the leader and registered to the Mesos master, while several other instances, presumably running on separate machines, serve as backups.

If the machine running one of the framework instances fails, or the framework service is otherwise unavailable, one of the standby instances can become the leader and reregister itself to the Mesos master. This usually requires some sort of external data store (such as ZooKeeper) for coordinating leadership among the multiple instances of the framework and maintaining a small amount of shared state between the various instances.

TIP   For more information on how ZooKeeper can be used for leader election, see http://zookeeper.apache.org/doc/current/recipes.html#sc_leader-Election.

Let's look at figure 4.4, which demonstrates what a framework failover might look like.

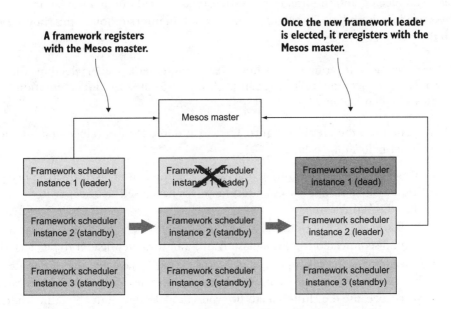

Figure 4.4   When a highly available framework scheduler fails, another instance can reregister to the Mesos master without interrupting any of the running tasks.

Let's break down the events in the figure:

1 Framework scheduler instance 1 is currently the leader, as decided by a prior leader election. It's registered to the leading Mesos master.
2 Framework scheduler instance 1 goes offline.
3 A leader election takes place among the framework scheduler instances. The new leader reregisters to the Mesos master with the same ID, and normal operation resumes.

This assumes that the framework scheduler is developed and deployed in a manner that allows for it to be highly available. Just because Mesos allows for a framework to reregister with the Mesos master doesn't mean that the framework is capable of doing so if its scheduler fails. But Mesos does provide a way for a scheduler to reregister to a new leading master in the event that the leading Mesos master fails. Let's take a look at this next.

MASTER FAILOVER

The Mesos masters all use ZooKeeper for leader election, with one master serving as the leader, and the remaining masters serving as backups or standby masters. Mesos slaves and frameworks also use ZooKeeper to determine the leading master. If a Mesos master fails (either due to a machine failure or a service failure), the frameworks and slaves detect that they've been disconnected from the master and use ZooKeeper to determine the new leading master. Once the new leading Mesos master has been elected and the framework reregisters, normal operation resumes and new tasks can be scheduled. This all happens without an interruption of the running tasks on the cluster.

> **TIP**   For more information on how Mesos implements leader election with ZooKeeper, see the following: http://mesos.apache.org/documentation/latest/high-availability.

Let's break down the events in figure 4.5, which demonstrates (albeit at a high level) what master failover looks like:

1 Mesos master 1 is currently acting as the leading master, as decided from a prior leader election. The slaves and frameworks have used ZooKeeper to determine that this is the leader.
2 Mesos master 1 goes offline. Slaves and frameworks have detected that they've been disconnected from the master, and wait for a new leader to be elected.
3 A leader election takes place, and Mesos master 2 is elected the leader. Remember that in this three-master scenario (quorum=2), no additional failures can take place, because the cluster needs two votes to make decisions about the leader.
4 Mesos slaves and frameworks detect the new leading master, reregister with the new leader, and resume normal operation. They can now receive resource offers.

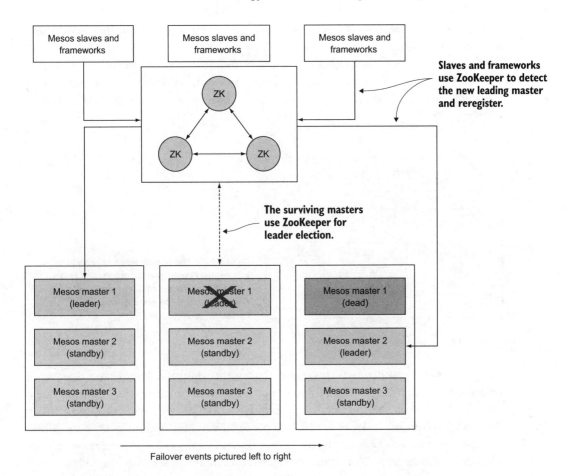

Figure 4.5 When the leading Mesos master fails, the surviving masters use ZooKeeper to elect a new leader. The slaves and frameworks use ZooKeeper to detect the new leader and reregister.

When performing cluster software upgrades, the Mesos masters need to be upgraded first, as documented in the upgrades section of chapter 3. If possible, it's a good idea to upgrade the standby masters first so that only one failover needs to take place in the Mesos master quorum in order for the upgrade to take effect.

SLAVE FAILOVER

Running (live) executors and tasks are capable of surviving a failure or restart/ upgrade of the mesos-slave daemon by checkpointing certain information about the tasks and executors to disk. It's worth remembering that in the event of a full system reboot, slave recovery isn't possible because the executors and tasks will have been killed along with the mesos-slave daemon. If the entire machine fails, the scheduler will detect the failure and reschedule the tasks on other machines in the cluster.

Otherwise, slave recovery is a useful feature for performing rolling upgrades of the Mesos cluster software.

The Mesos slave checkpoints information about the executors and tasks to disk, as shown in figure 4.6. If the `mesos-slave` daemon is unavailable, the executor automatically caches any status updates from the running tasks until the slave daemon starts again.

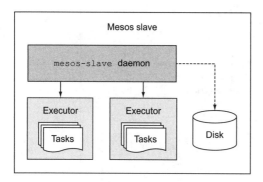

Figure 4.6 The Mesos slave checkpoints information about the executors and tasks to disk. This allows tasks to continue running, even if the slave daemon is restarted or upgraded.

Figure 4.7 walks you through the events that occur when the Mesos slave daemon is unavailable, either due to a scheduled upgrade or due to the process quitting unexpectedly (crashing). Note that this process is the default behavior of Mesos, which aims to keep running tasks up as much as possible. You may optionally have the Mesos slave process kill old executors by using the configuration option `--recover=cleanup`, which may also be useful for future, backward-incompatible software upgrades.

Let's break down the events in the figure:

1 The `mesos-slave` daemon is running and connected to its executors and tasks, providing regular updates to the Mesos master.
2 The `mesos-slave` daemon goes offline, for any number of reasons—the process could die from an unhandled error condition (crash), or perhaps the slave is being reconfigured or upgraded. Regardless, it loses the connection to its running tasks.
3 The tasks continue running for the duration of the `recovery_timeout` option, which defaults to 15 minutes. If the executors can't connect to the slave daemon within the allotted time, they will self-terminate. While the slave is offline, the executor driver caches status updates, and the frameworks and executors themselves continue operating normally.
4 The `mesos-slave` daemon comes back online, reads any information that was previously checkpointed to disk, and reconnects to the running tasks.

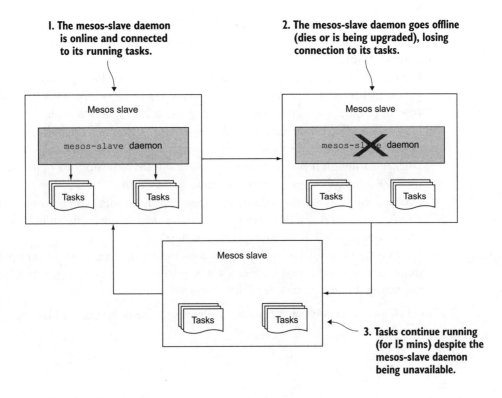

1. The mesos-slave daemon is online and connected to its running tasks.

2. The mesos-slave daemon goes offline (dies or is being upgraded), losing connection to its tasks.

3. Tasks continue running (for 15 mins) despite the mesos-slave daemon being unavailable.

Figure 4.7 Slave recovery allows tasks to continue running despite the `mesos-slave` daemon being unavailable.

NOTE For slave recovery to work, the `mesos-slave` daemon must reconnect to the master within 75 seconds. In Mesos 0.22.2, this is currently a hardcoded time-out, but will be configurable in future versions of Mesos (see https://issues.apache.org/jira/browse/MESOS-2110). Fortunately, modern service systems such as systemd and Upstart have options to automatically respawn failed processes. Alternately, you could use a tool such as Monit to ensure that the service is always running, or a configuration management tool such as Puppet, Chef, or Ansible to manage slave configuration, upgrades, and service restarts automatically.

4.4 Summary

In this chapter, you built upon the knowledge gained in the first three chapters of the book and learned how Mesos operates under the hood. Here are a few things to remember:

- Mesos slaves offer their resources to the leading Mesos master, which in turn offers resources to the registered frameworks. Frameworks can accept either all of the resources in the offer or a subset. If a subset of the resources is accepted, the remaining (unallocated) resources can then be offered to another framework.

- Various aspects of a Mesos slave can be customized, including resources, attributes, and roles. It's possible to create static resource reservations for a given role, but doing so could lead to decreased use of the system overall.

- On a given Mesos slave, using containers isolates multiple workloads. Examples of supported container technologies are Linux control groups (cgroups) and Docker. Although it isn't enabled by default, Mesos also supports per-container network monitoring and egress rate limiting on Linux.

- *Fault tolerance* is the ability of a system to gracefully handle (and recover from) a failure in one or more of its components. *High availability* is the ability for a system to be operational for long periods of time.

- Mesos is highly available and provides a fault-tolerant environment for applications. It can handle machine failures, service failures, and upgrades without impacting the overall health of the cluster.

The next chapter covers logging options and methods for debugging a Mesos cluster.

Logging and debugging

Now that you've learned what it takes to get a Mesos cluster up and running and how it provides a fault-tolerant environment for running applications, let's dive into how to debug and troubleshoot the services and workloads on a Mesos cluster. This chapter presents some of the logging options and log file locations for Mesos cluster nodes and frameworks. It then discusses methods and tools available for troubleshooting and debugging a Mesos cluster, using both the Mesos web interface and the command line.

This chapter is split into two main sections: logging and debugging. The first section covers the various log files, their locations, and options for configuring them. The second section builds on the first and teaches you how to debug issues and observe output from running tasks by using the Mesos web interface and command-line tools.

I've structured this chapter using a tutorial-like approach, walking you through the various methods to get information about the cluster. I hope you'll find this approach useful when you're attempting to troubleshoot cluster issues in your own environments.

5.1 *Understanding and configuring Mesos logging*

The log files that a service generates can be just as important as the service itself. Many times, log files aren't used; they're rotated away, or shipped to centralized logging services to be forgotten. But when problems arise, useful and detailed logging is invaluable to the troubleshooting process.

Luckily, Mesos is a great example of logging done right. The log files are helpful and provide enough information to inform systems administrators of exactly what's happening. For the more advanced operator or developer, Mesos logs even provide the filename and line of code that triggered the event to be logged in the first place.

> **NOTE** Although ZooKeeper is a service that Mesos depends on, it's still considered separate from Mesos itself. As such, this chapter doesn't include information on ZooKeeper cluster logging or debugging. You might consider consulting the ZooKeeper Administrator's Guide: http://zookeeper.apache .org/doc/current/zookeeperAdmin.html.

Let's take a look at the various log files available, for both Mesos cluster services and for a framework's tasks.

5.1.1 *Locating and interpreting log files*

Mesos provides system administrators a lot of flexibility when it comes to managing logs. Events can be written to Mesos-managed log files on disk or to the system log (syslog). The service scripts provided with Mesosphere's Mesos packages also ensure that the logs from the Mesos master and slave services are sent to syslog, thus allowing them to be easily collected and parsed by a log management service such as Logstash or Splunk.

In addition to service logs, Mesos provides two default log files in each task's sandbox: stdout and stderr. These two special files capture any console output to standard output (stdout) and standard error (stderr), respectively. This allows you to view a task's—or command's—console output without needing access to the console of the machine that the task is running on.

LOG FILES FOR MESOS SERVICES

Both the Mesos master and slave use the `--log_dir` configuration option to define where the log files for Mesos services are stored on disk. Typically, this is set to a value such as `/var/log/mesos`, but could alternately be omitted to log to standard error. If Mesos manages the log files for you, they're automatically rotated based on size, but you'll want to ensure that the old files are pruned on a regular basis.

> **TIP** Don't worry about the logging configuration for now; I'll cover it in the next section.

When the `mesos-master` or `mesos-slave` service first starts up, it outputs some information about the format of the log file. Let's take a look at the log file format now.

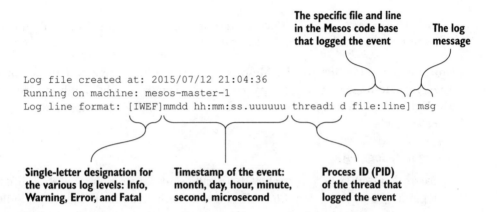

Following the format that was just described, here are a few lines from a log file on a Mesos slave:

```
I0713 00:35:04.730430  2217 containerizer.cpp:1123] Executor for container
    'cc538d82-c47b-4b9e-a050-6b6161f658c5' has exited
I0713 00:35:04.730542  2217 containerizer.cpp:918] Destroying container
    'cc538d82-c47b-4b9e-a050-6b6161f658c5'
```

In these two log file entries, you can see that a task has finished (the executor for a container has exited), and Mesos destroys the now-unused container. Each of these entries includes a timestamp, process ID, and the file and line number that performed the action.

LOG FILES FOR TASKS

As mentioned previously, Mesos automatically creates two files in a task's working directory, or sandbox: stdout and stderr. These files sit alongside the other files required by the task in the sandbox. You'll recall that the location of the Mesos slave's working directory on disk was configured by using the `--work_dir` configuration option, so if you configured the Mesos slave's `work_dir` to be `/var/lib/mesos`, the path to a task's sandbox will resemble the following:

```
/var/lib/mesos/slaves
└── <slave-id>/
    └── frameworks/
        └── <framework-id>/
            └── executors/
                └── <task-name>/
                    └── runs/
```

```
├─ <run-id>/
│    ├─ stderr
│    └─ stdout
└─ latest
```

TIP   The `latest` file mentioned in the preceding output is a symbolic link (symlink) to the full path of the last run ID.

Now unlike the log files for the Mesos services, these files are automatically pruned when the Mesos slave performs its garbage collection on old sandbox directories, which defaults to one week, but may occur more often based on the amount of disk space available.

5.1.2   *Configuring logging*

There are a number of approaches that systems administrators take when it comes to logging. Some have log files live on the individual host, being periodically cleaned up by a tool like Logrotate. Others have centralized logging collection systems such as Logstash, Splunk, or even just a centralized Rsyslog server. Mesos provides various options with which to configure its logging, thereby giving system administrators some flexibility in how the logs from a Mesos cluster are managed in their environments.

Let's take a look at some of these options, and when and why you might need to modify them:

- `log_dir`—Writes log files to a specific directory on disk. If not specified, no logs will be written to disk, but events will still be logged to stderr. This option applies to both the master and the slave, and has no default.
- `logging_level`—Only logs messages at (or above) this level of severity. Possible values (in increasing order of severity): `INFO`, `WARNING`, and `ERROR`. This option applies to both the master and the slave, and defaults to `INFO`.
- `work_dir`—When configured on the slave, specifies the location on disk for the frameworks' working (sandbox) directories, which contain the tasks' stdout and stderr log files. Defaults to `/tmp/mesos`.
- `external_log_file`—Specifies the path to an externally managed log file to display in the web interface and HTTP API. This could be useful if you're using the Logger utility to write messages to the system log, or log files not managed by Mesos. This option applies to both the master and the slave, and has no default.
- `quiet`—When specified, disables logging to stderr. This option applies to both the master and the slave, and isn't present by default.
- `logbufsecs`—Number of seconds to buffer log messages before flushing them to disk. This option applies to both the master and the slave, and defaults to `0` (flushes log messages to disk immediately).

Using these options, you can fine-tune the nature of Mesos service logging to fit well with your logging infrastructure, no matter what your preferred methods are. Personally, I like using the Elasticsearch, Logstash, and Kibana (ELK) stack to collect, parse, and index log entries, allowing you to easily search and visualize log entries as data.

Now that you've learned a bit about Mesos log file locations and the relevant configuration options, let's look at some methods and tools available for observing output, troubleshooting, and otherwise debugging a Mesos cluster.

5.2   *Debugging a Mesos cluster and its tasks*

Working with and troubleshooting distributed systems, especially those such as Mesos that can operate at scale, can be difficult. Generally speaking, the larger a cluster is, the harder it is to correlate events across all nodes. And as is Mesos's nature, larger clusters lead to better overall resource use and reduce static partitioning.

A quick note on centralized logging

Because Mesos clusters are made up of tens, hundreds, or even thousands of machines, and log files are stored on the various cluster nodes, troubleshooting issues can be a rather tedious process. Fortunately, a few options are available for the centralized processing and management of logs:

- Elasticsearch, Logstash, and Kibana (commonly referred to as ELK)
- Splunk
- Rsyslog forwarding to a central server

Each of these options runs a small service on each machine which then processes log files and forwards them to a centralized logging infrastructure. This allows you to store log files in a structured and searchable way, within a single data store, and easily search for and display log entries from a single console.

Setting up these tools is outside the scope of this text, but an internet search will quickly turn up numerous resources for online documentation and entire books written on these topics.

Although Mesos schedules resources and handles failure for you, at times you'll need to debug failures, or access information about the cluster and its workloads. It's helpful to know where to start debugging and what to check next. Figure 5.1 provides an example of one such troubleshooting workflow.

Before you even start debugging Mesos itself, you should ensure that the Mesos services are running and determine their current configuration. In the following example, I'm running both the master and the slave on the same machine, so both processes appear in the output of the commands `ps -ef` and `ps aux` (depending on your preference of arguments to `ps`). The configuration options have been omitted

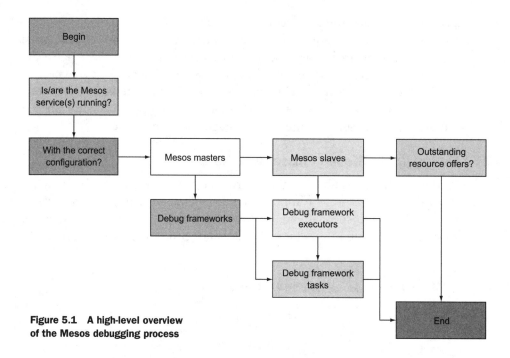

Figure 5.1 A high-level overview of the Mesos debugging process

for brevity, but would otherwise appear as arguments to the `mesos-master` and `mesos-slave` executables:

```
$ ps -ef | grep mesos
UID        PID  PPID  C STIME TTY          TIME CMD
root      2136     1  0 Jul12 ?        00:00:58 /usr/sbin/mesos-master ...
root      2195     1  4 Jul12 ?        00:14:58 /usr/sbin/mesos-slave  ...
```

If either the mesos-master or mesos-slave services fail to start, it's generally a good idea to start by looking in the system log for any problems. On RHEL (and derivatives), this is located at /var/log/messages; on Ubuntu, this is /var/log/syslog. With the Mesosphere packages having the Mesos services log to standard error by default, service start failures will appear in the system log and should point you toward the issue.

In addition to ensuring that the processes are up and running with the desired configuration and observing any service-related output in the syslog or systemd's journal, the remainder of this section teaches you the various tools and methods available to narrow down and troubleshoot problems.

5.2.1   *Using the Mesos web interface*

Mesos provides a web interface for administrators to gain insight into the state of the cluster, including its running and completed tasks. The web interface can be accessed on any of the masters by navigating to http://mesos-master.example.com:5050. If you happen to connect to a nonleading master, you'll receive a notification and automatically be redirected to the current leading master.

> **TIP**   Mesos also has a useful JSON-based REST API. You can find more information about the available endpoints by visiting http://mesos-master.example .com:5050/help on the masters and http://mesos-slave.example.com:5051/ help on the slaves. Chapter 6 provides more details on the endpoints available in this API.

The web interface contains various tabs, allowing you to observe the current state of the cluster or dig deeper into the current state of frameworks, slaves, and running and completed tasks. In the next few sections, you'll explore the information available so that you can quickly and successfully observe output from tasks and troubleshoot issues.

HOME

The main Mesos tab of the Mesos web interface shows active and completed tasks, in addition to cluster information and statistics. This page is where your web-based troubleshooting will begin; from this page, you can dig deeper into running frameworks, tasks, and slaves.

In figure 5.2, you can see two tasks in the state RUNNING. Other task states include STAGING, FINISHED, FAILED, KILLED, and LOST, and will appear throughout the web interface.

This particular page provides a lot of information about the state of your cluster. Let's look at the information available in the sidebar to the left of the page, starting at the top:

- *General cluster information*—Cluster name, version, build date, service start time, and leader election time
- *Log*—Opens a new window with live-updating logs from the Mesos master (assuming either the `log_dir` or `external_log_file` configuration options are set)
- *Cluster statistics*—A snapshot of the current cluster statistics, including number of active slaves, number of tasks (organized by their state), and cluster resources (total, used, offered, and idle CPUs and memory)

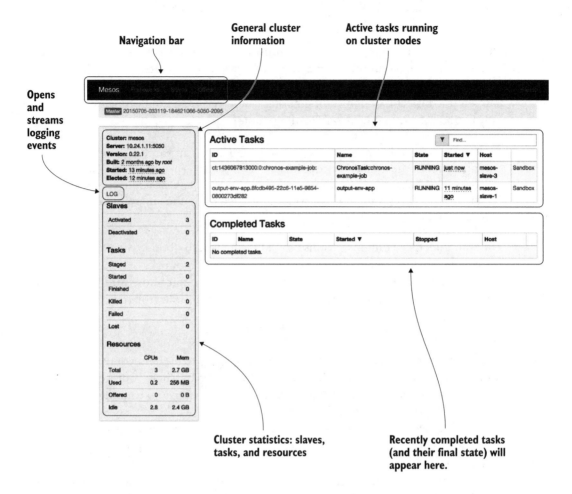

Figure 5.2   The main page of the Mesos web interface provides insight into the current state of the cluster.

In the main body of the page, you can observe active and completed tasks, as well as their states and links to their sandboxes. You can debug a specific task by clicking the link containing the task's ID. Or to have a look at the contents of the container, including console output, click the Sandbox link. I'll go over these two features in more detail a little later in this section.

FRAMEWORKS

The Frameworks tab lists active and terminated frameworks as well as their allocated and consumed resources. On this page, you can also see the date and time when the framework registered, or if it disconnected or failed over when it reregistered.

TIP By clicking any of the relative times in the web interface (such as "2 minutes ago"), the web interface will display the actual time instead of the relative time.

For example: in figure 5.3, you can see the Marathon framework is using 0.1 CPUs, 128 MB memory, and has 1 active task.

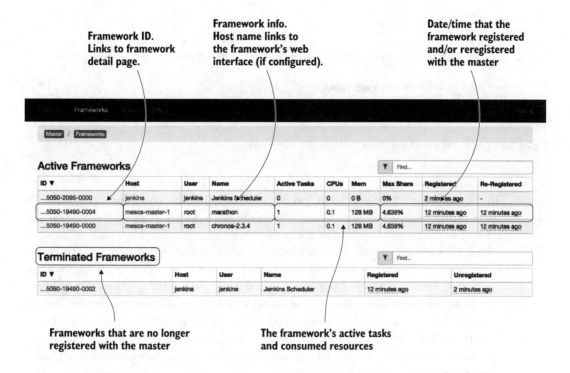

Figure 5.3   The Frameworks page shows registered and terminated frameworks. It also includes information about the number of active tasks, consumed resources, and the date and time that the framework registered.

Clicking the link for a particular framework ID takes you to another page listing the framework's tasks, along with their current or final state. If the framework registered a URL, clicking the link in the Host column will take you to that application's web interface.

TASKS

After navigating to the framework-level view, you'll observe active and completed tasks for that framework, in addition to framework information such as name, user, and web UI. Figure 5.4 shows an example.

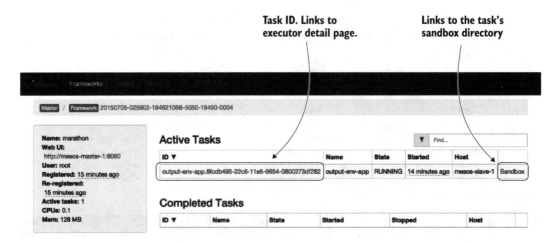

Figure 5.4   Active and completed tasks for a specific framework

To debug a particular task for a framework, click the link containing the task's ID. More information about the task appears in the sidebar to the left, including executor name and consumed CPU and memory resources.

Each task runs in a sandboxed environment or dedicated working directory, but still has access to tools and libraries available on the host system, with one notable exception: processes run in Docker containers have access only to the tools and libraries inside the container. When Mesos launches a Docker container, however, it automatically mounts the task's sandbox directory inside the container so that you can use features such as the Mesos fetcher to download files to the task's sandbox.

In the Mesos web interface, the Sandbox link for a particular task opens a graphical file browser, as shown in figure 5.5.

Clicking the stderr or stdout links brings up a new window with the log output updating in real time. To download the log files for further analysis with your favorite tools, click the Download link to the right.

SLAVES

The Slaves tab, shown in figure 5.6, lists the machines in the cluster that are offering resources to the cluster's frameworks. On this page, you can view the slaves registered with the cluster, and their aggregate resources.

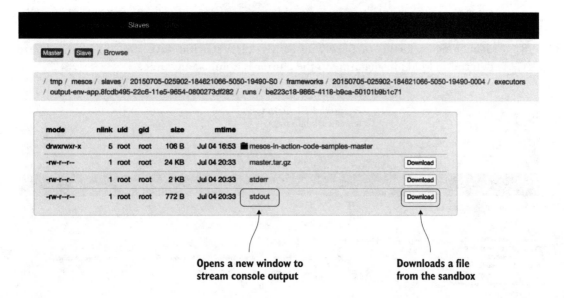

Figure 5.5   The Mesos web interface allows you to access a task's working directory, including the console logs.

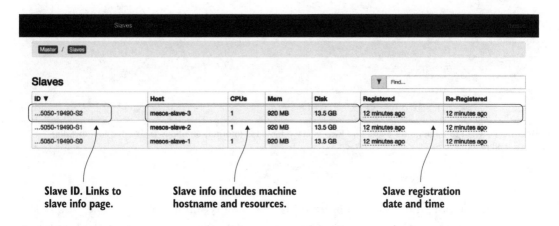

Figure 5.6   The Slaves page lists the Mesos slaves registered with the cluster. It includes the slave ID, hostname, resources, and the registration date and time.

Clicking a slave's ID takes you to another page, shown in figure 5.7, where you can view the frameworks actively using resources on that particular slave. This is useful for debugging problems or observing activity on a specific slave, and for being able to determine what any machine in the cluster is doing at any time.

Framework ID. Links to framework info page.

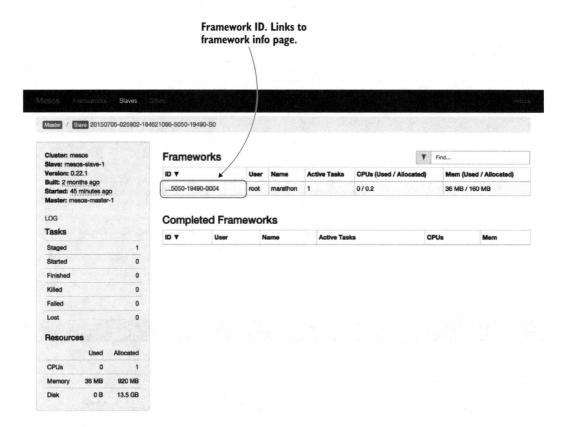

Figure 5.7   The status page for a specific Mesos slave includes information about the active frameworks, tasks, and resources.

In this case, the only framework using this slave is Marathon. If you click the link to Marathon's framework ID, you can look at the executors launched by the framework. Digging one level deeper, you can see the running tasks, their states, and the resources they're consuming (see figure 5.8).

Executor info

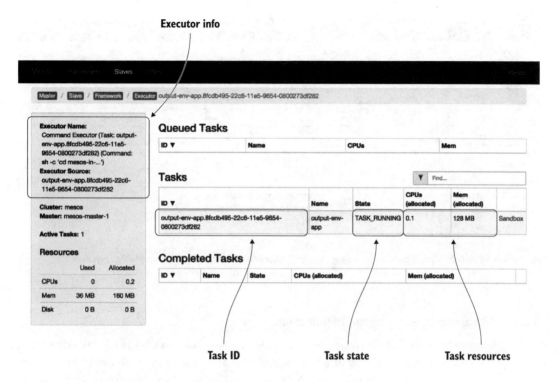

Figure 5.8 Executor/task detail page for a specific framework on a specific slave

OFFERS

The Offers tab lists outstanding offers on the cluster—resource offers that have been offered by the Mesos master to a framework, but haven't yet been accepted or declined by a framework's scheduler. You can see that the framework in figure 5.9, Bad-SchedulerExample, has been offered a number of resources that it hasn't yet accepted or declined.

Generally speaking, all the information you should need to observe a cluster's current state is available in the web interface. But for those of you who feel more comfortable working with the command line, Mesos also has command-line tools that provide roughly the same amount of information. Now that you've learned the general process for debugging a Mesos cluster and its frameworks using the web interface, let's look at some of the built-in command-line tools that are bundled with Mesos. These tools enable you to follow the same general debugging process, but from the command line instead of the web interface.

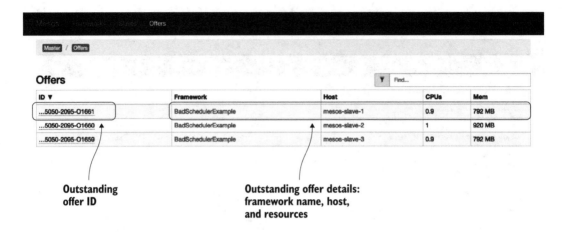

Figure 5.9 The Offers page lists outstanding resource offers that have not been accepted or rejected.

5.2.2 *Using the built-in command-line tools*

Mesos includes built-in command-line tools for those of you who prefer working from the command line instead of a web browser, in addition to the web interface and the HTTP API. It's worth noting that the tools that I'm about to cover in this section are available only if Mesos is also installed on the system.

OVERVIEW

Similar to their GNU core utilities (coreutils) counterparts, Mesos provides a small set of command-line tools for managing your cluster—and working with files and processes—from the console. These tools include the following:

- `mesos cat`—Concatenates and prints a file for a specific task.
- `mesos execute`—Launches a one-off command on the cluster.
- `mesos ps`—Similar to the Linux and UNIX tool `ps`, this command outputs a list of running tasks on the cluster.
- `mesos resolve`—Queries a master or ZooKeeper to determine the current leading master.
- `mesos scp`—Copies a local file (or files) to a remote directory on all the slaves known by the Mesos master.
- `mesos tail`—Similar to the UNIX `tail` command, concatenates and prints the last 10 lines of a file for a specific task.

For a complete list of available commands, run the command `mesos help`.

EXAMPLES

To better illustrate the use of some of these command-line tools, I thought it best to include a few real-world examples. In each of the commands that follow, both Zoo-Keeper and the Mesos master are running on the same host: mesos.example.com. Note that I've omitted the output from each command for brevity.

Output the currently running tasks on the cluster:

```
$ mesos ps --master=zk://mesos.example.com:2181/mesos
```

Determine the current leading master:

```
$ mesos resolve zk://mesos.example.com:2181/mesos
```

Launch a one-off command on the cluster, taking note of the framework ID that's output when the task is run. You'll need this framework ID for the next example:

```
$ mesos execute --command="echo 'Hello, Mesos'" --name=HelloMesos
➥ --master=$(mesos resolve zk://mesos.example.com:2181/mesos)
```

And finally, to observe the standard output from the command you just ran, run the following command. Be sure to replace the value of the --framework argument with the framework ID from the previous example:

```
$ mesos cat --master=$(mesos resolve zk://mesos.example.com:2181/mesos)
➥ --framework=20150712-210436-16842879-5050-2136-0002
➥ --task=HelloMesos --file=stdout
```

These built-in Mesos command-line tools are great if you prefer working in a terminal. But a few limitations exist, one being that Mesos must be installed on the system. In reality, most systems administrators prefer to debug systems from their individual laptop or workstation, and might not want to log in to production infrastructure to run some debugging tools, or to install Mesos locally.

Fortunately, the folks at Mesosphere have developed their own Mesos command-line tools that interact with Mesos remotely. These tools allow you to use the same commands you've learned about so far, but without needing to install Mesos. Let's take a look.

5.2.3 *Using Mesosphere's mesos-cli tool*

The team at Mesosphere has developed a Python-based, cluster-wide debugging tool for Mesos aptly named mesos-cli. It allows you to run commands against the Mesos cluster from your laptop or workstation, without needing to install Mesos itself. The tool reimplements some of the command-line tools mentioned in the preceding section in a more user-friendly way.

mesos-cli is available via the Python Package Index (PyPI), and you can install it on your workstation by running the following command:

```
$ sudo pip install mesos.cli
```

NOTE If the Python `pip` tool isn't already installed on your system, please refer to https://pip.pypa.io/en/stable/installing/ for instructions on how to install it.

After installation is complete, you'll have a new executable located at /usr/local/bin/mesos. As long as the directory /usr/local/bin appears early in your `$PATH`, the mesos-cli executable `mesos` should now supersede Mesos' built-in command-line tools. Now, let's take a look at some of the commands available in mesos-cli.

OVERVIEW

Similar to their coreutils counterparts and the relevant tools bundled with Mesos itself, I've included some of the popular mesos-cli subcommands here:

- `mesos cat`—Concatenates and prints a file for a specific task.
- `mesos config`—Configures the mesos-cli tool from the command line.
- `mesos events`—Chronologically streams master and slave logs in real time from nodes in the cluster.
- `mesos find`—Given a task ID, finds and lists files in the sandbox.
- `mesos head`—Similar to the Linux and UNIX equivalent, outputs the first several lines of a file.
- `mesos ls`—Similar to `mesos find`, lists all the files in a task's sandbox.
- `mesos ps`—Similar to the Linux and UNIX equivalent, outputs a list of running tasks on the cluster. Can also output inactive tasks using the `-i` argument.
- `mesos resolve`—Queries a master or ZooKeeper to determine the current leading master.
- `mesos scp`—Copies a local file (or files) to a remote directory on all the slaves known by the Mesos master.
- `mesos ssh`—Given a task ID, allows you to SSH directly to the sandbox of a particular task. Note that this command assumes you already have SSH access to the nodes in the cluster.
- `mesos state`—Outputs the current state of a master or slave in the cluster in JSON format.
- `mesos tail`—Similar to the Linux and UNIX equivalent, outputs the last several lines of a file.

TIP If you prefer to have these commands available for tab completion in your shell, you're in luck! For the Bash shell, add the following line to ~/.bash _profile: `complete -C mesos-completion mesos`

For a complete list of the available commands in mesos-cli, run the command `mesos help`.

EXAMPLES

To better illustrate the use of some of the command-line tools mentioned in the preceding section, I thought it best to include a few real-world examples. In each of the commands that follow, both ZooKeeper and the Mesos master are running on the same host: mesos.example.com. Note that I've omitted the output from each command for brevity.

> **TIP** You can get the usage for each of the commands mentioned previously by running `mesos <subcommand> --help`.

Configure the URL that mesos-cli will use to determine the leading master:

```
$ mesos config master zk://mesos.example.com:2181/mesos
```

Output the currently running commands on the cluster:

```
$ mesos ps
```

Launch a one-off command on the cluster within a Docker image:

```
$ mesos execute --command="cat /etc/redhat-release" --name="releaseTask"
➥ --master=$(mesos resolve) --docker_image="centos:7"
```

And finally, to observe the standard output from the command you just ran:

```
$ mesos cat releaseTask stdout
```

As covered here, the mesos-cli tool provided by Mesosphere builds upon the command-line tools, and allows you to interact with—and otherwise debug—a Mesos cluster and its workloads from the comfort and safety of your individual workstation. Being written in Python, and maintained outside the Mesos code base, it's also easy to customize to suit your needs.

5.3 Summary

In this chapter you learned the various methods and tools with which you can debug a Mesos cluster. This included log file locations, logging configuration options, the Mesos web interface, and various Mesos command-line tools. Here are a few things to remember:

- Mesos provides various configuration options around logging for both the masters and the slaves. You can configure the log locations and levels, and have externally managed (syslog) log files.
- Every Mesos task automatically gets two files: stdout and stderr. These files, located in the sandbox, capture output from stdout and stderr, respectively.
- Before you begin to debug issues, ensure that the `mesos-master` and `mesos-slave` services are running with the desired configuration. You can determine this by observing the output from `ps aux | grep mesos`.

- Mesos provides a web interface and HTTP API that are useful for determining the state of the cluster and assisting with debugging. You can reach the web UI by pointing your browser to http://mesos-master.example.com:5050. If you connect to a nonleading master, you'll automatically be redirected to the leader. The next chapter covers the API.

- Mesos includes built-in command-line tools to assist with debugging and troubleshooting. Mesosphere also provides a Python-based tool called mesos-cli, which can be downloaded from PyPI.

The next chapter finishes up part 2 of the book with information about running Mesos in production. It covers topics such as monitoring, security, and adding, removing, and replacing masters.

Mesos in production

6

This chapter covers

- Monitoring Mesos masters, slaves, and the ZooKeeper ensemble
- Navigating the Mesos REST API
- Adding, removing, and replacing Mesos masters
- Understanding and configuring authentication, authorization, and rate limiting

Congratulations! You've reached the last chapter in part 2 of this book. Up to this point, you've learned how Mesos provides a way to improve datacenter efficiency; how to install and configure Mesos, ZooKeeper, and Docker; how Mesos provides a fault-tolerant environment for applications to run on; and how to interact with and debug a running Mesos cluster.

This chapter—perhaps one of the most important in the book—covers the real world: the monitoring details, quorum changes, and access control rules that you'll need to know in order to fine-tune and run a production Mesos cluster. The content in this chapter will better prepare you and your environment for part 3, in which you'll launch long-running applications and scheduled tasks on the cluster by using the popular Marathon, Chronos, and Aurora frameworks.

6.1 Monitoring the Mesos and ZooKeeper clusters

As you learned previously, Mesos has two main services: `mesos-master` and `mesos-slave`. At the most basic level, you could configure a monitoring system to ensure that these processes are up and running on the systems that make up the Mesos cluster, but we all know that this level of monitoring usually isn't sufficient. Fortunately, Mesos has a rich JSON-based HTTP API that you can query for more information about the health of the cluster.

> **TIP** If you're looking to explore the JSON output from the Mesos API on the command line, you might consider using HTTPie, a human-friendly, cURL-like tool that includes features such as formatted and colorized output. For more information, check out the project at https://github.com/jkbrzt/httpie.

Considering that the Mesos project is under rapid development, it isn't practical to include every little detail about the API in this chapter. The following sections cover the most common—and perhaps most important—knowledge needed to monitor your Mesos and ZooKeeper clusters. You may also want to navigate to the following links to get additional information about endpoints that are available in your specific version of Mesos:

- http://mesos-master.example.com:5050/help
- http://mesos-slave.example.com:5051/help

Additional API reference material can be found in the Mesos online monitoring documentation at http://mesos.apache.org/documentation/latest/monitoring.

6.1.1 Monitoring the Mesos master

Monitoring the few machines that make up the Mesos master quorum is key to ensuring that your cluster continues to provide the level of service your users have come to expect, and that new tasks can be scheduled on the machines that make up the cluster. In many cases, this requires monitoring and metrics beyond basic host monitoring (CPU, memory, disk, network) and process monitoring (the `mesos-master` service).

Although there are many monitoring tools, this section limits coverage to monitoring the Mesos master with Nagios, a popular open source monitoring platform, and querying the Mesos REST API for its available metrics, which will be useful for developing your own monitoring checks.

Forwarding HTTP requests to the leading master

As you learned previously in this book, connecting to a nonleading master's web interface will cause you to be automatically redirected to the leading master. But what happens if you try querying the API of a nonleading master? As of Mesos 0.22.x, the behavior is somewhat unpredictable; chances are that you'll receive incorrect or incomplete data from the API.

To always ensure that you or your monitoring systems are getting accurate data from the leading master, you might consider putting a HAProxy instance in front of your Mesos masters for monitoring and administration purposes.

The following excerpt from a HAProxy configuration file adds each of the Mesos masters to a load-balancing pool. But it also adds a health check, one that only succeeds for the leading master. This way, you can ensure that requests are forwarded only to the leading master, whichever one of the three hosts it might be:

```
listen mesos-master 0.0.0.0:5050
    mode        http
    option      httpclose
    option      forwardfor
    option      httpchk GET /metrics/snapshot
    http-check  expect string "master\/elected":1
    server      mesos-master-1 mesos-master-1.example.com:5050 check
    server      mesos-master-2 mesos-master-2.example.com:5050 check
    server      mesos-master-3 mesos-master-3.example.com:5050 check
```

To ensure that HAProxy doesn't become a single point of failure in your infrastructure, you may want to deploy HAProxy in an active/passive configuration, using Keepalived and a floating IP address across the two instances. Alternately, if you don't want to put an instance of HAProxy in front of your masters, you can query the /master/redirect API endpoint. This endpoint will return an HTTP 307 redirect to the URL of the leading master.

MONITORING THE MESOS MASTER WITH NAGIOS

Nagios, an open source, battle-tested monitoring system, is typically ubiquitous with datacenter and service monitoring. Therefore, it seems only natural to discuss the Nagios options that are available to monitor Mesos.

The team over at OpenTable has created a Nagios check for monitoring a Mesos cluster. You can download the script from https://github.com/opentable/nagios-mesos. It's capable of monitoring the leading master for the following conditions:

- Basic health checks
- That a minimum number of slaves are registered
- That a given framework (or frameworks) is registered

To see a complete list of options, run check_mesos.py --help. Otherwise, the most basic way to use the check_mesos.py script is with the following example:

```
./check_mesos.py --host mesos-master.example.com
```

If you're looking for more information about the cluster or want to develop your own monitoring checks, look no further than the Mesos REST API. You'll explore the available endpoints and the data they return in the next section.

QUERYING THE MESOS MASTER API ENDPOINTS

Mesos provides an extensive REST API that provides information about the cluster. Some of this information includes (but isn't limited to) the following metrics:

- Utilized resources
- Framework messages received and processed (if authentication is enabled)
- System load
- Connected slaves

Because of the project's rapid development, listing all the available API endpoints isn't practical. Table 6.1 includes a few that are the most important.

Table 6.1 Select Mesos master API endpoints

Endpoint	Description
/help	Returns information about the available API endpoints
/metrics/snapshot	Returns a JSON object containing system metrics from the master
/master/health	Returns HTTP 200 (OK) if the master is healthy
/master/redirect	Returns an HTTP 307 (Temporary Redirect) redirect to the URL of the leading master
/master/slaves	Returns information about the connected Mesos slaves

For an extensive list of endpoints, you should visit the /help endpoint, or consult the official Mesos documentation for your particular version.

6.1.2 *Monitoring the Mesos slave*

Monitoring Mesos slaves is (arguably) a bit less critical than the masters because the slaves aren't necessarily responsible for maintaining a quorum and making decisions about where to schedule tasks across the cluster. Nevertheless, the monitoring of these worker machines is as important as any other machine running in production. Without proper monitoring in place for the slaves, you run the risk of running out of resources or filling your disks without so much as a warning.

There aren't any set-in-stone guidelines here; each organization and environment likely has particular thresholds for CPU, memory, and disk usage. Regardless, here are a few suggestions for monitoring checks to perform on any given Mesos slave:

- Ensure that the `mesos-slave` process is running (and that port 5051 is accessible)
- Ensure that the `docker` or `docker.io` process is running (if you're using Docker)
- Monitor basic CPU, memory, disk, and network use, ideally collected and graphed over time
- Monitor per-container metrics (CPU, memory, disk, network)

With the exception of per-container monitoring (covered later in this chapter), these are basic OS-level monitoring checks. Some of these metrics are also exposed over the Mesos slave's metrics endpoint for convenience. Let's now cover the information available to you and your monitoring system via the Mesos slave's REST API.

QUERYING THE MESOS SLAVE API ENDPOINTS

Just as with the Mesos master, the Mesos slave has an extensive REST API that you can query. Unlike the master, which returns cluster-wide metrics, the slave's endpoint returns only information about that particular slave. Because of the project's rapid development cycle, it isn't practical to include information about all the endpoints. Table 6.2 includes a few API endpoints that I find to be the most important for the purposes of this section.

Table 6.2   Select Mesos slave API endpoints

Endpoint	Description
/help	Returns information about the available API endpoints
/metrics/snapshot	Returns a JSON object containing system metrics from the slave
/monitor/statistics.json	Returns a JSON object about resources consumed by containers running on the slave

These endpoints can provide metrics on resource use that you'd normally expect from OS-level monitoring, plus insight into the running containers on a given Mesos slave. For an extensive list of endpoints, you should visit the /help endpoint, or consult the official Mesos documentation for your particular version.

6.1.3   *Monitoring ZooKeeper*

Although this book is predominantly about Mesos, ZooKeeper is critical for coordination and discovery. Therefore, it's important to ensure that ZooKeeper is sufficiently monitored for a stable Mesos deployment. Despite linking you to online ZooKeeper documentation in previous chapters, I thought it best to at least point you in the right direction in terms of ZooKeeper monitoring within this chapter.

> **NOTE**   The remainder of this section assumes you're using ZooKeeper 3.4.0 or later.

MONITORING AND MANAGING ZOOKEEPER WITH EXHIBITOR

To monitor and manage ZooKeeper installations, the team over at Netflix has developed and open sourced a tool they've named Exhibitor. Citing the project page, Exhibitor is "a supervisor system for Apache ZooKeeper." It provides system administrators cluster-wide management and monitoring features such as the following:

- Ensuring that an instance is up and responding to requests
- Performing backup and restore
- Managing cluster-wide configuration
- Exploring a tree of ZNodes via a web interface and REST API

For more information about Exhibitor, including installation and configuration instructions, check out the project page at https://github.com/Netflix/exhibitor.

MONITORING ZOOKEEPER WITH NAGIOS

In addition to Exhibitor, various monitoring scripts are distributed with ZooKeeper. If you installed ZooKeeper from source, or compiled Mesos from source and used the bundled version of ZooKeeper, the monitoring scripts can be found in the src/contrib/monitoring/ directory. Because we covered monitoring Mesos with Nagios already, we'll also cover monitoring ZooKeeper with Nagios.

> **TIP** If you installed ZooKeeper by using a package manager, the monitoring scripts weren't included. You can download the Nagios check for ZooKeeper from https://github.com/apache/zookeeper/tree/trunk/src/contrib/monitoring.

A Nagios check for ZooKeeper, check_zookeeper.py, can be found at src/contrib/monitoring/check_zookeeper.py. The script takes several arguments and can alert you if a particular metric is out of bounds. Example Nagios service configurations are also available in the nagios/ directory and can be used to configure your Nagios server.

   In the following example, I'll call the check_zookeeper.py script directly to illustrate how it works. It'll check a ZooKeeper node's outstanding requests, returning a warning status if the value reaches 10, and a critical status if the value reaches 25:

```
$ python check_zookeeper.py -o nagios -s zk.example.com:2181
➥ -k zk_outstanding_requests -w 10 -c 25
```

This is one example out of many of how you could monitor the health of a ZooKeeper instance. In addition to the number of example service checks provided within the nagios/ directory, you can get the full help and usage output by running the following command:

```
$ python check_zookeeper.py --help
```

You also can write your own Nagios monitoring script by using a series of built-in commands to query ZooKeeper, a few of which I'll cover next.

MONITORING ZOOKEEPER WITH FOUR-LETTER COMMANDS

ZooKeeper can provide certain information about an instance by using a series of four-letter commands issued to the server. Table 6.3 provides details on a select number of these commands that are useful for monitoring purposes.

Table 6.3   Select commands for monitoring ZooKeeper

Command	Description
ruok	Basic health check. Returns imok if the server is up and healthy.
mntr	Returns a tab-separated list of metrics used to monitor a ZooKeeper instance. Some of this information includes the server state (standalone, leader, follower), version, and latency.
srvr	Provides details about the server, including number of connections and mode (leader, follower, standalone).
stat	Returns a list of connected clients and some details on the state of the server.

The four-letter commands are typically sent to a ZooKeeper instance by using the Netcat tool. The following example demonstrates using Netcat to issue the ruok health check command to a ZooKeeper instance listening on port 2181:

```
$ echo 'ruok' | nc zk1.example.com 2181
imok
```

> **TIP**   For a complete list of ZooKeeper commands, see the ZooKeeper Administrator's Guide at http://zookeeper.apache.org/doc/current/zookeeper-Admin.html#sc_zkCommands.

6.2   *Modifying the Mesos master quorum*

At times you might find yourself needing to modify the number of Mesos masters running the cluster. Perhaps this is to replace failed hardware, rebuild a VM on a newer release of an operating system, or provision additional masters to improve your high-availability strategy. This section covers modifications to the number of Mesos masters running a given deployment.

> **Use caution when modifying the master quorum**
>
> Although this section provides instructions for modifying the number of masters and the master quorum size, it's worth taking the time to note a few areas of caution.
>
> The Mesos replicated log isn't capable of zero-downtime reconfiguration, so the masters need to be restarted in order to make changes to the cluster quorum via

(continued)

the --quorum configuration option. You'll learn how to perform this operation later in this section. For more information about online reconfiguration in future releases of Mesos, see https://issues.apache.org/jira/browse/MESOS-683.

Furthermore, Mesos doesn't implement a whitelist for masters that are participating in the quorum. To prevent corruption of the replicated log and potential split-brain scenarios, you need to ensure that the number of masters participating in the quorum doesn't exceed the corresponding quorum size (as referenced in table 6.4). As of Mesos 0.22.*x*, there's an outstanding feature request for Mesos to support such a whitelist. For more information, see https://issues.apache.org/jira/browse/MESOS-1546. To mitigate this risk, you might consider enabling authentication on the ZooKeeper ensemble that you're using for Mesos to prevent unauthenticated masters from joining the quorum.

Failure to follow these basic rules could result in service interruptions. As with any production service, be sure to test changes in a pre-production environment, and proceed with caution when making changes to a production system.

As a reminder from chapter 3, there needs to be an odd number of masters to maintain a quorum; a majority of masters is required to make decisions for the cluster. The quorum size is set on each of the Mesos masters with the --quorum configuration option. For ease of reference, the Mesos master quorum sizing table from chapter 3 is repeated here as table 6.4.

Table 6.4 Mesos master quorum size

Number of Mesos masters	Mesos master quorum	Number of failures tolerated
1	1	0
3	2	1
5	3	2
$2 \times N - 1$	N	$N - 1$

Now that you have some background information (and a few words of caution) about modifying the quorum size, let's go over what it takes to add masters to a cluster. Each of the following sections is presented in an example-like scenario and provides instructions about the steps to perform for each.

6.2.1 Adding masters

There might come a time when you want to increase the number of Mesos masters for additional failover capacity—for example, you might want to be able to tolerate two master machine failures instead of just one. In this scenario, I'll demonstrate how to increase the number of masters from three to five, thus allowing your cluster to tolerate the failure of two of its masters:

1. Currently, you have three Mesos masters running and configured with `--quorum=2`. Reconfigure each of the masters with `--quorum=3` and restart the `mesos-master` service on each of them by running `sudo service mesos-master restart`.

2. Provision two additional masters, also configured with `--quorum=3`, and start the `mesos-master` service by running `sudo service mesos-master start`.

TIP If ZooKeeper is running on the same machines as the Mesos masters, now would be a good time to increase the size of the ZooKeeper ensemble. Generally speaking, this involves configuring the new nodes to join the ensemble, followed by reconfiguring the existing followers, and finally reconfiguring and restarting the current leader. Also, be sure to update the ZooKeeper URL used by the Mesos masters, slaves, and frameworks to include the new members of the ensemble.

6.2.2 Removing masters

Although it's probably rare for someone to need to reduce the quorum size, it's possible to do so. In this scenario, you'll reduce the number of masters from five to three, thus decreasing the number of master machine failures your cluster can tolerate from two to one:

1. Currently, you have five masters running and configured with `--quorum=3`. Remove two of the masters from the cluster, ensuring they will never be brought back online.

2. Reconfigure the three remaining masters with `--quorum=2` and restart the `mesos-master` service on each of them by running `sudo service mesos-master restart`.

6.2.3 Replacing masters

If the need arises to replace one of the masters (removing one master and adding another in its place while maintaining the currently configured quorum size), you should be able to do so without any reconfiguration or downtime. In this scenario, you'll decommission an old master and replace it with a newly provisioned one:

1. Currently, you have three masters running and configured with `--quorum=2`. Remove the master you want to replace, ensuring that it will never rejoin the cluster (delete the virtual machine, wipe hard disks, and so forth).

2. Provision a new Mesos master and configure it with the same quorum value as the rest of the masters—in this case, `--quorum=2`.

3. Start the `mesos-master` service by running `sudo service mesos-master start` and allow the replicated log to catch up with that of the existing masters.

6.3   *Implementing security and access control*

A well-formed security strategy is critical to the security of an organization's infrastructure, and ultimately, its data. Today, we're seeing that a *security-in-layers* approach works best for this, where certain ideas for a given system—such as basic user authentication—are combined with more complex, overarching ideas—such as network segregation, or encryption between hosts and datacenters.

The security model implemented by Mesos can be divided into two discrete concepts that should already be familiar to most of you: *authentication* and *authorization*. Before continuing with this section, though, let's take a moment to clarify these terms.

> **Defining authentication and authorization**
>
> Authentication and authorization are two discrete concepts that play into the security model for controlling access to systems.
>
> An *authentication* mechanism provides a way to identify a user or service, typically (but not always) using a username and password. The credentials entered by the user (or service) are then compared with credentials stored in a database before the request is accepted.
>
> On the other hand, *authorization* is the process for enforcing access control policies. It's a way to define which actions an authenticated (or unauthenticated) user is allowed to perform on a given set of objects.

In Mesos, it's possible not only to enable authentication and authorization for users and systems administrators, but to enforce access control for frameworks and slaves as well. This section presents several features of Mesos that make up security and access control for the cluster: framework authentication and authorization, slave authentication, access control lists, and framework rate limiting.

6.3.1   *Slave and framework authentication*

The ability to authenticate machines and applications is important in any production system. In Mesos, authentication ensures that unauthorized slaves don't join the cluster and that unauthorized frameworks don't consume cluster resources.

Fortunately, Mesos provides a way to enable and configure authentication of slaves and frameworks. It uses the Simple Authentication and Security Layer (SASL) framework, with CRAM-MD5 as the authentication mechanism.

Although most of us are familiar with usernames and passwords for authentication, Mesos uses slightly different terms; usernames are called *principals*, and passwords are called *secrets*. It's worth noting, however, that the principal is different from the framework user (the Linux user running a framework's tasks) and the framework's role (used for resource reservations). This will become apparent a little later in this section.

Using these concepts of principal-secret and challenge-response authentication, let's explore how to configure authentication between masters, slaves, and frameworks. For any master-side security options you set here, you'll need to ensure the configurations are the same across the multiple Mesos masters.

SLAVE AUTHENTICATION

Mesos masters provide a few options for allowing Mesos slaves to participate in the cluster, including whitelisting a set of hosts or requiring slaves to authenticate with a principal and secret. These configuration options are listed in table 6.5.

Table 6.5 Configuration options for slave authentication

Configuration option	Description
whitelist	Takes a path to a file as a parameter. The target file has a list of slaves (one per line) that the master will advertise resource offers for.
credentials	A path to a file on disk containing usernames and passwords (for example, file:///path/to/file).
authenticate_slaves	If set to `true`, only authenticated slaves (those that have credentials present in the credentials file) are allowed to register with the master. The default is `false`, indicating that all slaves are allowed to register.

In addition to these master-side options, you'll also need to provide the Mesos slave with credentials to authenticate with the master. The `--credential` option takes a path to a file on disk containing the Mesos slave authentication credentials.

I thought it best to demonstrate how to configure slave authentication with a short example. On the Mesos master, create a credentials file on disk that resembles the following:

```
{
  "credentials": [
    {
      "principal": "slaveuser",
      "secret":    "slavepass"
    }
  ]
}
```

You can alternately create credential files by using whitespace-separated usernames and passwords, one pair per line:

```
$ echo -n "slaveuser slavepass" > /etc/mesos/secure/credentials
```

> **NOTE** Certain popular editors (Vim and Emacs) automatically insert newlines at the end of a file, which can lead to authentication failures. You can avoid this behavior by opening files in binary mode and explicitly setting the *noeol* option. Alternately, you can use JSON-formatted credentials files.

Then configure the master by using the `--credentials` configuration option and restart the service:

```
--credentials=file:///etc/mesos/secure/credentials
```

To provide the slave with authentication credentials, create a credentials file following the format mentioned earlier:

```
$ echo -n "slaveuser slavepass" > /etc/mesos/secure/slave-credentials
```

The configuration option on the Mesos slave is slightly different from that of the master; on the slave, you'll use the `--credential` configuration option to set the path to the slave's credentials file and then restart the service:

```
--credential=file:///etc/mesos/secure/slave-credentials
```

By following these instructions, you ensure that Mesos slaves can't join a particular cluster unless they've authenticated to the master first. Configuring authentication for frameworks follows a similar approach.

FRAMEWORK AUTHENTICATION

Just as you can require that a Mesos slave authenticate to the master, you can also enable authentication for frameworks as well. To enable authentication for frameworks registering with a Mesos cluster, you need to set a couple of configuration options on the master:

- `--credentials`—As mentioned previously, this option is a path to a file on disk containing usernames and passwords. Regardless of whether you're authenticating slaves or frameworks, all credentials are stored in a single file referenced by this configuration option.
- `--authenticate`—Set this option to `true` in order to allow only authenticated frameworks to register with the cluster.

To reiterate what we covered in the previous section for slave authentication, create a credentials file (or add to an existing credentials file) that resembles the following:

```
{
  "credentials": [
    {
      "principal": "frameworkuser",
      "secret":    "frameworkpass"
    }
  ]
}
```

Then configure the master by using the `--credentials` configuration option, and restart the `mesos-master` service:

```
--credentials=file:///etc/mesos/secure/credentials
```

TIP   Remember to pay attention to the owner, group, and permissions of your credentials files! Because Mesos currently requires that credentials are stored in plain text, you'll want to be sure that only administrators with root-level access can read these files.

The framework registering with the cluster then needs to provide a valid principal and secret in order to authenticate with the cluster. Let's not worry about configuring individual frameworks now, though; part 3 of this book covers that in more detail, when you'll learn about the Marathon, Chronos, and Aurora frameworks.

6.3.2   *Authorization and access control lists*

The Mesos master checks an access control list (ACL) to determine whether a request is permitted. These ACLs consist of a *subject* that can perform an *action* on a specific set of *objects*. The framework *principal* (or user), mentioned previously in the authentication section, is the same principal that you'll use in your ACLs. Consider the following in figure 6.1.

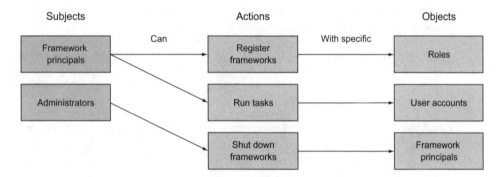

Figure 6.1   A Mesos ACL consists of a subject that can perform an action with specific objects.

For clarity, I didn't use the Mesos terms for the subjects, actions, and objects in the previous graphic, but hopefully you can understand what each is capable of performing. Building upon framework authentication, these ACLs will either permit or deny frameworks and users to perform certain actions on the cluster. In the next few sections, I'll provide some examples of how to write access control lists to define a framework's access to the cluster.

UNDERSTANDING ACCESS CONTROL LISTS

In contrast with some systems that default to least-privilege or most-privilege, Mesos ACLs are matched in the order they're defined: the first ACL that matches the request determines whether the request is authorized. Table 6.6 provides a list of subjects, actions, and objects that make up ACLs.

Table 6.6 Subjects, actions, and objects that make up Mesos ACLs

Subject	Action	Object
principals	register_frameworks	roles
	run_tasks	users
	shutdown_frameworks	framework_principals

As a fallback, it's also possible to provide a `permissive` option in your ACL; this option defines the default behavior in the event a request doesn't match any of the definitions in the ACL. This option defaults to `true`, meaning the action is permitted.

IMPLEMENTING ACCESS CONTROL LISTS

Access control lists are configured on the Mesos masters by using the `--acls` configuration option. This option accepts either a path to a file containing the ACLs (such as file:///etc/mesos/secure/acl) or the JSON-formatted ACL itself.

I believe that the best way to demonstrate the power of the Mesos access control lists is by example. The following examples include several ACL configurations, with short descriptions of what they're trying to accomplish, demonstrating how to limit access to the `run_tasks` and `register_frameworks` actions.

> **TIP**   ACL values are an array of strings, or the special types ANY and NONE. When used with the following ACL examples, ANY is generally permissive (permitting any framework to do something), and NONE is generally restrictive (prohibiting any framework from doing something).

Example 1: Permit the Jenkins framework to run tasks on Mesos slaves as the `jenkins` user on the underlying system. Note that the `jenkins` user must already exist on all of the Mesos slaves in order for this to work:

```
{
  "run_tasks": [
    {
      "principals": { "values": ["jenkins"] },
      "users":      { "values": ["jenkins"] }
    }
  ]
}
```

Example 2: Prevent frameworks from running tasks on Mesos slaves as the `root` user on a system:

```
{
  "run_tasks": [
    {
      "principals": { "type":   "NONE"   },
      "users":      { "values": ["root"] }
    }
  ]
}
```

Example 3: Create a whitelist of the framework principals that may register with a particular role. In this example, only `marathon` is allowed to register with the `prod` role; any requests from other frameworks to register with the `prod` role are rejected:

```
{
  "register_frameworks": [
    {
      "principals": { "values": ["marathon"] },
      "roles":      { "values": ["prod"]     }
    },
    {
      "principals": { "type":   "NONE"    },
      "roles":      { "values": ["prod"] }
    }
  ]
}
```

Example 4: Create a global whitelist for all frameworks across all roles. In this example, the only framework allowed to register with the master is `chronos`, and only with the `batch` role. Any other framework that attempts to register to the cluster, with any role, is denied.

```
{
  "permissive": false,
  "register_frameworks": [
    {
      "principals": { "values": ["chronos"] },
      "roles":      { "values": ["batch"]    }
    }
  ]
}
```

In addition to access control lists that authorize certain framework principals to perform certain actions, such as registering to the cluster with a specific role, Mesos also provides a means to rate-limit the messages coming from the frameworks.

6.3.3 *Framework rate limiting*

In any deployment that runs multiple frameworks, a single bad actor could flood the master with messages, thereby reducing throughput for higher-priority, "production-level" frameworks. Framework rate limiting in Mesos protects these higher-priority frameworks by limiting the number of queries per second—and the number of queued messages—for specific frameworks, as identified by their principal.

By restricting the number of messages processed per second for a given framework, you can be sure that the Mesos master can respond to other frameworks in a timely manner. And by restricting the number of messages that can be queued by the master, you can provide some guarantees about the master's memory usage. I'll explore these two ideas in a bit more detail throughout this section. For now, check

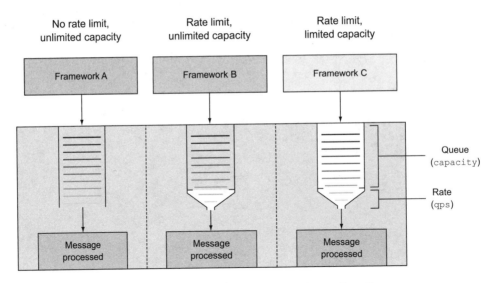

No rate limit,
unlimited capacity

Rate limit,
unlimited capacity

Rate limit,
limited capacity

Framework A

Framework B

Framework C

Queue
(capacity)

Rate
(qps)

Message
processed

Message
processed

Message
processed

Figure 6.2   Combinations of framework rate and capacity-limiting configurations

out figure 6.2, where you can visualize the various combinations of rate limiting and queue capacity.

When considering the monitoring and configuration sections that follow, it's important to keep in mind that the goal of framework rate limiting isn't necessarily to model a framework's behavior as accurately or precisely as possible, but instead to ensure that the throughput of higher-priority frameworks can't be negatively impacted by lower-priority frameworks.

Because frameworks without rate limiting configured will continue having their messages processed as soon as possible, it's perfectly reasonable to enable rate limiting on lower-priority frameworks first, letting you get an idea of how this functionality will work in your environment.

MONITORING FRAMEWORK AND MASTER BEHAVIOR

I recommend that you first observe the characteristics of any running frameworks before enabling rate limiting. Therefore, the first step in configuration framework rate limiting is to monitor the messages received and processed for each framework principal. These metrics can be obtained for each framework principal by querying the /metrics/snapshot API endpoint on the leading Mesos master.

To get an idea of how to monitor the messages being received and processed from each framework principal, let's take a look at this API endpoint. There will be a number of entries following the format frameworks/<framework-principal>. In the following example for marathon, you can see that the master has received and processed 254 messages:

```
"frameworks/marathon/messages_processed": 254,
"frameworks/marathon/messages_received": 254,
```

The values returned for `messages_received` and `messages_processed` should be equal (or about equal) when rate limiting is disabled (the default), because messages are processed as soon as they're received. You'll want to poll this API over a period of time to get an accurate representation of what your cluster activity looks like before enabling rate limiting.

> **TIP** You might consider writing a script to query this endpoint on a regular basis and store and visualize the metrics you wish to monitor using Graphite and Grafana, two popular (and open source) projects for storing and visualizing time series data.

It's also a good idea to look at the typical memory usage for the `mesos-master` process. You could do this with a monitoring tool that captures performance data as part of regular monitoring (such as Nagios), or a tool that focuses specifically on collecting time-series data from a system (such as Collectd). You could also get the physical memory use of the master (in KB) by running the following command:

```
$ ps -efo user,pid,rss,comm $(pidof mesos-master)
```

CONFIGURING FRAMEWORK RATE LIMITS

After observing and monitoring the behavior and resource consumption of the master and its frameworks, you can begin configuring rate limits for frameworks. But first, let's define the terms Mesos uses when configuring rate limiting:

- `principal`—Framework identifier (note: multiple frameworks can share a principal).
- `qps`—Rate limit, expressed as queries per second. If this field is omitted for a given principal, there will be no limit.
- `capacity`—Number of messages that can be queued on the master: messages received, but not yet processed. Effective only when used with qps.
- `aggregate_default_qps`—Aggregate rate limit for all frameworks not defined in the rate limits configuration.
- `aggregate_default_capacity`—Aggregate number of messages that can be queued on the master for all frameworks not defined in the rate limits configuration. Effective only when used with `aggregate_default_qps`.

Just as in the ACLs section, I think the best way to demonstrate rate limiting is with a couple of examples. Each of these configurations represents valid values for the `--rate_limits` master configuration option.

Example 1: Limit the `jenkins` framework to 100 queries per second, and to 6,000 messages in queue. All other frameworks aren't throttled and have unlimited queue capacity:

```
{
  "limits": [
    {
      "principal": "jenkins",
```

```
      "qps": 100,
      "capacity": 6000
    }
  ]
}
```

Example 2: Limit the chronos framework to 300 queries per second, with an unlimited queue capacity. The marathon framework has no throttling and an unlimited queue capacity. Any undefined frameworks (such as jenkins) will have an aggregate rate limit of 500 queries per second and a queue capacity of 4,500 messages:

```
{
  "limits": [
    {
      "principal": "chronos",
      "qps": 300
    },
    {
      "principal": "marathon"
    }
  ],
  "aggregate_default_qps": 500,
  "aggregate_default_capacity": 4500
}
```

If the framework exceeds its configured rate limit and subsequently exceeds its configured capacity, an error message is sent back to the framework. Framework developers can then use this event to trigger a behavior or action in their framework scheduler to handle the situation.

> **TIP**   Future releases of Mesos will have the ability to notify frameworks when their messages start to be queued up by the master. This way, frameworks can react accordingly as soon as messages begin to be queued, instead of waiting for their queue capacity to be exceeded. To track the progress of this feature, see https://issues.apache.org/jira/browse/MESOS-1664.

As you've seen in the previous few sections, combining framework, authentication, and rate limiting gives you a lot of control over the frameworks connecting to the cluster.

6.4   *Summary*

In this chapter, you learned about monitoring and managing Mesos clusters in a production environment. You explored topics such as monitoring Mesos and ZooKeeper, adding and replacing Mesos masters, and implementing access control lists. Here are a few things to remember:

- Both the Mesos masters and slaves provide a JSON-based REST API that contains valuable information about the cluster or individual node. For a list of available endpoints, see http://mesos-master.example.com:5050/help and http://mesos-slave.example.com:5051/help.

- To ensure that your monitoring requests are always going to the leading Mesos master, you might consider following the HTTP redirects offered by the master's /master/redirect endpoint. Alternately, you could put a HAProxy instance between your monitoring system and your Mesos masters.

- To manage and monitor ZooKeeper clusters, Netflix has created—and open sourced—a tool named Exhibitor. ZooKeeper can also be monitored with a set of four-letter commands, such as `ruok` and `mntr`. The project maintainers also include various monitoring scripts in the project's src/contrib/ directory.

- When adding Mesos masters to an existing cluster, be sure to resize the cluster quorum before bringing the new masters online.

- In addition to slave and framework authentication, access control lists (ACLs) define which *subjects* can perform certain *actions* on a set of *objects*. In the context of frameworks, the ACLs ensure that only approved frameworks matching a given set of criteria can register with the master.

- Framework rate limiting in Mesos protects higher-priority, production-level frameworks by limiting the number of messages processed for other frameworks. These metrics are exposed in the /metrics/snapshot API endpoint, and identified by their *principal*.

This concludes the second part of this book. Part 3 covers some popular open source frameworks that allow you to run applications and scheduled tasks on a Mesos cluster, and also introduces the Mesos API and provides guidance for developing your own Mesos framework.

In the next chapter, you'll learn about the popular Marathon framework for running applications and Docker containers on top of a Mesos cluster.

Part 3

Running on Mesos

Now that you've learned how to deploy Mesos in a production environment, part 3 covers how to use some popular (and open source) Mesos frameworks to deploy applications and scheduled jobs. You'll learn about service discovery within the cluster, and how to load-balance incoming user traffic. Finally, I introduce the Mesos APIs and some examples of how to develop your own Mesos framework.

Deploying applications with Marathon

This chapter covers

- Installing and configuring Marathon
- Deploying applications and Docker images
- Using HAProxy for service discovery and routing

In parts 1 and 2 of this book, you learned about the Apache Mesos project and how to configure a Mesos cluster for production use. In part 3, which begins with this chapter, you'll start putting your Mesos cluster to work by deploying applications and scheduled tasks on a Mesos cluster.

This chapter introduces you to Marathon, a popular, open source Mesos framework developed by Mesosphere that can be used for deploying long-running services and applications—including Docker containers. This chapter is structured in a way that enables you to become familiar with Marathon and application management by using real-world examples.

7.1   *Getting to know Marathon*

Up to this point, you've explored Mesos in the context of running multiple different frameworks and have seen how to achieve better datacenter utilization when you don't need to statically partition the datacenter. You know that certain Mesos-enabled applications—such as Jenkins and Spark—can connect directly to the cluster and run tasks, but what about a more typical application, or an application contained in a Docker image?

If you consider Mesos to be analogous to the kernel of an operating system, Marathon is the equivalent of the service management system; in Linux, this is commonly referred to as the *init* system. Marathon deploys applications as long-running Mesos tasks, both in Linux cgroups and Docker containers. Perhaps more correctly, it can also be considered a private platform as a service (PaaS) on which to deploy applications. Marathon does this by launching instances of an application as long-lived Mesos tasks, as you can see in figure 7.1.

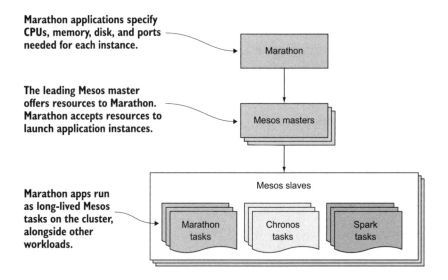

Figure 7.1   Marathon launches application instances as long-lived Mesos tasks.

Marathon allows you to specify the resources needed for each instance of an application, and then the number of instances you'd like to run. Similar to modern service managers such as systemd and Upstart, Marathon automatically respawns failed tasks by using available cluster resources. If a Mesos slave fails, or an instance of your application crashes or exits, Marathon will automatically start a new instance to replace the failed one. Marathon also allows users to specify dependencies on other services and applications during deployment, so you can be certain that an application instance can't start before its database instance is up and passing health checks.

NOTE This chapter covers Marathon version 0.10.1.

Marathon contains an extensive list of features that should satisfy the needs of most application management scenarios. Some of the most noteworthy features include the following:

- Managing applications and groups of applications, with dependencies and health checks
- Rolling application upgrades with specific capacity requirements
- A powerful web interface and REST API
- High availability (using ZooKeeper for leader election and coordination)

The next few sections introduce you to the most popular of these features and show how Marathon manages applications and application deployments. You'll learn how to combine Marathon with tools such as HAProxy and Mesos-DNS to handle service discovery and routing, both from other applications and from your users.

7.1.1 Exploring the web interface and API

To get familiar with Marathon, let's first discuss the two main ways of interacting with it: the web interface and the REST API.

EXPLORING THE WEB INTERFACE

Marathon has an intuitive web interface for both managing applications and observing deployment status. Let's take a quick tour of the main Apps page of the web interface by looking at figure 7.2.

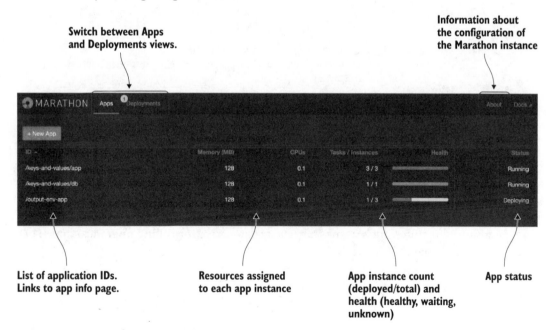

Figure 7.2 Overview of the Marathon web interface

Despite the fact that the web interface is helpful for visualizing and managing your applications and deployments, it's somewhat limited: you can't use the web interface to launch Docker containers, or use the more advanced features such as minimum health capacity or health checks. For those features, you need to manage your applications by using Marathon's API.

EXPLORING THE REST API

Considering that many organizations are embracing continuous integration (CI) and continuous delivery (CD) to automate their application deployments, Marathon's rich JSON-based REST API makes it easy to deploy new apps or deploy new versions of existing apps. Table 7.1 includes important Marathon API endpoints and the HTTP methods for operating on them. You'll use these select endpoints throughout the rest of the chapter. Because the result of each endpoint is different, based on the HTTP method used, the table includes multiple behaviors for each endpoint with the method in parentheses.

Table 7.1 Select Marathon API endpoints

API endpoint	Description
/v2/apps	Query for all applications on a Marathon instance (GET) or create new applications (POST)
/v2/apps/<app-id>	Query for information about a specific app (GET), update the configuration of an app (PUT), or delete an app (DELETE)
/v2/groups	Query for all application groups on a Marathon instance (GET) or create a new application group (POST)
/v2/groups/<group-id>	Query for information about a specific application group (GET), update the configuration of an application group (PUT), or delete an application group (DELETE)
/v2/info	Query for information about the Marathon instance (GET)
/v2/leader	Query Marathon for the hostname and port of the current leader (GET), or cause the leader to abdicate and trigger a leader election (DELETE)

The full documentation for Marathon's REST API can be found under Marathon's /help endpoint, or online at https://mesosphere.github.io/marathon/docs/rest-api.html. This documentation includes more information about some of Marathon's more advanced features, such as minimumHealthCapacity (for rolling upgrades) and HTTP and TCP-based health checks.

TIP The API-based examples throughout this chapter show you how to submit JSON to the API directly. If you're interested in a higher-level implementation, there's a great Python client library for Marathon. For more information, see https://github.com/thefactory/marathon-python.

I'll cover some practical application management scenarios a little later in this chapter. For now, let's cover how the various services that make up modern application architectures can communicate with each other. For the purposes of this book, I'll refer to this as *service discovery and routing*.

7.1.2 *Service discovery and routing*

Modern applications are typically composed of multiple services, or layers. Perhaps most commonly, a load balancer is responsible for forwarding requests from users to a few web servers. The front-end web application typically consumes a RESTful API, which may also be running on servers behind a load balancer. In turn, these API servers act as an abstraction to one or more back-end databases.

Needless to say, it's crucial that these services can all communicate with each other. But what's relatively easy in the traditional world—associating services with a specific hostname—becomes rather complex in the Mesos world. Because containers can run anywhere in the cluster with available compute resources, it's difficult to know where instances of a particular application are located so that load-balancer configurations can be updated.

In the Mesos and Marathon ecosystem, we refer to this problem (and the solution, for that matter) as *service discovery*. Fortunately, though, multiple tools are available to handle service discovery and application routing. This section covers two of the most popular options: HAProxy and Mesos-DNS.

SERVICE ROUTING WITH HAPROXY

As covered earlier in the chapter, Marathon provides information about running instances of applications (tasks) via its REST API. With a bit of tooling, you can use this information to dynamically create configurations for HAProxy, a popular, lightweight, open source HTTP and TCP load balancer.

In contrast to a traditional load balancer that primarily handles user traffic, you can deploy HAProxy on each of the Mesos slaves in the cluster, and then have your applications connect to a port on the local host, depending on which service it needs to communicate with. Figure 7.3 demonstrates using HAProxy in two distinct ways: as a means for intra-cluster communication, and as a means for handling inbound connections from users.

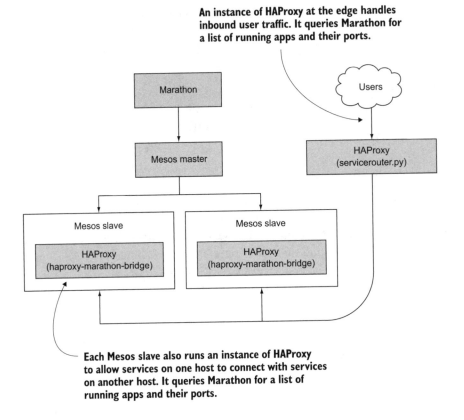

An instance of HAProxy at the edge handles
inbound user traffic. It queries Marathon for
a list of running apps and their ports.

Each Mesos slave also runs an instance of HAProxy
to allow services on one host to connect with services
on another host. It queries Marathon for a list of
running apps and their ports.

Figure 7.3   At a glance: service routing with HAProxy

Perhaps due to HAProxy's popularity and stability, Marathon is distributed with two
scripts that can periodically (via Cron) query the Marathon API for information about
running application instances. It can then use this information to build HAProxy configurations and reload the service. These scripts include the following:

- *haproxy-marathon-bridge*—A small shell script that builds an HAProxy configuration based on application information within Marathon. It automatically reloads
  the HAProxy service when changes are made.
- *servicerouter.py*—Similar to the aforementioned script, but allows much more
  control over the generated HAProxy configuration.

Each of these scripts is available in the Marathon project repository, located at https://
github.com/mesosphere/marathon/tree/v0.10.1/bin, and each serves a slightly different purpose, depending on how much control you want or need to have over the
generated HAProxy configurations. Don't worry about downloading them yet, though;
you'll learn how to deploy HAProxy for service routing later in this chapter.

SERVICE DISCOVERY WITH MESOS-DNS

Mesos-DNS—an open source project developed by Mesosphere—is a stateless Domain Name System (DNS) service for Mesos clusters. Much like a typical DNS server, it allows applications and services to find other applications and services by using a predictable naming convention and name lookups, publishing both A and SRV records for running Mesos tasks (see figure 7.4).

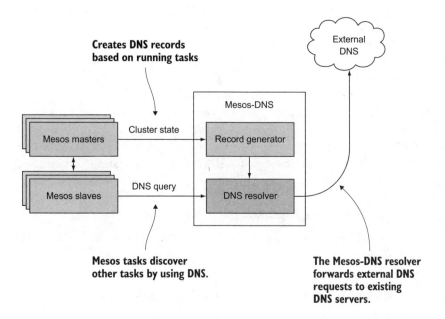

Figure 7.4   At a glance: Mesos-DNS

Unlike the HAProxy method mentioned previously, Mesos-DNS works with Mesos directly and doesn't depend on Marathon. This makes it a good method for services to use to communicate with each other even across different Mesos frameworks.

> **TIP** Figure 7.4 demonstrates using Mesos-DNS as a resolver, which forwards external (unknown) DNS queries. If you already have a DNS infrastructure in place, it's also possible to do the opposite: configure existing DNS infrastructure to forward DNS queries for the .mesos domain (the default) to Mesos-DNS.

Although this section covered both HAProxy and Mesos-DNS, DNS is a familiar enough concept to most, so I'm going to proceed with demonstrating service routing with HAProxy throughout the remainder of this chapter. If you're interested in learning more about the Mesos-DNS project, you can check out its project page at http://mesosphere.github.io/mesos-dns.

7.2   Deploying Marathon and HAProxy

All workloads running on a Mesos cluster run as individual tasks inside containers. The reduced overhead of running applications in containers means that you'll use datacenter resources more efficiently. But to deploy applications and services, you need a way to manage application instances as if they're long-running Mesos tasks.

Marathon provides a way to easily scale an application from 1 instance to 100 (and beyond), ensuring that each task is up and running as much as possible. If a task or a node fails, Marathon automatically restarts it based on incoming resource offers from Mesos, which means application instances are automatically moved to a new node if needed. When you combine the power of Marathon with HAProxy, you have a powerful platform for deploying applications and services, ensuring that they can communicate with any other dependent services in a scalable way.

In this section, you'll prepare your Mesos cluster to run applications by deploying Marathon for application management and HAProxy for service discovery, routing, and load balancing. You'll deploy Marathon in a highly available manner and deploy HAProxy on each of the Mesos slaves, ensuring that application instances can easily load-balance connections to other dependent services. Let's get started.

7.2.1   Installing and configuring Marathon

To deploy Marathon, certain prerequisites must be met. As of version 0.10.1, these include the following:

- Java 1.7 or later
- Mesos 0.22.2 or later (0.22.2 is the recommended version as of this writing)
- ZooKeeper (for leader election, and to maintain state)

For Marathon to be highly available, you need to deploy it on a number of nodes, just as you deployed an odd number of Mesos masters in chapter 3. Deploying three Marathon instances is probably fine for most environments, and each of these instances will use a ZooKeeper ensemble for leader election and to maintain state.

For a simpler installation, you could consider deploying Marathon on the same machines as the Mesos masters themselves. To make the examples in this section easier to understand, let's assume you'll be installing Marathon on the Mesos masters that you deployed in chapter 3.

> **A single DNS name for Marathon**
>
> In a highly available Marathon deployment, multiple instances are deployed across a number of hosts. For administration and automated application deployment purposes, you might consider creating a single record in DNS to point at your Marathon cluster. Fortunately, Marathon has a feature whereby any requests that are sent to a nonleading Marathon instance are transparently proxied to the leader.

You can take two approaches to connect to the Marathon cluster by a single name:

- *DNS load balancing*—Create a single DNS name with multiple A or CNAME records pointing to each Marathon instance
- *HTTP load balancing*—Use a load balancer (such as HAProxy) to forward connections to Marathon, and create a single DNS name pointing to the load balancer

Each option has advantages and disadvantages. For example: DNS load balancing is simple to configure, but if one of the Marathon instances is unavailable, failed connection attempts could result. On the other hand, adding a HAProxy load balancer automatically removes failed instances from the pool, but at the expense of adding a service between the client and Marathon.

Let's proceed with installing and configuring Marathon.

INSTALLING MARATHON

The easiest way to install Marathon is by using Mesosphere's package repositories, which you already installed and configured during the Mesos installation in chapter 3. Based on your Linux distribution, run one of the following commands to install Marathon:

- On RHEL and CentOS: `sudo yum install marathon-0.10.1-1.0.416.el7`
- On Ubuntu: `sudo apt-get install marathon= 0.10.1-1.0.416.ubuntu1404`

Although it's possible to download and install Marathon from the source code, the procedure is more involved than using the package manager. As a result, this book doesn't go over the build instructions. But if you're interested in going that route, check out the project's "Getting Started" documentation (http://mesosphere.github.io/marathon/docs) for up-to-date instructions.

CONFIGURING MARATHON

Similar to Mesos, Marathon has a few configuration conventions, depending on your deployment method and preference. Because Mesosphere develops and packages Marathon, its file-based configuration (similar to that of Mesosphere's Mesos packages) is probably the easiest and most straightforward to get started with. Marathon can be configured by creating text files under the /etc/marathon/conf/ directory.

Marathon has several configuration options, as specified at https://mesosphere.github.io/marathon/docs/command-line-flags.html. Table 7.2 details the configuration options that I find to be most noteworthy.

Table 7.2   Select Marathon configuration options

Configuration option	Description
master	The ZooKeeper URL used by the Mesos masters. If /etc/mesos/zk is present (Marathon is deployed on a Mesos master), the value in that file will automatically be used.
zk	The ZooKeeper URL for Marathon to use for leader election and state. For example: zk://host1:2181/marathon. If /etc/mesos/zk is present (Marathon is deployed on a Mesos master), Marathon will use the same ZK hosts and ports as Mesos, but create its own /marathon znode instead.
hostname	The DNS name or IP address for a given Marathon instance.
mesos_role	If set, registers Marathon to the Mesos cluster with a specific role (see chapter 6).
mesos_authentication_principal	The Mesos principal used for framework authentication (see chapter 6).
mesos_authentication_secret_file	The path to a file containing the secret for framework authentication (see chapter 6).

Marathon also supports SSL and basic authentication. I've intentionally left this feature out of the previous table because some users might prefer to set up authentication on a load balancer in front of multiple Marathon instances instead. If you're interested in enabling SSL and authentication for the instance of Marathon itself, see https://mesosphere.github.io/marathon/docs/ssl-basic-access-authentication.html.

> **TIP** Some users on the mailing lists have experienced issues with Mesos scheduler drivers binding to an incorrect network interface, which can result in connectivity problems between the Mesos master and the framework. By default, the Mesos native library will bind to the IP address that maps to the system's FQDN, as provided by the command hostname -f. To ensure that the scheduler driver binds to the correct interface, be sure that the host's DNS record (or the entry in /etc/hosts) is properly configured, or manually set the $LIBPROCESS_IP environment variable for the service to the IP address of the network interface you wish to advertise to the Mesos master.

After Marathon has been installed and configured on each of the Mesos masters, you can start the service by running sudo service marathon start. Once the service is up and running, you should be able to access the Marathon web interface at http://mesos-master.example.com:8080.

7.2.2   *Installing and configuring HAProxy*

Building on our previous coverage of service discovery and routing, you'll handle network traffic between various applications and services by installing and configuring HAProxy on each Mesos slave in the cluster. The haproxy-marathon-bridge script that's distributed with Marathon will dynamically generate HAProxy configuration files based on information available from Marathon. This will permit Marathon applications to connect to a port on the local host and automatically have access to a running instance of a dependent service.

In addition, you'll also need to consider how to handle the inbound user traffic. For the purposes of this text, I assume that the HAProxy instance running servicerouter.py will be a separate machine tasked with handling inbound user traffic. This allows me to go into the best level of detail about how to deploy the load balancer.

INSTALLING HAPROXY

To maintain compatibility with the scripts provided with the Marathon project, you'll want to install the latest version of HAProxy in the 1.5.*x* series on each of the Mesos slaves. The easiest way to do this is by using the operating system's package manager.

> **NOTE**   To install HAProxy 1.5.*x* on Ubuntu 14.04, you'll first need to enable the `trusty-backports` repository by uncommenting the relevant lines in /etc/apt/sources.list. After you've done this, be sure to update the package list by running `sudo apt-get update`.

To install HAProxy on Enterprise Linux or Ubuntu, run one of these commands:

- On RHEL and CentOS—`sudo yum install haproxy`
- On Ubuntu—`sudo apt-get -t trusty-backports install haproxy`

DYNAMICALLY CONFIGURING HAPROXY WITH HAPROXY-MARATHON-BRIDGE

To facilitate communication between services within the cluster, you'll use the haproxy-marathon-bridge script provided with Marathon to dynamically create HAProxy configurations, and automatically reload the service when changes occur. By installing HAProxy on each node and automatically and dynamically reconfiguring the service, you allow applications to communicate with other applications in a scalable way by connecting to the application's `servicePort` on `localhost`. To visualize this concept, take a look at figure 7.5.

To install haproxy-marathon-bridge on a given system, download the script from the Marathon GitHub repository and use its built-in `install_haproxy_system` function:

```
$ curl -LO https://raw.githubusercontent.com/mesosphere/marathon/
➥ v0.10.1/bin/haproxy-marathon-bridge
$ chmod +x haproxy-marathon-bridge
$ ./haproxy-marathon-bridge install_haproxy_system <host1> [host2] [...]
```

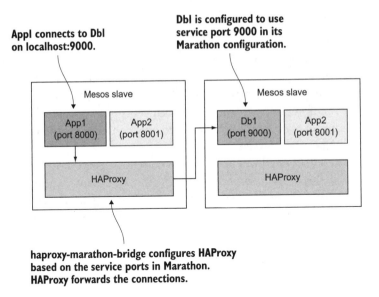

Appl connects to Dbl on localhost:9000.

Dbl is configured to use service port 9000 in its Marathon configuration.

haproxy-marathon-bridge configures HAProxy based on the service ports in Marathon. HAProxy forwards the connections.

Figure 7.5   Deploying HAProxy for routing intra-cluster network traffic

NOTE   For Debian-based systems, the haproxy-marathon-bridge script assumes that you have aptitude installed on the system. If you don't, you can install it by running `sudo apt-get install aptitude`.

As executed here, you've just accomplished the following:

- Installed the script to /usr/local/bin/haproxy-marathon-bridge
- Added `host1`, `host2`, and any additional Marathon hosts to the configuration file located at /etc/haproxy-marathon-bridge/marathons
- Created a Cron job at /etc/cron.d/haproxy-marathon-bridge that runs the script every minute
- Created or modified the HAProxy configuration file located at /etc/haproxy/haproxy.cfg and restarted the service

The script adds application instances to the HAProxy configuration file. If no tasks are running, the file will be empty. Otherwise, HAProxy will be used to load-balance connections between applications.

If a Mesos slave goes offline or a task (an instance of an application) fails within the one-minute window between Cron running the script, HAProxy's health checks will automatically detect the failure and stop sending traffic to that instance. The failed instance will then be removed from the HAProxy configuration the next time the Cron job runs.

DYNAMICALLY CONFIGURING HAPROXY WITH SERVICEROUTER.PY

Another script included with Marathon is servicerouter.py, which is intended to be a more full-featured replacement for haproxy-marathon-bridge. It configures HAProxy more as you'd expect from a typical load balancer, with features such as SSL termination, HTTP-to-HTTPS redirection, and virtual hosts. Despite our previous example of using servicerouter.py on the edge node that handles user traffic, you could also use this in lieu of haproxy-marathon-bridge on each of the Mesos slaves.

Configuration for this script resides within the Marathon application configuration itself in the form of environment variables. servicerouter.py also permits an administrator to override the templates built into the script by using a templates/ directory relative to the location where the script resides. This can be useful for modifying the HAProxy configuration to suit your specific environment, including certain information such as paths to SSL certificates, or preferred load-balancing policies.

To use the script on a given system, download it from Marathon's GitHub repository to a well-known location on disk. In this example, you'll download it to /usr/local/servicerouter/servicerouter.py:

```
$ sudo mkdir -p /usr/local/servicerouter
$ sudo curl -L -o /usr/local/servicerouter/servicerouter.py
➥ https://raw.githubusercontent.com/mesosphere/marathon/v0.10.1/bin
➥ /servicerouter.py
$ sudo chmod +x /usr/local/servicerouter/servicerouter.py
```

To use the script, you'll pass in some command-line arguments, specifying the URLs to the various Marathon instances and the location to save the haproxy.cfg file:

```
$ ./servicerouter.py --marathon http://marathon.example.com:8080
➥ --haproxy-config /etc/haproxy/haproxy.cfg
```

For full usage, run the following command:

```
$ ./servicerouter.py --longhelp
```

After you have the script building HAProxy configurations to your liking, it's a good idea to create a local Cron job to ensure that this script runs on a predictable schedule. Although HAProxy will automatically remove unhealthy instances from its load-balancing pool, it's important to ensure that the configurations always have the latest data from the Marathon API.

Let's create a Cron job at /etc/cron.d/servicerouter that resembles the following:

```
* * * * * root /usr/local/servicerouter/servicerouter.py <args>
```

Now that you've completed installing and configuring Marathon and HAProxy and have covered haproxy-marathon-bridge and servicerouter.py, let's dive into creating and deploying your first applications with Marathon.

7.3   *Creating and scaling applications*

One of the many problems that SysOps and development teams have to tackle is application management. How do you deploy new applications? How do you update existing ones? How do you easily scale an application up as demand increases, or down as it decreases? How do you ensure that your front-end application doesn't come up before the API service that it consumes, and that the API service doesn't come up before the database that backs it?

Marathon helps operations and development teams by providing a platform on which to run applications. Instead of the traditional approach of provisioning servers, deploying apps, and getting paged at 3 a.m. when a service goes down or when hardware (inevitably) fails, Marathon runs each instance of the application as a task on the Mesos cluster, automatically restarting the instance if it should fail. Marathon does this by ensuring that the workflow begins with the application, not with the server. Create the application, define the resources each instance will need, and specify the number of instances to run. Marathon and Mesos take it from there.

Following the concept that infrastructure should exist to serve applications, Marathon makes it easy to deploy your apps by using the container support built into Mesos. Let's get started by looking at what it takes to deploy applications with Marathon, using both Linux and Docker containers.

7.3.1   *Deploying a simple application*

In Marathon's own terms, an *application deployment* is defined as a set of actions that accomplishes the following:

- Starting (creating) or stopping (destroying) one or more applications
- Scaling application instances up or down (n > 1), or suspending them altogether (n = 0) without destroying the application configuration itself
- Upgrading (modifying the configuration of) one or more applications and rolling those changes out across your infrastructure

When writing this chapter, I thought it was best to provide somewhat real-world scenarios for deploying applications. The supplementary materials for this book include an example application named OutputEnv. This simple Ruby web application outputs the environment variables for a given application instance (Mesos task) as a web page.

DEPLOYING THE OUTPUTENV EXAMPLE APPLICATION

Because OutputEnv is a simple application (it doesn't run in Docker, nor does it have any dependencies on external services, health checks, or host constraints), let's deploy this particular application by using Marathon's web interface.

> **NOTE** Because OutputEnv doesn't run in Docker, you must have Ruby (version 1.9.3 or later) and Bundler installed on each of the Mesos slaves in order to deploy this application. Ruby can be installed using your system's package manager, and Bundler can be installed by running sudo gem install bundler.

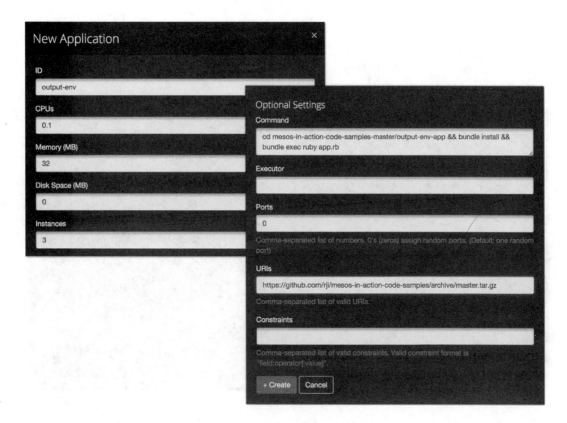

Figure 7.6 Creating the OutputEnv application in the Marathon web interface

From the main Apps page that you saw earlier in the chapter, clicking the New App button brings up a dialog box like the one in figure 7.6.

Here, you can give the application a name, set the required resources for each instance, and set the number of instances. In the Optional Settings portion, you provide a URI to download the application, and the command that you use to run it. By entering the settings in figure 7.6, you can download the OutputEnv application from this book's GitHub repository and run it on your Mesos cluster. If you specify an archive file (for example, zip or tar.gz) in the URIs field, the Mesos fetcher will automatically extract the archive for you in the sandbox. Click the Create button to start deploying the application.

MANAGING THE OUTPUTENV EXAMPLE APPLICATION

After creating the app, you'll arrive back at the main Apps page. Clicking the OutputEnv application will take you to an application management page, which lists all of the Mesos tasks for the application, as shown in figure 7.7.

Application
ID and status

Scale to N app
instances, or
suspend app
(scale to 0).

Switch between
Tasks and
Configuration
views.

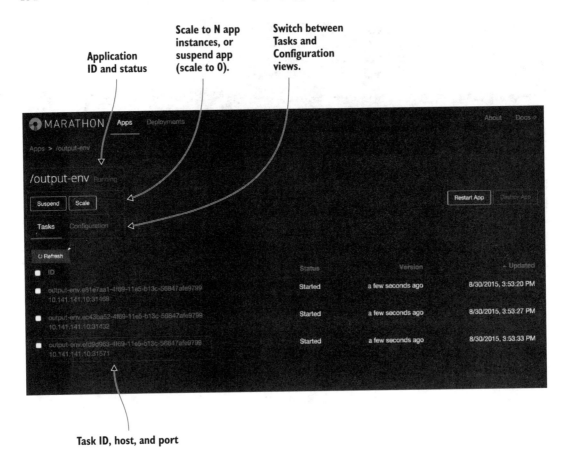

Task ID, host, and port

Figure 7.7 Marathon application details and management page for output-env

As shown in the previous graphic, you get a fair amount of information about the running application, as well as a few controls for scaling the number of instances up or down, redeploying the application, or destroying it altogether. By clicking the Scale button, you can enter application instances (Mesos tasks) you wish to deploy for a particular application, allowing you to easily scale it up as load increases, or down as load decreases. Furthermore, you could connect your monitoring system to the Marathon API and scale applications automatically, knowing that your HAProxy load-balancer configuration is being dynamically generated and updated every minute.

Clicking any of the task IDs provides additional information about that particular task, and clicking the hostname and port takes you to that particular application instance in your web browser (assuming your workstation has network connectivity to the Mesos slave the task is running on).

Unfortunately, as of this writing, the Marathon web interface is rather limited; you can't use it to modify an application's configuration, perform rolling upgrades, or deploy Docker containers. But now that you've seen how to create and deploy an application via the web interface (in this case, by running `bundle exec ruby app.rb`), let's take a look at some of the more advanced operations available in Marathon by using the REST API.

7.3.2 *Deploying a Docker container*

As covered earlier in this book, Docker provides a great way to package both application code and dependencies in a way that you can run it on any infrastructure, on premises, and in the cloud. Fortunately, both Marathon and Mesos are capable of running applications and services inside Docker containers. But as of this writing, you'll need to rely on Marathon's REST API in order to deploy them. That's not a problem, though; this section covers how to do so.

> **TIP** Docker images are typically pushed to Docker Hub, a web-based repository provided by Docker, Inc. If you prefer to host your own internal repository using Docker Registry, you'll need to take a few additional steps when deploying your applications. For instructions on how to set this up, see https://mesosphere.github.io/marathon/docs/native-docker-private-registry.html.

To get started, let's take a look at deploying the official Nginx Docker image as a new Marathon application.

DEPLOYING THE NGINX DOCKER IMAGE

Just in case you aren't already familiar with Nginx, it's a high-performance web server, reverse proxy, and load balancer that supports various protocols. The project's maintainers publish an official Nginx image to Docker Hub, which can be found at https://hub.docker.com/_/nginx/.

Deploying Docker images on Marathon works by adding a `container` field to the JSON object that defines your application. Let's take a look at the docker-nginx application definition in the following listing.

Listing 7.1   Deploying the Nginx Docker image in Marathon

```
{
    "id": "docker-nginx",              ◁   Marathon
    "instances": 1,                        application ID
    "cpus": 0.5,
    "mem": 64.0,
    "container": {
        "type": "DOCKER",                  Docker container
        "docker": {                    ◁   info, specifying
            "image": "nginx:1.9",          the image and
            "network": "BRIDGE",           networking mode
            "portMappings": [          ◁
                {                          Bridge containerPort
                    "containerPort": 80,   80 to the ephemeral
                    "hostPort": 0          hostPort used by
                }                          Mesos and Marathon
```

```
          ]
        }
      }
    }
}
```

This basic application definition deploys one instance of the Nginx Docker container, bridging port 80 within the container (the port that Nginx is listening on) to the randomly assigned port provided by Mesos and Marathon.

Assuming the previous JSON object was saved as docker-nginx.json, the following cURL command will launch the `nginx:1.9` Docker image as a new Marathon application:

```
$ curl -H 'Content-Type: application/json' -d @docker-nginx.json
➥ http://marathon.example.com:8080/v2/apps
```

If you navigate to the Marathon web interface or query Marathon's /v2/apps/docker-nginx API endpoint, you'll get information about the application and each of its running instances (tasks), including the hostname and port that each instance of the container is running on. If you navigate to one of these instances, you should see the default Nginx welcome page.

7.3.3 *Performing health checks and rolling application upgrades*

Despite Mesos's ability to use the currently running process to provide a task's status (such as running, finished, failed, and killed, among others), application instances warrant an additional level of monitoring. Traditionally, this is where a monitoring and alerting system such as Nagios might come into play, but the Marathon developers decided that something more dynamic was needed. Therefore, Marathon provides optional HTTP- and TCP-based health checks for each of the instances of a particular application.

In the event that an instance starts failing its health checks—either by returning an HTTP error code or by failing a TCP connection—the task will be reported as unhealthy. After a certain number of failed health checks, Marathon will restart the unhealthy task. The parameters of these health checks are all configurable, and I'll cover them shortly.

These health checks also allow you to perform rolling upgrades of an application or service, ensuring a minimum level of service, or *capacity*, so that new instances come up healthy before the upgrade proceeds. Combine these features with dynamically configured load balancers, and Marathon allows for zero-downtime deployments of new versions of applications.

Let's begin by taking a look at how health checks are implemented; you'll learn about rolling upgrades later in this section.

ANATOMY OF A HEALTH CHECK

Health checks can be implemented for any Marathon application. As of this writing, three methods, or *protocols*, are available for performing health checks of an application instance:

- HTTP—Issues a layer 7 HTTP request to a specific port and path
- TCP—Attempts to open a TCP socket connection to a specific port
- COMMAND—Runs an arbitrary command to determine health (not currently compatible with tasks running in Docker containers)

In addition, you can customize the interval, grace period, time-out, and number of consecutive failures allowed for the health check. Let's take a look at the following listing for a couple of examples of application health checks in Marathon.

Listing 7.2 Examples of Marathon application health checks

❶ Specifies health-check protocol. Valid values are **HTTP, TCP,** and **COMMAND.**

❷ Path to query (HTTP only)

❸ Index of the port to query in the application's ports array

Seconds between health checks

Health check time-out

Number of consecutive failures allowed before the task is killed

Ignores health-check failures within *N* seconds of the task being started.

```
"healthChecks": [
    {
        "protocol": "HTTP",        ←❶
        "path": "/ping",            ←❷
        "portIndex": 0,             ←❸
        "gracePeriodSeconds": 3,
        "intervalSeconds": 30,
        "timeoutSeconds": 10,
        "maxConsecutiveFailures": 3
    },
    {
        "protocol": "COMMAND",
        "command": {
            "value": "curl -f -X GET http://$HOST:$PORT0/ping"
        },
        "maxConsecutiveFailures": 3
    }
]
```

This example specifies an HTTP health check ❶ that queries a specific path ❷, but instead of repeating the port in the application definition, you use the portIndex field to specify the index of the service port in the ports array ❸. By default, this is 0, which is the first port in the array.

Health checks are a powerful way to ensure that the various instances, or tasks, for a given application are all up and healthy at the application layer. They play a crucial role in allowing Marathon to perform rolling upgrades of a given application—deploying a new version of an application with zero downtime.

PERFORMING HEALTH-BASED ROLLING UPGRADES

During an upgrade, Marathon will, by default, bring up the total configured tasks for the new version of an application before it starts killing tasks belonging to the old version. This ensures that all instances of the new version of the application are running and healthy before completely switching over. But as most things in Marathon, this is highly customizable, depending on the strategy that works best for your team, organization, and infrastructure. Let's explore the upgrade strategy configuration a bit more with a few examples.

The upgrade strategy, consisting of a minimum health capacity and a maximum "over capacity," can be configured for a Marathon application like this:

```
"upgradeStrategy": {
    "minimumHealthCapacity": 1.0,
    "maximumOverCapacity": 0.2
}
```

Percentage of tasks to remain online during an upgrade

Percentage of additional tasks to bring up during an upgrade

Because these two options aren't immediately clear, let's consider an example application upgrade scenario: a given app has 100 instances (tasks) serving users, and you'd like to deploy a new version of the app with Marathon. With a `minimumHealthCapacity` of `1.0` (100%), Marathon will maintain a minimum of 100 tasks during the upgrade. If this number is set lower (say: `0.9`, or 90%), Marathon will kill 10 of the existing tasks to make room for the new tasks to start.

The other configuration option worth paying attention to is `maximumOverCapacity`. This option allows Marathon to replace a given percentage of tasks at a time during the upgrade. In this example, Marathon will bring up 20 tasks of the new version and wait for them to become healthy before killing off any of the existing tasks.

These values can be modified to meet the SLAs for your individual applications, or fine-tuned based on the available resources you have in the cluster. If you've specifically granted a fixed amount of resources to a given application, you could set `minimumHealthCapacity` to `0.9` and `maximumOverCapacity` to `0.0`, causing the app to maintain 90% of its configured instances throughout the upgrade (and thus replacing 10 instances at a time).

As I mentioned earlier in the chapter when introducing Marathon's REST API, you can update the configuration of an existing Marathon application by using the HTTP PUT method against the /v2/apps/<app-id> endpoint. If you have an application named test-app and your Marathon application definition lives in your code repository or on disk as marathon.json, you can run the following cURL command to upgrade it:

```
$ curl -H 'Content-Type: application/json' -X PUT -d @marathon.json
  http://marathon.example.com:8080/v2/apps/test-app
```

When rolling upgrades are combined with the dynamic HAProxy configuration generated by haproxy-marathon-bridge and servicerouter.py, it allows new instances to enter the pool—and old instances to be removed—throughout the upgrade, ensuring a seamless transition between application versions, and zero downtime for your users.

Now that you know a bit about deploying simple applications, health checks, and rolling upgrades, let's go over how to create application groups and service dependencies as a single Marathon deployment. Because application groups are made up of individual applications, much of the content covered in this section also applies in the next section (even if I don't necessarily repeat it).

7.4 Creating application groups

Although the examples in the previous section help demonstrate the power of Marathon, chances are that your applications are composed of multiple services and/or Docker images. Up to this point, I've showed you how to deploy multiple instances of single, standalone Marathon applications, using both the web interface and the REST API. The real power of Marathon starts to appear when you look at defining your applications—and their dependent services—in the form of application groups.

7.4.1 Understanding the anatomy of an application group

Marathon deployments are made up of standalone *applications*, or applications contained in *application groups*. Application groups can contain either applications or other application groups. Additionally, applications and application groups can have dependencies on other applications or application groups. Before delving too far into what application groups can look like, let's consider the application groups, as shown in figure 7.8.

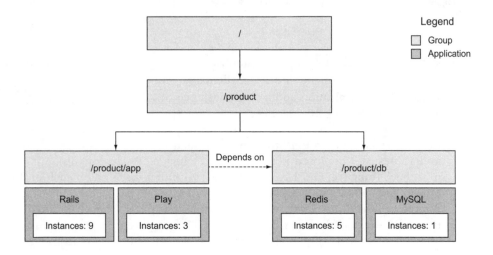

Figure 7.8 Marathon application groups containing multiple individual applications

Using application groups, you can model complex applications—and their dependencies—all within a single JSON payload. This allows you to easily define dependencies, deploy updates, and scale entire application stacks running on Marathon, both by the individual application and by the entire application group. Now that you understand a bit more about how an application group is composed, let's take a look at a more real-world scenario.

7.4.2 Deploying an application group

To best illustrate how to deploy an application that depends on a database, let's deploy an example application (Keys and Values) included with the supplementary materials for this book. You'll start by taking a look at figure 7.9 to see what this Marathon application group looks like at a high level.

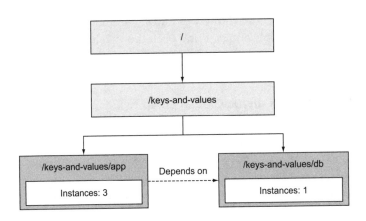

Figure 7.9   Overview of the Keys and Values application deployment

Keys and Values is a Ruby web application (written using the Sinatra framework) that allows a user to manipulate entries in a Redis key/value database. You'll run several instances of the application and a single instance of Redis, using HAProxy to handle communication between the services.

> **NOTE**   Just like the OutputEnv app mentioned earlier in this chapter, Keys and Values isn't deployed here as a Docker image. To deploy this app, you must have Ruby (version 1.9.3 or later) and Bundler installed on each of the Mesos slaves. Ruby can be installed using your system's package manager, and Bundler can be installed by running sudo gem install bundler. This is to illustrate a point: Docker makes it easy to distribute applications and dependent libraries to systems, without any intervention from a systems administrator.

DEPLOYING THE KEYS AND VALUES EXAMPLE APPLICATION

Listing 7.3 brings together everything you've learned up to this point to create a Marathon application group called `keys-and-values` that will ensure that Redis is available before the application. Note that you must be running haproxy-marathon-bridge on each machine in the cluster so that the application can connect to the database.

Listing 7.3 Deploying the Keys and Values app in Marathon

```
{
    "id": "keys-and-values",          ID of the
    "apps": [                         application group
        {
            "id": "app",              ID of the application
            "instances": 3,           inside the application
            "cpus": 0.1,              group
            "mem": 128.0,
            "disk": 0.0,
            "uris": [
                "https://github.com/rji/
mesos-in-action-code-samples/archive/master.tar.gz"
            ],
            "cmd": "cd mesos-in-action-code-samples-master/keys-values-app
&& bundle install --retry 3 && bundle exec ruby app.rb",
            "ports": [
                8080                  The servicePort that
            ],                        Marathon will
            "env": {                  advertise to HAProxy
                "REDIS_HOST": "localhost",
                "REDIS_PORT": "9000"  Environment variables
            },                        for the app; connects to
            "dependencies": [         Redis on localhost:9000
                "/keys-and-values/db"
            ]                         Ensures the database is
        },                            available before the app.
        {
            "id": "db",               ID of the database
            "instances": 1,           service inside the
            "cpus": 0.1,              application group
            "mem": 128.0,
            "disk": 0.0,
            "container": {
                "type": "DOCKER",
                "docker": {
                    "image": "redis:3.0.3",     Bridge port 6379
                    "network": "BRIDGE",        inside the container
                    "portMappings": [           to Marathon's
                        {                       random hostPort
                            "containerPort": 6379,  3
                            "hostPort": 0,
                            "servicePort": 9000,    HAProxy should
                            "protocol": "tcp"       forward connections
                        }                           on port 9000 to
                    ]                               this app.
                }
            }
        }
```

```
        },
        "healthChecks": [
            {
                "protocol": "TCP",
                "portIndex": 0,
                "maxConsecutiveFailures": 3
            }
        ]
    }
]
}
```

> Establishes a TCP
> health check on the
> Marathon hostPort.

Assuming that the previous JSON object was saved as keys-and-values.json, the following cURL command will launch this application group in Marathon, starting with Redis:

```
$ curl -H 'Content-Type: application/json' -d @keys-and-values.json
➥ http://marathon.example.com:8080/v2/groups
```

If you navigate to the Marathon web interface or query the /v2/groups/keys-and-values API endpoint, you'll get information about the application group and each of its apps. If you navigate to one of these instances, you should be able to interact with the application.

Additionally, take note of the ports array specified in /keys-and-values/app. This service port will be used by haproxy-marathon-bridge and/or servicerouter.py to populate a HAProxy load-balancer configuration file. If you've set up a load balancer by using one of these scripts, you should be able to access it by navigating to http://load-balancer.example.com:8080.

7.5   *Logging and debugging*

Despite the fact that Marathon is a Mesos framework, the logging messages provided by Mesos stop with the Mesos API. The Mesos master won't know a whole lot about what's happening with Marathon outside of resource offers, launching tasks, and framework registration and re-registration. Therefore, the logs provided by a Mesos-native application are as important as any other application that runs in a datacenter.

The log messages provided by Marathon can be useful for troubleshooting an issue or observing common behavior from the service itself. The log messages include information such as API endpoints accessed, resource offers that are accepted and declined, status updates from tasks, and scaling applications up and down. You'll observe these messages during your day-to-day interactions with the Marathon service.

This section covers how Marathon handles logging, and what configurations are available.

7.5.1   *Configuring logging for Marathon*

By default, the startup script that comes with Marathon uses the logger interface for adding entries to the system log. It does so at an INFO-level of verbosity by default, which provides a decent amount of information regarding the API endpoints being accessed and the state of deployed Marathon applications. As with most things, the log level can be configured, and Rsyslog can be customized to better suit the environment. Let's take a look at what's required to modify each of these.

MODIFYING THE LOGGING LEVEL

Marathon provides a configuration option to modify the logging level of the application. Using the `--logging_level` configuration option (or by creating a file with the value at /etc/marathon/conf/logging_level), you can set logging to be one of the following values, listed in increasing severity: `all`, `trace`, `debug`, `info`, `warn`, `error`, `fatal`, and `off`. By default, Marathon is distributed with its logging level set to `info`.

REDIRECTING MARATHON LOGS FROM SYSLOG TO A DEDICATED LOG FILE

By default, Marathon sends logs at—and above—the configured logging level to the system log. For some, this may be desirable: a centralized logging infrastructure such as Logstash or Splunk can easily consume the syslog entries and structure them in a way that can be easily queried later. For others, it's incredibly tedious to look through the syslog file at /var/log/messages or /var/log/syslog (depending on your distribution) and try to filter out Marathon's logging messages to troubleshoot a problem.

If you aren't planning to centralize your logging, or you'd prefer to filter Rsyslog and have the log entries for Marathon written to their own log file, create the file /etc/rsyslog.d/10-marathon.conf with the following content:

```
if $programname == "marathon" then {
    action(type="omfile" file="/var/log/marathon.log")
}
```

> **TIP** For more information on the available filter conditions for Rsyslog, check out the official documentation at www.rsyslog.com/doc/v8-stable/configuration/filters.html.

As always, if you're planning to write logs to a dedicated file on disk, you should take care to create some Logrotate rules to ensure that the log files don't grow too large and fill the logging partition on the local system.

7.5.2 Debugging Marathon applications and tasks

Because instances of a Marathon application are simply long-running Mesos tasks, most of the logging and debugging content already covered in chapter 5 applies here. It's important to quickly revisit this and add some information about debugging Docker containers.

REFRESHER ON DEBUGGING MESOS TASKS

Each task running on a Mesos cluster is visible from the Mesos web interface, located at http://mesos-master.example.com:5050. If you navigate to a nonleading master, you'll automatically be redirected to the leader. From here, you'll be able to view the sandbox for a running task. Two files will be automatically created in each sandbox (stdout and stderr) to capture any console output for that particular task.

The process (task) will continue running until it's killed, lost, or exits, at which point it will update the state of the task with Mesos. If the loss of a task means that a Marathon application isn't operating at 100% capacity, Marathon will automatically restart the failed task, no questions asked.

In the case of Marathon, application instances can be defined as either shell commands (such as `bundle exec ruby myapp.rb`) or Docker containers (by adding a `container` section to the application's JSON object). There's an important distinction here: standalone commands will be launched using the Mesos command executor, whereas Docker images will be launched using the built-in Docker executor. Because of this distinction, it's worth covering a common failure mode when launching Docker containers on a Mesos cluster: failed tasks with empty log files in the sandbox.

DEBUGGING DOCKER CONTAINERS LAUNCHED BY MARATHON AND MESOS

If the application within the Docker container is configured to log to standard output and standard error, logging entries will appear in the Mesos sandbox in the stdout and stderr files, respectively. This is pretty typical of tasks running on a Mesos cluster. Sometimes, though, a Docker container will fail to run via Marathon, and the log files within the sandbox will be completely empty. What gives? Let's take a look at one such situation.

Let's say you created and deployed an application to Marathon named docker-invalid-container-example that was configured to pull down and run the Docker container fake-org/thisisnotmybeautifulcontainer. The only problem: this container doesn't exist. When you observe that your application isn't failing to start and navigate to the Mesos UI to figure out what's wrong, you find both the stdout and stderr log files are completely empty.

When taking a look one level deeper—at the Marathon logs—all you manage to find is this rather cryptic entry:

```
Oct 18 21:24:48 mesos marathon[1335]: [2015-10-18 21:24:48,434] INFO
Received status update for task docker-invalid-container-example.a753e2af-
75de-11e5-a1ac-56847afe9799: TASK_FAILED (Abnormal executor termination)
(mesosphere.marathon.MarathonScheduler$$EnhancerByGuice$$417430f8:100)
```

Unfortunately, you haven't learned much more than you already knew: the task failed. In this particular case, the real failure cause is logged in the /var/log/mesos/mesos-slave.INFO file on the machine that attempted to launch the Docker container. If you investigate a bit further, you'll find the following error:

```
E1018 21:24:48.423717 18610 slave.cpp:3112] Container '978cc82b-6838-4c2a-
8487-3516357a8641' for executor 'docker-invalid-container-example.a753e2af-
75de-11e5-a1ac-56847afe9799' of framework '20150930-024708-16842879-5050-
1180-0000' failed to start: Failed to 'docker pull fake-
org/thisisnotmybeautifulcontainer:latest': exit status = exited with status
1 stderr = Error: image fake-org/thisisnotmybeautifulcontainer:latest not
found
```

Aha! The reason that the sandbox logs are blank is that the executor is failing to launch (because the Docker container doesn't exist), which means no log entries are written to the sandbox. Correcting the error in the application definition should resolve the issue.

This scenario is exactly where a centralized logging solution like the open source Elasticsearch, Logstash, and Kibana (ELK) stack, or a commercial product like Splunk, start to become valuable additions to your infrastructure. Instead of figuring out which Mesos slave the container failed to run on and then logging into the host and looking through logs, you could easily search them from a single interface. For more information on Logstash, check out the documentation at www.elastic.co/guide/en/logstash/current/introduction.html. For more information on Splunk, see www.splunk.com/en_us/products/splunk-enterprise.html.

Now, if you want to have more control over Docker container logging and to specifically enable use of the `docker logs` command on the Mesos slave, I suggest you take a look at the following documentation:

- Configuring Docker logging drivers: https://docs.docker.com/reference/logging/overview/
- Passing arbitrary Docker parameters via Marathon: http://mesosphere.github.io/marathon/docs/native-docker.html#privileged-mode-and-arbitrary-docker-options

I've only touched the tip of the iceberg when it comes to logging and inspecting the state of Docker containers. Other options are available, such as structured logging with JSON, or sending Docker container logs to the system log. Besides reading over the official Docker documentation, you may also be interested in picking up a copy of *Docker in Action* by Jeff Nickoloff (Manning, 2016).

7.6 Summary

In this chapter, you learned about deploying services and applications on Marathon. The chapter covered topics such as installation, configuration, application deployments, application dependencies, and service discovery and routing. Here are a few things to remember:

- Marathon is a private platform as a service (PaaS) for Mesos. It deploys long-running applications or services as Mesos tasks, and automatically restarts them if they fail. It's commonly referred to as the Mesos equivalent of the init system of a traditional Linux operating system.
- Service discovery and routing can be handled using HAProxy and the included haproxy-marathon-bridge and servicerouter.py scripts, or Mesos-DNS.
- Application deployments can be composed of standalone *applications*, or applications contained in *application groups*. Application groups can contain either applications or other application groups.

- Health checks can be implemented using HTTP, TCP, or COMMAND, ensuring that the application is up and responsive. You can also configure the allowed number of consecutive failures, the maximum check time-out, and the interval between checks, on a per-application basis.
- To ensure that new versions of applications can be rolled out without interrupting users, Marathon allows for rolling upgrades of existing applications using the minimumHealthCapacity field in an application's JSON object. Combined with health checks, Marathon can ensure that a new version of the application is coming up properly before proceeding with tearing down the old version.
- Within an application group, Marathon applications can have dependencies on other applications or services, in addition to minimum health requirements (such as a Rails application depending on a certain number of instances of a database).

Although this chapter provided several in-depth examples, Marathon has many more features than I can cover in this book—and more are being added in every release. For the latest documentation, check out https://mesosphere.github.io/marathon/docs/.

In the next chapter, you'll go over the popular Chronos framework for running scheduled tasks—also known as Cron jobs—on a Mesos cluster.

Managing scheduled
tasks with Chronos

8

This chapter covers

- Installing and configuring Chronos
- Creating scheduled tasks
- Observing task output and alerting on failures

In a traditional Linux operating system, the Cron daemon is responsible for time-based execution of commands or scripts, commonly referred to as *Cron jobs*. If you consider Mesos to be the "distributed systems kernel" as it's described on the project's website, Chronos is the Mesos equivalent of the Cron system: it handles time-based scheduling of jobs (tasks) on a Mesos cluster. If you want to have an arbitrary command run on the Mesos cluster, you need to specify the schedule and the amount of CPU and memory the job needs.

This chapter introduces you to Chronos, a popular, open source Mesos framework originally developed at Airbnb to handle its complex data analysis pipelines. It was designed to be highly available, to automatically retry jobs when they fail, and to be as flexible as possible: that is, to be a Mesos equivalent of the Cron daemon, and not simply used for data analysis.

Chronos can be used to schedule commands or scripts, and uses the built-in containerizers in Mesos; it comes with out-of-the-box support for running commands in Linux control groups (cgroups) and Docker containers. With the Chronos feature set, you can easily and reliably create standalone schedule-based jobs, as well as complex dependency-based jobs and pipelines, simply by specifying the schedule and resources (which are offered up by the Mesos slaves) that the job requires. This allows you to be sure that your time-based jobs are running on time while continuing to use datacenter resources as efficiently as possible.

8.1 Getting to know Chronos

Up to this point, you've explored Mesos in the context of running multiple different frameworks, and learned how to achieve better datacenter utilization without worrying about managing multiple, statically configured machines. With Chronos, I'm going to shift this approach a bit to discuss how running scheduled tasks on a Mesos cluster can make for a more resilient, scheduled job-execution system. In fact, deploying Chronos as a robust replacement to running a Cron job on a lone server somewhere in a datacenter was among one of the first things I did when I started using Mesos. Let's consider the differences between running Cron jobs on a single machine and running them on a Mesos cluster by taking a look at figure 8.1.

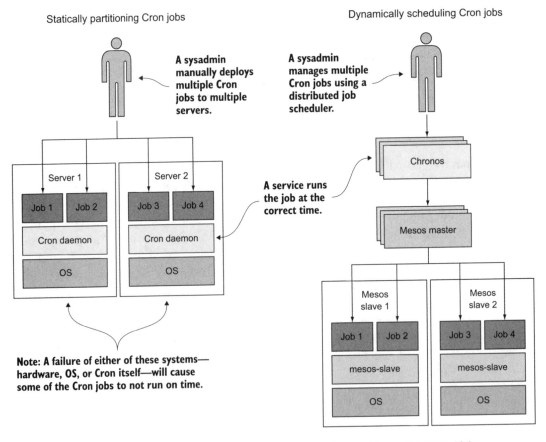

Figure 8.1 Mesos and Chronos provide a dynamic, fault-tolerant environment to run time-based jobs.

I've depicted how systems administrators might traditionally deploy scheduled jobs, and how they might do the same thing using Chronos and Mesos. Sure, you could deploy several new VMs and create Cron jobs on them, but at the end of the day you don't need to concern yourself with which jobs run on which servers; instead, you need to be concerned with the CPU, memory, and disk resources that your jobs need to run.

Chronos allows you to schedule tasks by using available resources on a Mesos cluster. It's fault tolerant and uses the available resources on the Mesos cluster, meaning you won't have to worry about failures in hardware, the OS, or the Cron daemon itself. It's also highly available, which means you won't need to concern yourself with a single instance of the Chronos framework failing; a new instance will be elected leader, and chances are that you and your users won't even notice that a failover took place.

Combined with the Mesos container-based approach to resource isolation (covered in chapter 4), each of these jobs can run alongside other jobs or applications on a Mesos cluster without any interference.

> **NOTE** This chapter covers Chronos version 2.4.0.

Chronos contains an extensive list of features that builds upon the basic features of the Cron daemon (specifying schedules and users to run commands). These features allow you to do the following:

- Execute jobs on a schedule
- Create complex parent/child dependencies between jobs
- Run commands in Docker containers
- Automatically retry failed jobs

The next few sections provide a tour of the Chronos web interface and REST API, before diving into deploying Chronos and creating scheduled jobs.

8.1.1 Exploring the web interface and API

Chronos has a rich web interface for managing scheduled jobs and gathering information about them, with a REST API underneath. This allows you to store your Chronos job configurations as JSON objects in version control, and use a CI system (such as Jenkins or TeamCity) to deploy changes when they occur. You'll learn about the REST API a little later in this section. For now, let's get started by taking a look at the web interface.

EXPLORING THE WEB INTERFACE

Similar to Marathon (covered in chapter 7), Chronos provides a web interface for managing scheduled jobs and displaying information about them. Some of this information includes the state (success/failure) of the job, run durations, and a job

List of jobs, showing
success/failure and
current state

View the job
dependency graph

Create a
new job

Job operations: edit, run,
duplicate, view dependency
graph, and delete

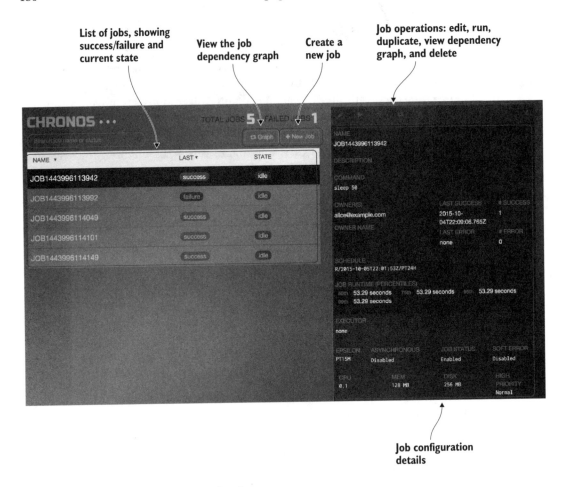

Job configuration
details

Figure 8.2   Overview of the Chronos web interface

dependency graph. Let's take a quick tour of the main page of the web interface, shown in figure 8.2.

As you can see, the web interface provides functionality to do the following:

- Create, configure, and delete jobs
- View existing jobs and their current state and last-run status
- View dependencies between jobs using a built-in dependency graph

Despite the web interface being helpful for creating simple tasks and viewing their dependencies, it's somewhat limited: you can't (currently) use the web interface to launch Docker containers, nor can you access some of the more advanced features, such as using the Mesos fetcher to download files to the sandbox, specifying a time zone, or setting environment variables. For this reason, this chapter covers the API in a fair amount of detail.

EXPLORING THE **REST API**

The JSON-based REST API in Chronos makes it simple to create, update, or remove jobs. To get started, table 8.1 lists some important Chronos API endpoints and the HTTP methods for operating on them. Because the result of each endpoint is different based on the HTTP method used, I've included multiple behaviors for each endpoint, with the method in parentheses. You'll use these endpoints throughout the rest of the chapter to create increasingly complex jobs.

Table 8.1 Select Chronos API endpoints

API endpoint	Description
/scheduler/jobs	Query for all jobs on a Chronos instance (GET).
/scheduler/iso8601	Create (POST) or modify (PUT) a job that runs on a schedule.
/scheduler/dependency	Create (POST) or modify (PUT) a job that runs after a parent job completes.
/scheduler/job/<job-id>	Perform operations on an existing job: manually run the job (PUT) or delete it (DELETE).

The full documentation for the Chronos REST API—including additional features not mentioned in this text—can be found online at http://mesos.github.io/chronos/docs/api.html.

> **TIP** In the API-based examples throughout this chapter, you'll see how to submit JSON to the API directly. If you're interested in a higher-level implementation, an open source Python client library for Chronos wraps the various API endpoints and HTTP methods required to operate on them. For more information, see https://github.com/asher/chronos-python.

You'll learn about creating tasks by using both the web interface and the REST API later in this chapter. For now, let's go over how to deploy Chronos.

8.2 *Installing and configuring Chronos*

The previous section introduced you to the Chronos project and provided a brief overview of its web interface and REST API. Now, let's prepare the Mesos cluster for handling scheduled jobs by installing and configuring Chronos.

8.2.1 *Reviewing prerequisites*

To deploy Chronos to your infrastructure, the following prerequisites must be met on the systems that it will run on. As of version 2.4.0 (and for the purposes of this book), these dependencies include the following:

- Java 1.7 or later
- Mesos 0.22.2 or later
- ZooKeeper

For Chronos to be highly available, you need to deploy it on a number of nodes, just as you deployed an odd number of Mesos masters in chapter 3. Deploying three Chronos instances is probably fine for most environments, and each of these instances will use a ZooKeeper ensemble for leader election and to maintain state.

For a simpler deployment, you could consider deploying Chronos on the same machines as the Mesos masters, or run Chronos as an application on Marathon. To make the examples in this chapter easier to understand, let's assume that you'll be installing Chronos on the same machines as the Mesos masters that you deployed in chapter 3.

> **A single DNS name for Chronos**
>
> In a highly available Chronos deployment, multiple instances are deployed across a number of hosts. For administration purposes, you might consider creating a single record in DNS to point at your Chronos cluster. Fortunately, Chronos has a feature whereby any requests sent to a nonleading Chronos instance are transparently proxied to the leader.
>
> You can take two approaches to connect to the Chronos cluster by a single name:
>
> - *DNS load balancing*—Create a single DNS name with multiple A or CNAME records pointing to each Chronos instance
> - *HTTP load balancing*—Use a load balancer (such as HAProxy) to forward connections to Chronos, and create a single DNS name pointing to the load balancer
>
> Each option has advantages and disadvantages. For example, DNS load balancing is simple to configure, but if one of the Chronos instances is unavailable, failed connection attempts could result. On the other hand, adding a HAProxy load balancer automatically removes failed instances from the pool, but at the expense of adding a service between the client and Chronos.

Now, let's proceed with installing and configuring Chronos.

8.2.2 Installing Chronos

The easiest way to install Chronos is by using Mesosphere's package repositories, which you already installed and configured during the Mesos installation in chapter 3. Based on your Linux distribution, run one of the following commands to install Chronos:

- On RHEL and CentOS:

```
$ sudo yum install chronos-2.4.0-0.1.20151007110204.el7
```

- On Ubuntu:

```
$ sudo apt-get install chronos= 2.4.0-0.1.20151007110204.ubuntu1404
```

Although it's possible to download and install Chronos from the source code, the procedure is more involved than using the packages provided by Mesosphere. In the interest of brevity, this book doesn't detail the build instructions. But if you want to go that route, check out the project's "Getting Started" documentation (http://mesos.github.io/chronos/docs/getting-started.html) for the most up-to-date instructions.

8.2.3 Configuring Chronos

Like Marathon, Chronos has a few configuration conventions, depending on your deployment method and preference. Because Mesosphere continues to develop Chronos and provides packages for the community, its file-based configuration (similar to that of Mesosphere's Mesos and Marathon packages) is probably the easiest and most straightforward to start with. Chronos can be configured by creating text files under the /etc/chronos/conf/ directory. You may need to create the parent directory (/etc/chronos/conf) on your system.

Chronos has various configuration options, as specified at http://mesos.github.io/chronos/docs/configuration.html. Table 8.2 details the configuration options that I find to be most noteworthy and that you'll most likely need to configure when deploying Chronos yourself.

Table 8.2   Select Chronos configuration options

Configuration option	Description
master	The ZooKeeper URL used by the Mesos masters. If /etc/mesos/zk is present (Chronos is deployed on a Mesos master), the value in that file will automatically be used.
zk_hosts	A comma-separated list of ZooKeeper hosts for Chronos to use for leader election and state. If /etc/mesos/zk is present (Chronos is deployed on a Mesos master), Chronos will use the same ZK hosts and ports as Mesos, but create its own /chronos/state znode instead.
hostname	The DNS name or IP address for a given Chronos instance.
mesos_role	If set, registers Chronos to the Mesos cluster with a specific role (see chapter 6).
mesos_authentication_principal	The Mesos principal used for framework authentication (see chapter 6).
mesos_authentication_secret_file	The path to a file containing the secret for framework authentication (see chapter 6).
mail_from	The From email address for Chronos email notifications.

Table 8.2 Select Chronos configuration options *(continued)*

Configuration option	Description
`mail_server`	The SMTP server used for sending email. Combine with `mail_user` and `mail_password` if the server requires auth, and `mail_ssl` to encrypt connections to the mail server.
`slack_url`	The webhook URL for sending notifications to Slack.

In addition, Chronos supports basic authentication and SSL. I've intentionally left this out of the previous table because some users might prefer to set up authentication and SSL termination on a load balancer in front of multiple Chronos instances. If you're interested in enabling SSL and authentication for Chronos itself, you might want to check out the `ssl_keystore_path` and `ssl_keystore_password` configuration options in the project's configuration documentation, located at http://mesos.github.io/chronos/docs/configuration.html.

After Chronos has been installed and configured on each of the Mesos masters and the service is up and running, you should be able to access the Chronos web interface at http://chronos.example.com:4400.

8.3   *Working with simple jobs*

This chapter classifies Chronos jobs into two categories: *simple* and *complex*. First, let's take a moment to clarify what I mean by this:

- I use the term *simple job* throughout this chapter to refer to a standalone, schedule-based Chronos job. This job won't have any parent or child dependencies on other Chronos jobs. This might be something like sending an email every day, or performing a database backup nightly.
- I use the term *complex job* beginning in section 8.4 to refer to at least one schedule-based Chronos job, followed by one or more dependency-based jobs (a job that runs only after its parent job(s) completes successfully). This might be something like a series of extract-transform-load (ETL) pipelines for data analysis that could be run hourly, daily, and weekly.

To get started with Chronos, you'll begin with a single, standalone job, not unlike one you'd expect to find configured with the traditional Cron daemon.

8.3.1   *Creating a schedule-based job*

Let's face it: in every organization, there's a need to run something on a schedule. Whether that's submitting billing data to a payment processor each night, rotating log files every hour, or running an ETL pipeline every 30 minutes, there are clearly use cases for running a task on a schedule and expecting it to be reliably scheduled and launched on time.

Compared to the traditional Cron daemon that most of us are familiar with, Chronos allows you to schedule resources on a Mesos cluster and run a scheduled job within a container. Instead of wasting time and resources by manually provisioning individual machines (that are also single points of failure!) to run Cron jobs, Mesos and Chronos provide a way to reliably launch jobs with available resources on the cluster, and automatically retry them when they fail.

Let's start by taking a look at the limitations of the traditional Cron daemon before jumping into creating your first Chronos job.

ANATOMY OF A TRADITIONAL CRON JOB

The following example represents the most basic form of a schedule-based job in Cron. Every minute, run a command as the user `alice` that sleeps for 30 seconds:

```
* * * * * alice /bin/sh -c 'sleep 30'
```

This example should be familiar enough. This Cron job is typically deployed to a single machine, and will run as long as the machine—and the Cron daemon—are both alive and healthy. Regardless of how simple this example is, consider the drawbacks of the Cron system itself for a moment:

- The job must be manually deployed to a specific system running the Cron daemon.
- The job can't run more often than once per minute.
- The job isn't capable of having parent/child dependencies on other jobs.
- The standard Cron syntax may be counterintuitive to some.

Sure, you could argue that tools like Anacron allow you to schedule missed jobs if the system experiences some downtime, and, yes, you could execute a command that handles the relationships between multiple jobs for you. But at the end of the day, you're still left administering another machine in the datacenter, and the Cron jobs located on it.

ANATOMY OF A SCHEDULE-BASED CHRONOS JOB

In contrast, a schedule-based job in Chronos is represented as a JSON object containing, at a minimum, the following parts:

- Schedule
- Name (also referred to as an ID)
- Command

The job schedule is composed of three parts, each separated with a / (forward slash):

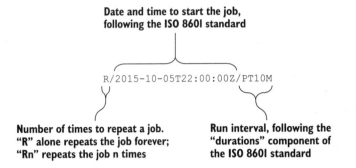

After you become familiar with the Chronos job schedule format, you can easily understand the date and time that the job first begins, how often it runs from that date and time, and the number of times (including infinity) that it should repeat. The previous example runs the job every 10 minutes beginning October 5, 2015 at 10 p.m. UTC, and repeats an infinite number of times.

> **TIP** For more information regarding the ISO 8601 date/time standard, check out https://en.wikipedia.org/wiki/ISO_8601.

Now that you've seen how Chronos differs from the traditional Cron daemon and understand how its schedules are formatted, let's go over how to create a simple schedule-based job by using the Chronos web interface.

CREATING A SCHEDULE-BASED JOB BY USING THE WEB INTERFACE

The web UI provides various fields when creating a job; these include name, description, command, and schedule. For the most part, they're self-explanatory. In figure 8.3, you create a simple job that sleeps for 60 seconds and exits.

Clicking the advanced options link for a job allows you to set additional options, such as the epsilon (the amount of time Chronos will wait for a resource offer from Mesos) and the resources required to run the job (CPUs, memory, disk, and so forth). For now, the defaults are fine, and you shouldn't need to modify those options. I'm showing them here in the interest of completeness.

Unfortunately, the web interface doesn't have all of the job options available in Chronos. To use some of the more advanced features, you need to turn to the REST API.

Basic job configuration:
name, description, and
command

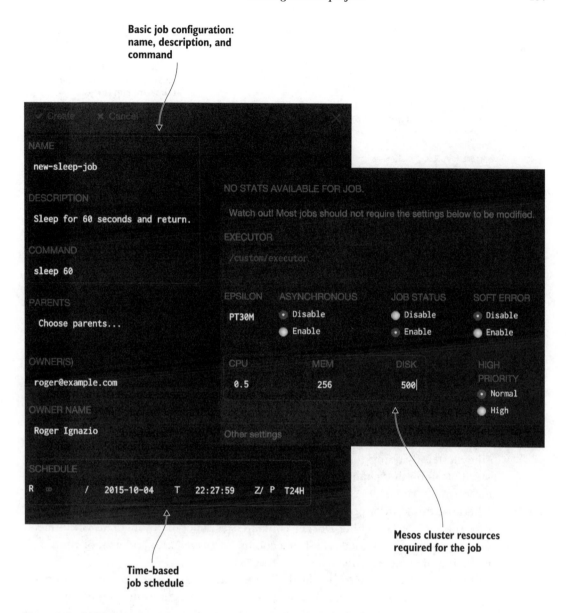

Figure 8.3 Defining the configuration for a Chronos job using the web interface

Mesos cluster resources
required for the job

Time-based
job schedule

CREATING A SCHEDULE-BASED JOB BY USING THE REST API

The REST API includes features that aren't present in the web UI, such as Docker container information, time-zone support, and the ability to use the Mesos fetcher to download files into the task's sandbox. The following listing presents the same job as in figure 8.3, but created using the REST API instead.

Listing 8.1   A simple sleep job in Chronos

The schedule includes the start date, run interval, and number of times to run the job.

```
{
  "schedule": "R/2015-10-04T22:57:59Z/PT24H",
  "name": "new-sleep-job",
  "description": "Sleep for 60 seconds and return.",
  "cpus": 0.5,
  "mem": 256,
  "disk": 500,
  "command": "sleep 60"
}
```

A unique identifier for the job

A human-readable description for the job

The command to run

Assuming the previous JSON was saved as simple-sleep.json, the following cURL command creates the job `new-sleep-job` in Chronos:

```
$ curl -H 'Content-Type: application/json' -d @simple-sleep.json
  http://chronos.example.com:4400/scheduler/iso8601
```

If you navigate to the Chronos web interface at this point, you'll see information about the job, including its last-run result, current status, and historical run durations.

8.3.2   Creating a schedule-based job using Docker

As covered in part 1 of this book, using Docker containers allows you to package your code—along with its dependencies—and distribute it as a single artifact to any node in the cluster. By doing so, you're able to build and distribute Docker images at will instead of submitting change requests for installing dependencies on every node that your job might run on.

Because this kind of portability is valuable, the Chronos maintainers have built in native support for launching Docker containers as scheduled jobs. This could mean launching Docker containers that run a command (using CMD) and exit, or running a command within a container (using ENTRYPOINT).

One useful feature here is that the Mesos task's sandbox directory is automatically mapped to a path within the container, so you can continue to use features in Mesos—such as the fetcher—to download any files or scripts you need for your scheduled job. Let's take a look at how to use the Mesos fetcher to download a script into the sandbox, and then run the script inside a Docker container that comes with Python 3.

CREATING THE JOB BY USING THE REST API

One of the common use cases for Cron (and Chronos, for that matter) is automatically sending emails on a set schedule. I've included an example script along with the supplementary materials for this book: email-weather-forecast.py. This script emails the user the latest weather forecast for their area by specifying a U.S. zip code. Let's take a look at how you deploy this job by using the Chronos REST API in the next listing.

Listing 8.2 Running a script within a Docker container

```
{
  "schedule": "R/2015-10-28T00:00:00.000Z/PT24H",
  "name": "daily-forecast-97201",
  "description": "The daily NWS weather forecast for Portland, OR",
  "container": {
    "type": "DOCKER",
    "image": "python:3.4.3"
  },
  "cpus": 0.1,
  "mem": 128.0,
  "owner": "user@example.com",
  "uris": [
    "https://raw.githubusercontent.com/rji/
    ➥ mesos-in-action-code-samples/master/email-weather-forecast.py"
  ],
  "command": "cd $MESOS_SANDBOX && python3 email-weather-forecast.py",
  "environmentVariables": [
    { "name": "TO_EMAIL_ADDR",   "value": "user@example.com"    },
    { "name": "FROM_EMAIL_ADDR", "value": "weather@example.com" },
    { "name": "ZIP_CODE",        "value": "97201"               },
    { "name": "MAIL_SERVER",     "value": "mail.example.com:25" },
    { "name": "MAIL_USERNAME",   "value": "weather@example.com" },
    { "name": "MAIL_PASSWORD",   "value": "ItsTopSecret!"       }
  ]
}
```

The ContainerInfo; here we use the Docker container python:3.4.3.

Download the example from this book's GitHub repository.

Chronos will send emails to the owner if the job fails.

Change into the sandbox directory and run the script.

Specify environment variables that will be used by the script.

Assuming the JSON in the previous code listing was saved as simple-docker.json, the following cURL command creates the job daily-forecast-97201 in Chronos:

```
$ curl -H 'Content-Type: application/json' -d @simple-docker.json
➥ http://chronos.example.com:4400/scheduler/iso8601
```

TIP You can update an existing job's configuration by resubmitting the same JSON using the HTTP PUT method instead of POST. If you're using cURL, this can be accomplished by adding the argument -X PUT to the command.

Although these standalone, schedule-based jobs have demonstrated how Chronos provides a more full-featured Cron for Mesos, you see its real power when you start working with complex jobs—a mix of schedule-based and dependency-based jobs.

8.4   *Working with complex jobs*

The preceding section covered simple, standalone jobs that run on a schedule, much like the Cron daemon that most of us are familiar with. Chronos also has the ability to create a dependency-based job: a job that runs only when its parent job(s) has completed successfully. Although many use cases exist for this, one that stands out is an ETL job, typically associated with data processing and analytics.

8.4.1   *Combining schedule-based and dependency-based jobs*

At their core, ETL jobs do the following:

- *Extract* data from one or more data sources
- *Transform* that data to be stored in a format more suited for analysis
- *Load* data into the destination store

In Chronos, dependency-based jobs don't contain a `schedule` field, but instead specify one or more parent jobs (using the `parents` field) that must complete before that job will run. Figure 8.4 shows how an ETL job might look in Chronos. Note the difference between the `schedule` field and the `parents` field.

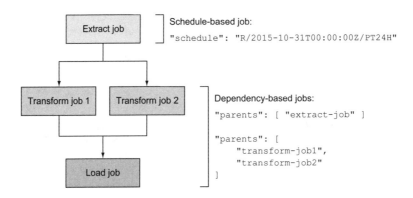

Figure 8.4   A complex Chronos job that runs when parent job(s) have completed successfully

In the previous figure, `extract-job` must complete successfully before `transform-job1` or `transform-job2` can begin. By establishing these dependencies between jobs, you can develop more-complex scheduled jobs. Combined with your external data stores, Chronos gives you a reliable way of scheduling jobs on a Mesos cluster.

Let's look at one such example: scheduling an ETL job that counts the words in Leo Tolstoy's *War and Peace*.

AN EXAMPLE: GETTING THE TOP 20 WORDS IN *WAR AND PEACE*

To illustrate how you can combine schedule-based and dependency-based jobs within the context of an ETL job, I've included an example of a Chronos job made up of a single schedule-based job and two dependency-based jobs. This example also uses HDFS and Spark, covered briefly in chapter 2. You can find the source code for this example with the supplementary materials included with this book.

> **TIP** To run the Spark job with Chronos, I've installed Cloudera's CDH 5.3 Hadoop distribution and Apache Spark on a Mesos cluster. Installation instructions are available at www.cloudera.com/content/www/en-us/documentation/ enterprise/5-3-x/cloudera-homepage.html and http://spark.apache.org/ downloads.html.

To visualize how this might look, consider figure 8.5.

Although this looks like it might normally be a complex task, Chronos allows you to create smaller, individual jobs and chain them together by creating a dependency graph. In listing 8.3, you begin the first job in the chain by downloading *War and Peace* from Project Gutenberg and storing the resulting text in HDFS for later use.

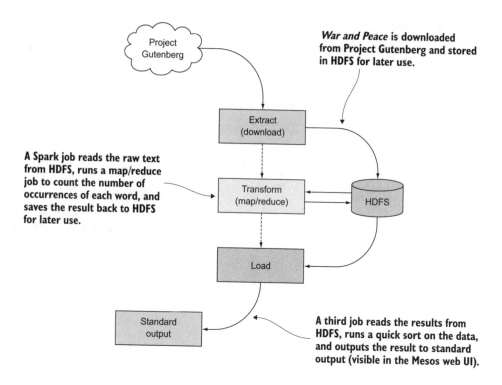

Figure 8.5 Visualizing the *War and Peace* ETL job as three Chronos jobs

Listing 8.3 A Chronos job to download *War and Peace*

```
{
  "name": "download-war-and-peace",
  "description": "Download the text of War and Peace.",
  "schedule": "R1//PT1M",                                          ◄─┐  Run this job
  "command": "hadoop fs -mkdir -p ${basepath} && hadoop fs -put -f    │  once on a
            ➥ pg2600.txt ${basepath}/warandpeace.txt",               │  schedule.
  "uris": [ "http://www.gutenberg.org/cache/epub/2600/pg2600.txt" ],
  "environmentVariables": [
    { "name": "basepath", "value": "/tmp/warandpeace" }
  ]
}
```

In the next step of your ETL job, you need to run a Spark map/reduce job that processes the text and counts the number of times each word appears. In the following listing, you create a second Chronos job, this time specifying the previous job (download-war-and-peace) in the parents field.

Listing 8.4 Running a Spark job to count the words in *War and Peace*

```
{
  "name": "war-and-peace-wordcount-spark-job",
  "description": "Use Spark to count all the words in War and Peace",
  "parents": ["download-war-and-peace"],                              ◄─┐
  "command": "/opt/spark/bin/spark-submit                              │
              ➥ mesos-in-action-code-samples-master/wordcount-example/
              ➥ war-and-peace-wordcount_2.10-0.1.0.jar ${basepath}",
  "uris": [
    "https://github.com/rji/mesos-in-action-code-samples/archive/
    ➥ master.tar.gz"
  ],
  "environmentVariables": [
    { "name": "basepath", "value": "/tmp/warandpeace" }
  ]
}
```

Run this job when
download-war-and-peace has
completed successfully.

The Spark job in the previous code listing reads the text from HDFS and then stores the word counts alongside the text. To display the output in the Mesos UI, let's read the results from the Spark job in listing 8.5, sort them, and get the first 20 lines. As in the code in listing 8.4, you also specify the parents field to establish a dependency on the previous job.

Listing 8.5 Loading the results and outputting the top 20 words

```
{
  "name": "load-war-and-peace-word-counts",
  "description": "Read the output from HDFS and send it to stdout",
  "parents": ["war-and-peace-wordcount-spark-job"],
  "command": "hadoop fs -cat ${basepath}/result/part-* |
        ➥ sort -t, -rnk2 | head -20",
  "environmentVariables": [
    { "name": "basepath", "value": "/tmp/warandpeace" }
  ]
}
```

Run this job when war-and-peace-wordcount-spark-job has completed successfully.

That's it! Those three jobs will run the ETL pipeline required to process the text of *War and Peace* and output the top 20 words. To illustrate this as quickly as possible, a small script that deploys these three jobs is in the GitHub repository for this book. If Spark and HDFS are set up on your Mesos cluster, you can try it by running the following command:

```
$ complex-etl-job/create-jobs.sh http://chronos.example.com:4400
```

The script creates three jobs, as defined in listings 8.3 through 8.5. Assuming that everything works as intended, you should be able to navigate to the Mesos web interface and view the output from the load-war-and-peace-word-counts job. It should display the top 20 words in the book.

8.4.2 *Visualizing job dependencies*

Chronos has a useful feature for visualizing dependencies between various jobs. Instead of trying to track complex job dependencies by hand, you can view a dynamically generated graph, right from within the Chronos web interface. Look at figure 8.6, which shows the job dependencies from the ETL pipeline created in the previous section.

The other helpful aspect of the dependency graph is that it highlights which jobs are successful and which fail, allowing you to quickly discover and resolve failures in increasingly complex jobs.

> **TIP** If you'd rather retrieve the contents of the DOT file instead of the rendered graph, check out the /scheduler/graph/dot API endpoint.

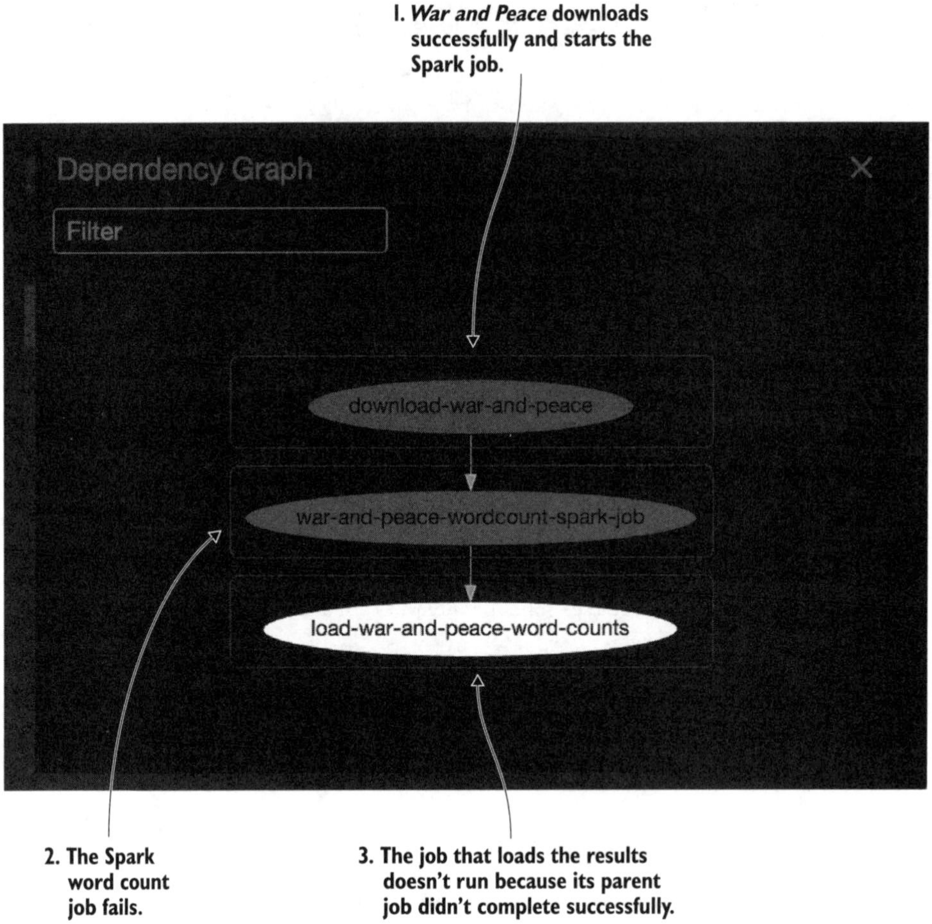
1. *War and Peace* downloads successfully and starts the Spark job.
Dependency Graph
Filter
download-war-and-peace
war-and-peace-wordcount-spark-job
load-war-and-peace-word-counts
2. The Spark word count job fails.
3. The job that loads the results doesn't run because its parent job didn't complete successfully.

Figure 8.6 A Chronos dependency graph for jobs that have a parent/child relationship. The success of the first job causes the second job to run, but because the second job fails, the third job never runs.

8.5 Monitoring the output and status of Chronos jobs

It's not a matter of *if* something will fail; it's a matter of *when*. Even the most well-designed systems will suffer some sort of failure or service degradation eventually. The key is to ensure that the system fails or degrades gracefully and notifies the system's owner with relevant information when it occurs.

This section covers how to enable job-failure notifications in Chronos for both email and Slack, the popular group-messaging service. The section also covers how to monitor jobs to determine whether they're in a healthy or a failed state and observe job output when further debugging is required.

8.5.1 *Job failure notifications and monitoring*

Depending on your organization, team, and preferred medium for receiving alerts and notifications, you might prefer email notifications on job failures, Slack notifications for your team, or a monitoring system like Nagios to periodically check the status of your jobs via the REST API. Fortunately, solutions exist for each of these.

EMAIL NOTIFICATIONS ON JOB FAILURE

To enable email notifications, Chronos must first be configured to connect to a mail server. Although we first covered this during the installation and configuration section, the options you need to set within /etc/chronos/conf are as follows:

- `mail_from`—The email address from which to send notifications, such as chronos@example.com
- `mail_server`—The mail server to connect with, specified as the server and port (such as mail.example.com:25)
- `mail_user`—Optional; the username to use when authenticating to the mail server
- `mail_password`—Optional; the password to use when authenticating to the mail server
- `mail_ssl`—Optional; enables SSL connections to the mail server

After the Chronos instance is configured to connect to a mail relay, each job can specify the email addresses of one or more owners. As with the To field in an email, multiple owners for a job can be entered; just be sure to separate them with commas. This option is on a per-job basis, and is configurable both via the web interface and the `owner` field first covered in listing 8.2.

SLACK NOTIFICATIONS ON JOB FAILURE

Slack is a popular group-messaging platform that allows for instant communication between team members. Considering that a large portion of a team's communication could be happening via instant messaging, email might not necessarily be the best option to be notified of a failure and be able to respond quickly. Fortunately, Chronos has built-in support for sending a notification to a Slack channel when a job fails.

> **NOTE** As mentioned earlier, the Slack support in Chronos requires that you provide a Slack webhook URL using the `--slack_url` configuration option. This can be accomplished by creating the file /etc/chronos/conf/slack_url for each of the deployed Chronos instances.

As of this writing, the Slack implementation has a limitation in Chronos: because it's implemented as a configuration option for the Chronos instance and not the job within Chronos, all notifications must go to one channel. In some cases, sending these notifications to #general or #sysops should be fine. Figure 8.7 shows an example Slack notification sent to the #general channel.

chronos-notifications BOT 10:18 PM
[Chronos] job 'periodic-user-account-audit' failed!:
'2015-11-03T06:18:29.911Z'. Retries attempted: 2.
Task id: ct:1446531489797:2:periodic-user-account-audit:
The scheduler provided this message:

Command exited with status 1

**Figure 8.7   An example of a Chronos
notification in a Slack channel**

As you can see in the screenshot, the job failed and a Slack notification was sent. This notification includes the name of the job, the timestamp, the number of retries that were attempted, the task ID (for debugging in the Mesos UI), and the error message.

MONITORING A JOB'S STATUS VIA THE REST API

Chronos provides the /scheduler/jobs API endpoint, which allows you to get information about all of the jobs within Chronos, their configurations, and information about the jobs' successes and failures. By iterating over the items in the JSON array, you're able to check the status of all jobs by making a single HTTP request.

Just as you might write a script for your monitoring system to check on the status of a Cron job, you can do the same thing for Chronos jobs. Of particular note are the following fields within a given job's JSON hash, as provided in table 8.3.

Table 8.3   Select job metrics available for monitoring purposes

Field	Description
errorsSinceLastSuccess	The number of times the job has failed since the last successful run
lastSuccess	The date and time of the last successful run, in ISO 8601 format
lastError	The date and time of the last failed run, in ISO 8601 format
successCount	Successful run count over the history of the job
errorCount	Failed run count over the history of the job

Given this information, you could write a check for your monitoring system of choice. Some alerting use cases that come to mind include the following:

- Alerting that a job is in an error state: errorsSinceLastSuccess will be 0 if the last run of the job was successful. If this is positive, the job is currently in a failed state.
- Alerting that the timestamp of a job's last successful run is outside a given SLA: lastSuccess could be used to escalate an alert to an engineering manager or product manager if a business-critical data processing job that should run every hour hasn't been successful in the last 3 hours.
- Alerting on the failure rate of a particular job: you could create a check that uses the formula failure_pct = errorCount / (errorCount + successCount) to determine how often a job completes successfully.

8.5.2 Observing standard output and standard error via Mesos

Because Chronos jobs run as Mesos tasks, the easiest way to observe output from these jobs is by using the Mesos web interface, as covered in chapter 5. To provide a refresher, two files are automatically created in a task's sandbox: stdout and stderr, as shown in figure 8.8. These files capture output from a task's standard output and standard error, respectively.

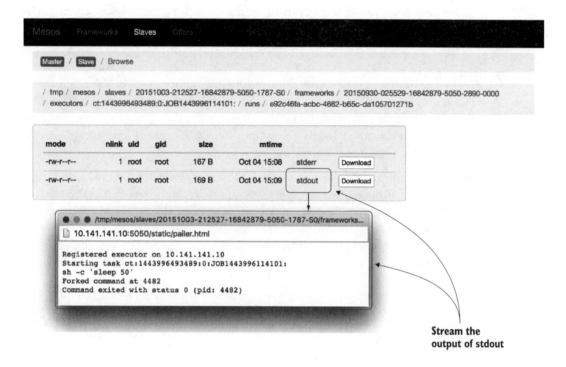

Figure 8.8 Observing the output from a Chronos job in the Mesos web interface

Clicking either the stdout or stderr link within a task's sandbox opens a new window, allowing you to live-stream the logs from the job to your web browser. This makes it easy to keep an eye on long-running Chronos jobs or determine why a job failed without needing to log in to a machine.

8.6 Summary

In this chapter, you learned about deploying scheduled jobs on Chronos. You explored topics such as installation and configuration, jobs and job dependencies, and monitoring. Here are a few things to remember:

- The schedule for a Chronos job is broken into three parts, separated by a forward slash: the number of times the job repeats, the start time of the job (in ISO

8601 format), and a run interval (following the format of the "durations" component in the ISO 8601 standard).

- Jobs that run on a schedule and don't have any parent/child dependencies are *simple jobs. Complex jobs* have one parent job that runs on a schedule, and one or more child jobs that run only if their parent job completed successfully.

- When using Docker images, the Mesos task's sandbox is automatically mapped within the container. This allows you to use the Mesos fetcher to download files that need to be present in the sandbox before the Docker container is even launched.

- When creating jobs that are dependent on a parent job, the schedule field is omitted; instead, you need to use the parents field.

- You can monitor jobs, send notifications on failure, and observe output in numerous ways: notifications can currently be sent via email and Slack; a job's status—including success and failure counts and times—can be gathered using the REST API; and to observe the output from a job, check out the stdout and stderr files within a task's sandbox.

Although this chapter provided several in-depth examples with the most commonly used parameters, Chronos has many more features than can be covered in this book—and more are being added in every release. For the latest documentation, check out https://mesos.github.io/chronos.

The next chapter covers the popular Apache Aurora project. Aurora allows you to deploy applications and scheduled jobs on Mesos, all within a single framework.

Deploying applications and managing scheduled tasks with Aurora

This chapter covers

- Building, installing, and configuring Aurora
- Deploying applications and Docker containers
- Creating scheduled tasks

In the preceding two chapters, you learned about Marathon and Chronos, two popular Mesos frameworks that allow you to deploy applications and run scheduled tasks on a Mesos cluster. In this chapter, I'll cover Apache Aurora, a Mesos framework developed by Twitter to simplify its operations around deploying applications and Cron jobs.

Although Aurora is arguably more difficult to configure and deploy than Marathon or Chronos, this book covers Aurora to provide you with options for frameworks to deploy on your own cluster. For example, Marathon and Chronos both provide an easy-to-use, JSON-based REST API, but they don't provide user-access control. On the other hand, Aurora provides multi-user access control, but with the added complexity of its own Python-based language. Of course, you should evaluate each in a development or preproduction environment and determine which suits your team and organization the best. Although Aurora is complex, it's also powerful.

Before proceeding with Aurora, you should be comfortable compiling software, writing your own service scripts, and (optionally) building your own packages. Because I already covered running applications and Cron jobs in chapters 7 and 8, I won't necessarily repeat all of that information here, instead opting to cover the Aurora-specific bits using the examples you're already familiar with. If you haven't read through chapters 7 and 8 and are interested in how Mesos handles application deployments and scheduled tasks, I recommend you read those first. Otherwise, let's get started!

9.1   *Introducing Aurora*

Aurora began as a project at Twitter in 2010, around the same time the company was adopting Mesos to scale its infrastructure and put an end to the "Fail Whale." As one of the first Mesos frameworks, Aurora allowed Twitter to simplify its operations by providing self-service application and job management to its large team of developers.

Twitter open sourced this work, and Aurora became a top-level project at the Apache Software Foundation, alongside Mesos. It's safe to say that Aurora has been battle-tested in a large-scale production environment, and supports hundreds of software engineers deploying applications and Cron jobs on a daily basis.

NOTE   This chapter covers Aurora 0.9.0.

Because Aurora grew out of a necessity to support multiple users, it isn't (in some cases) as full-featured as other Mesos frameworks. But you can rest assured that the features built into Aurora are stable and robust. Let's take a moment to compare Aurora to the other frameworks discussed previously (Marathon and Chronos) by taking a look at table 9.1.

Table 9.1   Comparing features of Aurora, Marathon, and Chronos

	Aurora	Marathon	Chronos
Configuration DSL	Yes	No	No
Deploy long-running applications	Yes	Yes	No
Deploy scheduled (Cron) jobs	Yes	No	Yes
Docker support	Experimental / incomplete	Yes	Yes
HA deployment	Yes	Yes	Yes
Packages available	No	Yes	Yes
REST API	No	Yes	Yes
Support for user auth and resource quotas	Yes	No	No

Despite the framework generally being referred to by the Aurora name, it's made up of several components:

- Scheduler
- Client (two—one for users and one for administrators)
- Executor
- Observer

Together, these components make up a platform for running applications and scheduled jobs on a Mesos cluster. The scheduler serves as the main interface into an Aurora cluster, and a command-line client provides a way for users to create, update, and delete jobs. The executor and observer provide a consistent execution environment for running and monitoring tasks, and an admin client allows operators to administer the cluster. Let's take a look at each of these components in a bit more detail.

9.1.1 *The Aurora scheduler*

Like any other Mesos scheduler, the Aurora scheduler is responsible for registering to the Mesos master, accepting or declining resource offers, and launching tasks on the cluster. Similar to other frameworks that you've learned about in this book, the scheduler is the component responsible for providing the overall Aurora service to users. When users need to deploy new services or scheduled jobs, it's the scheduler that handles dispatching the process to a machine in the cluster.

The scheduler itself is written in Java, and, during the build process, bundles all its dependencies into a single JAR (with the exception of libmesos and the JVM itself; these must already be present on the system). Like Mesos and other Mesos frameworks, Aurora uses ZooKeeper for replica detection, leader election, and to publish service discovery information. By using a distributed database like ZooKeeper, Aurora can be deployed in a highly available manner.

Most of the operations in Aurora either start with or flow through the scheduler. The command-line clients connect with the scheduler and are used for managing both user jobs and the cluster itself. The scheduler is also capable of supporting multiple users via the Apache Shiro security framework, which I'll cover later in this chapter. Finally, the scheduler also provides a web interface for viewing job configurations and an application's configuration and deployment status.

9.1.2 *The Thermos executor and observer*

You learned earlier in the book that Mesos launches a task on a slave in the cluster by using an executor. One of the built-in executors in Mesos, the `CommandExecutor`, launches commands using a shell (/bin/sh). But Mesos also provides an API to develop custom executors that can launch, monitor, and kill tasks. Thermos, the executor used in Aurora, is an example of a custom, Python-based executor for Mesos that provides a consistent execution environment for tasks launched by the Aurora scheduler.

> **TIP** The next chapter covers custom executors in more detail.

Thermos is made up of two parts:

- *Executor*—A Mesos executor that launches and manages Aurora's tasks and health checks
- *Observer*—A separate service (one instance per Mesos slave) that monitors tasks launched by a Thermos executor

When the Aurora scheduler accepts a resource offer to launch a task on a slave, it does so by first launching the executor. Once the executor registers with the Mesos slave, it can launch the process that the user requested, whether that's launching an instance of an application or running a scheduled job.

The observer in Aurora is unique in that it monitors each executor and provides a web interface on each Mesos slave participating in an Aurora cluster. This provides a way for users to interact with a monitoring service on each of the cluster nodes without requiring shell access to the Mesos infrastructure itself. As you may recall from chapter 7, Marathon displays some basic task information, but for any additional details, you need to switch back to the Mesos web interface (at least as of this writing). The close integration between the Aurora scheduler's web interface and that of the Thermos observer provide for a more consistent user experience, at the cost of a more complex deployment overall.

9.1.3   *The Aurora user and admin clients*

The Aurora project provides two separate, Python-based command-line clients that I refer to as the *user client* and the *admin client.* Just as the names imply, the user client can be distributed to application developers for deploying services and scheduled jobs on an Aurora-enabled Mesos cluster. The admin client, on the other hand, is distributed to systems administrators and is used for common tasks such as cluster maintenance and managing users.

You'll learn more about how to use these clients a little later in this chapter. For now, I'll provide a brief overview of some of the capabilities that each of these clients provides.

THE USER CLIENT

The first of the two command-line clients, the Aurora user client, is typically deployed to users and engineering teams so that they can manage their own services and scheduled jobs on a common cluster. A few noteworthy capabilities of this client, which you'll see throughout the remainder of this chapter, include the following:

- job—Create, kill, restart, and list services and ad hoc jobs.
- cron—Create, modify, remove, and manually start Cron jobs.
- update—Start, abort, pause, and resume a rolling update of a service or job.

There's a lot more functionality built into the client than we have time to cover here, and the Aurora project is still being actively developed. For the complete list of subcommands, including detailed usage and help, run aurora -h or refer to the official project documentation at http://aurora.apache.org/documentation/latest/client-commands.

THE ADMIN CLIENT

The second of the two command-line clients, the Aurora admin client, is tailored toward the systems administrators responsible for maintaining the Aurora cluster. It allows you to perform operations across a given Aurora cluster from the comfort of your laptop or workstation. It includes features such as the following:

- *Backup and restore*—Perform a backup of the scheduler's state, and restore from a backup.
- *Maintenance*—Put hosts into (and remove them from) maintenance mode, including draining tasks from a specific host or set of hosts.
- *Quotas*—Create and modify the amount of production quota granted to a specific user.
- *SLAs*—Probe a specific host for its tasks, and calculate a projected SLA should the host go offline.

Just as with the user client, a large amount of functionality is built into the admin client, and I probably don't need to repeat it all in this text. To get a complete list of all of the subcommands, run `aurora-admin -h`. I'll cover some of the main functionality, specifically host maintenance and user management, later in this chapter.

9.1.4 *The Aurora domain-specific language*

Unlike Marathon and Chronos, the two Mesos frameworks covered in chapters 7 and 8, Aurora provides its own Python-based domain-specific language (DSL) for writing job configurations in lieu of a JSON-based API. Each configuration file is maintained by the team deploying the application or job, and is suffixed with .aurora.

The Aurora language has a few primitives that are worth understanding:

- `Process`—The command that's executed on a system. One or more `Process` objects make up a `Task`.
- `Task`—An object that contains one or more processes. There are also two variations of this primitive: `SimpleTask` and `SequentialTask`.
- `Job`—A collection of `Tasks` that can be launched on a Mesos cluster.

These configuration files are processed by the Aurora client and deployed to the cluster. Each job has a unique identifier, referred to as the *job key*. Each job key follows this format:

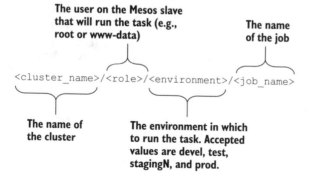

The user on the Mesos slave that will run the task (e.g., root or www-data)

The name of the job

```
<cluster_name>/<role>/<environment>/<job_name>
```

The name of the cluster

The environment in which to run the task. Accepted values are devel, test, stagingN, and prod.

An Aurora job is referred to in the configuration file by its job key, and contains one or more Processes, Tasks, and Jobs. I cover some examples of jobs written in the Aurora DSL a little later in this chapter. For the complete configuration reference and best practices around creating configuration files and working with the Aurora DSL, please refer to the official documentation:

- The configuration tutorial provides step-by-step instructions for using the DSL: http://aurora.apache.org/documentation/latest/configuration-tutorial.
- The configuration reference provides detailed information about the entire schema: http://aurora.apache.org/documentation/latest/configuration-reference.

Now that you're familiar with the components that make up Aurora—the scheduler, the executor, the observer, the two command-line clients, and the job configuration DSL—let's go over how to build, install, and configure Aurora to work with your Mesos cluster.

9.2   *Deploying Aurora*

Similar to Mesos and other Mesos frameworks, Aurora can be deployed in various ways. It can be installed as a single instance (for development purposes), highly available (for production purposes), or if you're just looking to test it out in a development environment, you can use the Vagrant file located inside the Aurora download at aurora.apache.org to provision a single-node Aurora cluster right on your laptop.

Before continuing, it's important to learn how each component in Aurora interacts with the others by studying figure 9.1.

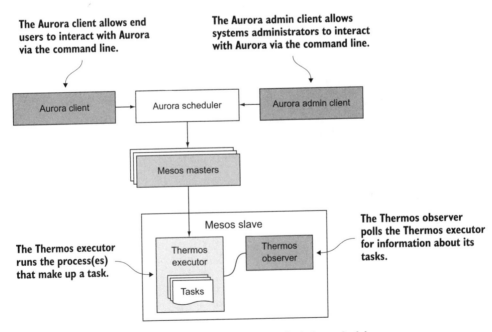

Figure 9.1   The components that make up Apache Aurora include a scheduler.

Similar to the scheduler of any other Mesos framework, Aurora's scheduler registers with the Mesos master and launches tasks on a slave. The Aurora command-line clients are responsible for deploying applications, creating Cron jobs, and administering the cluster. When the scheduler has work to be run on the cluster, it accepts a resource offer from the leading Mesos master, and launches one or more tasks.

This section discusses how to get up and running with Aurora in a development (Vagrant) environment, and also how to deploy it to a production-ready Mesos cluster such as the one that you first learned to create in chapter 3.

9.2.1 Trying out Aurora in a development environment

The easiest way to get started with Aurora in development is to use the Vagrant environment included in the project's Git repository. In case you aren't familiar with Vagrant, it's an open source tool that provides a simple way to share development environments with others. You can find more information, including download links, at www.vagrantup.com.

The Vagrant file included with Aurora sets up the Mesos master, Mesos slave, and Aurora, all on a single virtual machine. This allows you to test out Aurora and deploy some applications and Cron jobs from the comfort of your laptop or workstation. If you're interested in trying out Aurora locally first, great! If not, feel free to skip ahead to section 9.2.2, where you'll install Aurora in a more production-like manner.

SETTING UP THE VAGRANT ENVIRONMENT

The Vagrant environment is commonly used for setting up Aurora for development purposes. You can clone Aurora from its Git repository hosted by the Apache Software Foundation by running the following commands:

```
$ git clone git://git.apache.org/aurora.git
$ cd aurora
$ git checkout rel/0.9.0
```

When Aurora has finished cloning and you've checked out the version of Aurora that we cover in this chapter, bring up the Vagrant machine by running the following command:

```
$ vagrant up
```

> **WARNING** The Vagrantfile included with Aurora 0.9.0 installs Mesos 0.22.0, which has some known issues with recent versions of Docker. After the Vagrant machine is up and running, you should add the Mesosphere package repository (instructions available in chapter 3 and at https://mesosphere.com/downloads), and upgrade Mesos to version 0.22.2 before proceeding. After upgrading Mesos, be sure to restart each of the services by running `service mesos-master restart` and `service mesos-slave restart`. Without upgrading Mesos, the `mesos-slave` daemon will refuse to start, and you won't be able to schedule any tasks.

You should now be able to access Mesos and Aurora at the following URLs:

- Mesos master: http://192.168.33.7:5050
- Aurora scheduler: http://192.168.33.7:8081/scheduler
- Thermos observer: http://192.168.33.7:1338

9.2.2 *Building and installing Aurora*

As you did with Mesos, you need to deploy the Aurora scheduler on a number of machines. For production workloads, deploying three or five instances of the Aurora scheduler should be sufficient. To keep the deployment simple, assume that you're deploying Aurora on the same machines as the Mesos masters themselves. The Aurora project doesn't maintain packages for both RHEL and Ubuntu, at least at the time of this writing, so I've opted to demonstrate how to build Aurora from the source code available at aurora.apache.org.

> **TIP** Although Aurora packages aren't available at the time of writing, efforts are underway to build and distribute official packages. You can find the latest code at https://git-wip-us.apache.org/repos/asf?p=aurora-packaging.git;a=tree. But for now, you'll need to write your own service scripts for your service manager or supervisor of choice (systemd, upstart, supervisord, and so forth), or try to adapt the scripts in the packaging repo to meet your needs.

To facilitate the building of the various Aurora components, and to keep the build instructions in the text to a minimum, I've included a build script for Aurora in the chapter09 directory of the GitHub repository that accompanies this book. The script is capable of building the Aurora components on both RHEL / CentOS 7 and Ubuntu 14.04.

BUILDING AURORA

To build all of the components that make up Aurora, first clone this book's Git repository by running the following commands:

```
$ git clone https://github.com/rji/mesos-in-action-code-samples
$ cd chapter09
```

Next, use the aurora-build.sh script to compile all of the components. The script will also install any prerequisite packages needed to build Aurora:

```
$ ./aurora-build.sh all
```

The build script will take a few minutes to complete. When it's done, all of the built components will be available in the apache-aurora-0.9.0/dist directory. I'll refer to the individual components during the installation instructions in the next several sections.

INSTALLING THE AURORA SCHEDULER

As I mentioned previously, let's assume that you'll install an instance of the scheduler on each of the Mesos masters. In the previous build step, a zip file containing the scheduler code can be found in your current working directory at apache-aurora-0.9.0/dist/distributions/aurora-scheduler-0.9.0.zip. Go ahead and copy this file to each of the Mesos masters:

```
$ scp apache-aurora-0.9.0/dist/distributions/aurora-scheduler-0.9.0.zip
➥ user@mesos-master-1.example.com:
```

Next, extract the Aurora distribution from your home directory to your location of choice. For the purposes of this book, let's install it to /usr/local, and create a symlink to the installation at /usr/local/aurora-scheduler. This will allow you to easily upgrade Aurora in the future by placing a newer version of Aurora within /usr/local and updating the target of the symlink:

```
user@mesos-master $ sudo unzip aurora-scheduler-0.9.0.zip -d /usr/local
user@mesos-master $ sudo ln -fns /usr/local/aurora-scheduler-0.9.0
➥ /usr/local/aurora-scheduler
```

With the Aurora scheduler code in place on each of the masters, let's move on to cover the installation of the remaining Aurora components. I'll cover the configuration of each of the components in the next section (9.2.3).

INSTALLING THE THERMOS EXECUTOR AND OBSERVER

To install the Thermos executor and observer, you'll need to copy a couple of executables to each machine in the Mesos cluster. For large installations, this is where a configuration management tool like Puppet, or an orchestration tool like Ansible, really comes in handy.

Copy thermos_executor.pex and thermos_observer.pex from the apache-aurora-0.9.0/dist directory on your local machine to each of the Mesos slaves by running the following commands:

```
$ scp -p apache-aurora-0.9.0/dist/thermos_{executor,observer}.pex
➥ user@mesos-slave-N.example.com:
```

Next, just as you did for the Aurora scheduler, move them to a location on disk that makes sense for your environment and then create symlinks pointing to the current version. This will allow you to upgrade the executor and observer code by updating the target of the link:

```
user@mesos-slave $ sudo mkdir /usr/local/aurora-executor-0.9.0
user@mesos-slave $ sudo mv thermos_{executor,observer}.pex
➥ /usr/local/aurora-executor-0.9.0/
user@mesos-slave $ sudo ln -fns /usr/local/aurora-executor-0.9.0
➥ /usr/local/aurora-executor
```

> **NOTE** The Aurora executor code must be available at the same location on every slave in the cluster. You'll need to provide this path when configuring the Aurora scheduler in the next section.

After copying the Aurora code to the Mesos masters and slaves, you're almost ready to start deploying applications and creating Cron jobs. But before you can do that, you need to build and install the command-line clients that allow you to do so.

INSTALLING THE AURORA CLIENT

Aurora provides a separate command-line client for managing jobs and services from developer workstations, providing a great self-service model for small to large engineering organizations. After aurora-build.sh has finished building all of the components, you'll find a file named aurora.pex located in the apache-aurora-0.9.0/dist directory. Move this file to a suitable location on your workstation by running the following commands:

```
$ sudo mv apache-aurora-0.9.0/dist/aurora.pex
➥ /usr/local/aurora-client-0.9.0.pex
$ sudo ln -fns /usr/local/aurora-client-0.9.0.pex /usr/local/bin/aurora
```

If all is well, you should be able to run the command aurora --version and have it return 0.9.0. If not, ensure that /usr/local/bin appears on your $PATH.

BUILDING AND INSTALLING THE AURORA ADMIN CLIENT

The second command-line tool that comes with Aurora, the Aurora admin client, is designed for systems administrators and provides several tools for performing cluster maintenance and overall cluster administration. To install the aurora-admin command-line tool to /usr/local/bin/aurora-admin, run the following commands:

```
$ sudo mv apache-aurora-0.9.0/dist/aurora_admin.pex
➥ /usr/local/aurora-admin-0.9.0.pex
$ sudo ln -fns /usr/local/aurora-admin-0.9.0.pex
➥ /usr/local/bin/aurora-admin
```

Now that you've built and installed the components that make up Aurora, let's start configuring each of them.

9.2.3 Configuring Aurora

Each component in Aurora, especially the scheduler, is highly configurable based on your specific wants, needs, and environment. This section provides examples of how you might configure Aurora, including the required (and some recommended) configuration options for doing so.

CONFIGURING THE SCHEDULER

Aurora's scheduler is responsible for interfacing with Mesos, launching tasks, and allowing users to submit jobs, so it's safe to say that most operations rely on it being up and running. Let's begin configuring Aurora by first configuring the scheduler and ensuring the service is up and running.

> **NOTE** Aurora expects to be run by an external supervisor process, such as systemd, upstart, or supervisord. You should keep this in mind when building and deploying Aurora in your own environment.

Table 9.2 includes the required configuration options, plus a few other important options you might need when deploying the Aurora scheduler for your Mesos cluster. For a complete listing of the configuration options available, you can also run the following command:

```
$ /usr/local/aurora-scheduler/bin/aurora-scheduler -help
```

Table 9.2 Required (and important) configuration options for the Aurora scheduler

Configuration option	Description
-cluster_name	An arbitrary name used to identify the Aurora cluster.
-mesos_master_address	The ZooKeeper URL for detecting and connecting to the Mesos master. For example: zk://zk1:2181,zk2:2181,zk3:2181/mesos
-serverset_path	ZooKeeper ServerSet path used for registration. For example: /aurora/scheduler
-zk_endpoints	A list of servers in the ZooKeeper ensemble to be used with Aurora. For example: zk1:2181,zk2:2181,zk3:2181
-native_log_quorum_size	The quorum size for the Aurora schedulers. If deploying the Aurora schedulers on the same machines as the Mesos masters, this would be the value of /etc/mesos-master/quorum.
-native_log_file_path	The location on disk for the Mesos replicated log used by Aurora to maintain state.
-backup_dir	The directory in which Aurora will store its backups.
-thermos_executor_path	The path to the Thermos executor on a slave. The executor must be located at the same path on all slaves in the cluster.
-thermos_executor_flags	Additional options to pass to the Thermos executor.
-allowed_container_types	The containerizers that can be used by Aurora. For our cluster, this will be DOCKER, MESOS.
-framework_authentication_file	Mesos authentication principal and secret (see chapter 6).
-zk_digest_credentials	A file containing credentials used to authenticate with ZooKeeper (optional). Follows the format username:password

To maintain state across each of the scheduler instances, Aurora uses an instance of the replicated log present in Mesos. Therefore, you need to initialize a new replicated log—dedicated to Aurora—on each of the Mesos masters. Running the following command will initialize the log file at /var/db/aurora:

```
$ sudo mkdir -p /var/db && sudo mesos-log initialize --path=/var/db/aurora
```

NOTE   The location for the Mesos replicated log for Aurora is completely arbitrary, but it must match the value for the -native_log_file_path configuration option passed to the Aurora scheduler.

Because Aurora's configuration and startup is much more involved than that of Marathon or Chronos (or, in some cases, even Mesos), I thought it best to include an example script that can be used to launch the Aurora scheduler service. The script in the following listing also includes some sane values for the configuration options covered in table 9.1.

Listing 9.1   Example Aurora scheduler startup script

```
#!/bin/bash

AURORA_SCHEDULER_HOME=/usr/local/aurora-scheduler
export LIBPROCESS_PORT=8083
export JAVA_OPTS="-Djava.library.path=/usr/lib -Xms2g -Xmx2g"

AURORA_OPTS=(
    -zk_endpoints=$(cut -d / -f 3 /etc/mesos/zk)
    -mesos_master_address=$(cat /etc/mesos/zk)
    -native_log_quorum_size=$(cat /etc/mesos-master/quorum)
    -cluster_name=aurora-cluster
    -http_port=8081
    -serverset_path=/aurora/scheduler
    -native_log_zk_group_path=/aurora/replicated-log
    -native_log_file_path=/var/db/aurora
    -backup_dir=/var/lib/aurora/backups
    -vlog=INFO
    -logtostderr
    -allowed_container_types=DOCKER,MESOS
    -thermos_executor_path=/usr/local/aurora-executor/thermos_executor.pex
    -thermos_executor_flags="--announcer-enable
    --announcer-ensemble $(cut -d / -f 3 /etc/mesos/zk)"
)

exec "${AURORA_SCHEDULER_HOME}/bin/aurora-scheduler" "${AURORA_OPTS[@]}"
```

The port used by the Mesos scheduler driver (libmesos) to communicate with the master

JVM options; in this case we specify the heap size and the location to libmesos.

Note that the script in this listing is just one example of how you could configure this service. Depending on how you configured Mesos, or if you're deploying Aurora to machines that aren't also running the Mesos master daemon, this could be different for your environment. In addition, you could also modify the previous script to take the approach that Marathon and Chronos use, whereby all configuration options exist as files on disk and the service script reads them in as arguments when the script is executed. Either way, you then need to combine this with your service manager of choice to run the scheduler.

Because you have many deployment options and a lot of them come down to personal preference, let's fire up the Aurora scheduler as a background process so you can move forward. Assuming you saved the script from listing 9.1 as aurora-sched-uler.sh, start the scheduler by running the following command:

```
$ chmod +x aurora-scheduler.sh
$ sudo ./aurora-scheduler.sh > /dev/null 2>&1 &
```

If all is well, you should see a framework registered with the name TwitterScheduler in the Mesos web interface. Note that for brevity, all logging output in the previous command is being redirected to /dev/null. When you adapt this script to your service manager of choice, be sure to redirect logs to a sane location for your system or centralized logging solution.

CONFIGURING THE THERMOS EXECUTOR AND OBSERVER

Out of the box, the Thermos executor doesn't require any additional configuration; it just needs to be deployed to the same path on every Mesos slave. But at the same time, you can use numerous configuration options to fine-tune the executor. Because these are options used for fine-tuning the executor and aren't required for normal operation, I won't cover them here. For a complete list of configuration parameters, run the following command:

```
$ /usr/local/aurora-executor/thermos_executor.pex --long-help.
```

The Thermos observer, on the other hand, is a service separate from the executor that runs on each of the Mesos slaves. The observer provides information about the running executors and tasks and requires some light configuration. Table 9.3 lists the configuration options that you'll need to set for the observer.

Table 9.3   Thermos observer configuration options

Configuration option	Description
--root	The root directory to search for the Thermos executor's tasks. Defaults to /var/run/thermos.
--mesos-root	The Mesos root directory that Thermos executor sandboxes are contained in. This should be set to the same directory as --work_dir on the Mesos slaves. Defaults to /var/lib/mesos.
--port	The port that the observer will listen on. Defaults to 1338.
--polling_interval_secs	The interval between polling attempts of the Thermos executor's tasks. Defaults to five seconds.

The previous table listed the most important options, but as with the executor, there are additional options to fine-tune the observer that I won't go into detail here. For a complete listing of all available configuration parameters, run the following command:

```
$ /usr/local/aurora-executor/thermos_observer.pex --long-help
```

Depending on your preferences and environment, you'll want to use an external supervisor system to start the service and automatically respawn it if it fails. But to get everything up and running as quickly as possible, you can fire up the Thermos observer by running the following command:

```
$ sudo /usr/local/aurora-executor/thermos_observer.pex --port=1338
➥ --log_to_disk=NONE --log_to_stderr=google:INFO > /dev/null 2>&1 &
```

Now, let's create the configuration file that will be used by the Aurora command-line clients.

CONFIGURING THE CLIENT

The Aurora clients use JSON-formatted configuration files, where you define one or more cluster configurations. By default, the client reads a file named clusters.json, located at /etc/aurora/clusters.json or ~/.aurora/clusters.json. The structure of clusters.json resembles the following:

```
[
  {
    "auth_mechanism": "UNAUTHENTICATED",
    "name": "aurora-cluster",
    "scheduler_zk_path": "/aurora/scheduler",
    "slave_root": "/var/lib/mesos",
    "slave_run_directory": "latest",
    "zk": "mesos-master-1,mesos-master-2,mesos-master-3"
  }
]
```

Multiple Aurora clusters can be specified in a single file by creating additional hashes in the top-level array, each with a unique cluster name. The example here is enough to get you up and running, but for the complete client configuration reference, see http://aurora.apache.org/documentation/latest/client-cluster-configuration.

> **NOTE** The ZooKeeper hosts list in clusters.json assumes that each ZooKeeper instance is listening on the default port: 2181. Although an additional zk_port option is available, I've intentionally left it out of the example; Aurora 0.9.0 has a bug in the client whereby a custom port would be used only for the last host in the list. For more information, see https://issues .apache.org/jira/browse/AURORA-1405.

At this point, all of the Aurora components should be built, configured, and deployed to your Mesos cluster and workstation. You should navigate to the following URLs to ensure that the scheduler and observer services are up and running, and that their web interfaces are accessible:

- Aurora scheduler: http://mesos-master.example.com:8081/scheduler
- Thermos observer: http://mesos-slave.example.com:1338

Assuming all is well, let's start running through some practical examples of deploying applications and scheduled jobs on Aurora.

9.3 Deploying applications

Today, more and more organizations are turning to technology to operate their business more effectively. Whether that means delivering application enhancements to users (internal and external), building data analysis pipelines for better insight into user behavior, or building the next killer app, it's important to have robust tools that help you deploy changes quickly.

Increasingly, individual engineering teams are tasked with deploying changes to production—usually by an automated system that builds, tests, and deploys code—to reduce delivery time. As a result, the typical "over the wall" approach to application deployment is removed altogether; no longer does a developer need to wait for an application administrator or systems administrator to deploy their new code.

Aurora provides this sort of self-service application management to engineering teams. Engineers are responsible for building their own Aurora configuration files and—using Aurora's command-line tools—deploying changes in a way that makes sense for the given application. Aurora allows you to define an application's configuration and the number of instances that should be running, and perform rolling upgrades of running applications to minimize downtime to users.

Service discovery when using Aurora

Service discovery with Aurora is a bit more complicated than the solutions you learned about in chapters 7 and 8. Let's take a moment to consider a few possible ways to allow services to communicate with each other when using Aurora to deploy them.

First, Aurora includes a built-in mechanism for allowing its executors to advertise services into a ServerSet in ZooKeeper. Because this requires writing additional code and services, I've intentionally left it out of this book. But more information on this topic, including implementation details, is readily available at http://aurora.apache .org/documentation/latest/user-guide/#service-discovery.

Second, TellApart has written a service named Aurproxy that has knowledge of Aurora's service-discovery mechanism. Aurproxy allows you to load-balance traffic to application instances running on Aurora by using Nginx running in a Docker container. For more information about Aurproxy, see https://github.com/tellapart/aurproxy.

Finally, as I first mentioned in chapter 7, Mesos-DNS is a DNS-based service-discovery mechanism for Mesos that creates A and SRV records based on the information about running tasks from Mesos itself. As such, Mesos-DNS automatically supports Aurora, and makes for a great generic, multiframework solution to service discovery. More information about Mesos-DNS can be found at http://mesosphere.github.io/ mesos-dns.

In contrast to the JSON-based REST API provided by Marathon and Chronos, Aurora provides a powerful Python DSL that allows you to create and manage applications as code. Because these definitions can use the full power of the Python programming language, you can also create and reuse templates within and across teams. The next few sections provide examples of how to configure and deploy applications by using the Aurora DSL and command-line client.

> **TIP**   If you're interested in learning how Twitter uses Aurora for its application deployments, check out Bill Farner's talk "Generalizing Software Deployment" from MesosCon 2015: www.youtube.com/watch?v=y1hi7K1lPkk.

9.3.1   *Deploying a simple application*

As I first introduced when covering Marathon in chapter 7, the supplementary materials for this book include an example application named OutputEnv. This simple Ruby web application outputs the environment variables for a given instance of the application (a single Mesos task) as a formatted web page.

To deploy this application on Aurora, you first need to create a configuration file by using the Aurora DSL. In this file, you'll define the role, environment, and job that you want to deploy, and which cluster the application should run on. The following listing shows how you might deploy this application using Aurora.

Listing 9.2   Aurora configuration for the OutputEnv application

```
tarball = 'https://github.com/rji/mesos-in-action-code-samples/       ⟵ Download the
➥ archive/master.tar.gz'                                                 supplementary
                                                                         code for this
download = Process(                                                      book from
    name='download', cmdline=' '.join(['curl -LO', tarball]))            GitHub.

extract = Process(name='extract', cmdline='tar zxf master.tar.gz')    ⟵ Extract the tarball.

run = Process(name='run', cmdline="""
    cd mesos-in-action-code-samples-master/output-env-app && \        ⟵ Run the
    bundle install --retry 3 && \                                        commands to
    PORT={{thermos.ports[http]}} bundle exec ruby app.rb""")            launch the app,
                                                                        substituting in
task = SequentialTask(                                                   an available
    processes=[download, extract, run],                                  port.
    resources=Resources(cpu=0.1, ram=128*MB, disk=1*GB))

jobs = [
    Service(
        cluster='aurora-cluster',
        role='www-data',          ⟵ Create a new Service definition for a specific cluster, role, and environment.
        environment='prod',
        name='outputenv',
        task=task,                ⟵ Create a new SequentialTask that executes the download, extract, and run processes.
        instances=3)
]
```

The cluster name that you use in the configuration file must match an entry in your Aurora client's clusters.json file so that the Aurora command-line client knows how to connect to that particular Aurora cluster. Assuming the following was saved as outputenv.aurora, running the following command will deploy the application on the cluster:

```
$ aurora job create aurora-cluster/www-data/prod/outputenv outputenv.aurora
```

If the application was deployed successfully, you should see output in your terminal that resembles the following:

```
INFO] Creating job outputenv
INFO] Checking status of aurora-cluster/www-data/prod/outputenv
Job create succeeded: job url=http://mesos-master:8081/scheduler/
www-data/prod/outputenv
```

In the output from the Aurora client, you'll see a job URL that you can navigate to in order to get more information about the job that was just created. Let's briefly explore the Aurora web interface to get a bit more information about this application and where it's running in the cluster.

> **NOTE** As you may recall from chapter 7, Ruby and Bundler must be present on each Mesos slave for the OutputEnv application to run. This was used to illustrate the difference between requiring dependencies on each of the slaves in the cluster and bundling an application's dependencies in a Docker image.

EXPLORING THE WEB INTERFACE

By using your web browser to navigate to the job URL link provided by the command-line client, you'll arrive at a job configuration page that looks similar to the one shown in figure 9.2. This page provides an overview of the configuration for the job that was just deployed, and information about each of the running instances of the job.

In the event that you updated the configuration for an already-deployed job, Aurora will perform a rolling upgrade of the application, ensuring that each new instance passes its health checks before an old instance is torn down. This process, commonly referred to as a *blue/green deployment*, will display the new instances in green until the update is complete. You would then be able to view the configurations side by side to observe the differences between the two versions of the job.

By clicking the link specified in the Host column for a particular instance, you can open the page to the Thermos observer for the Mesos slave that the task is currently

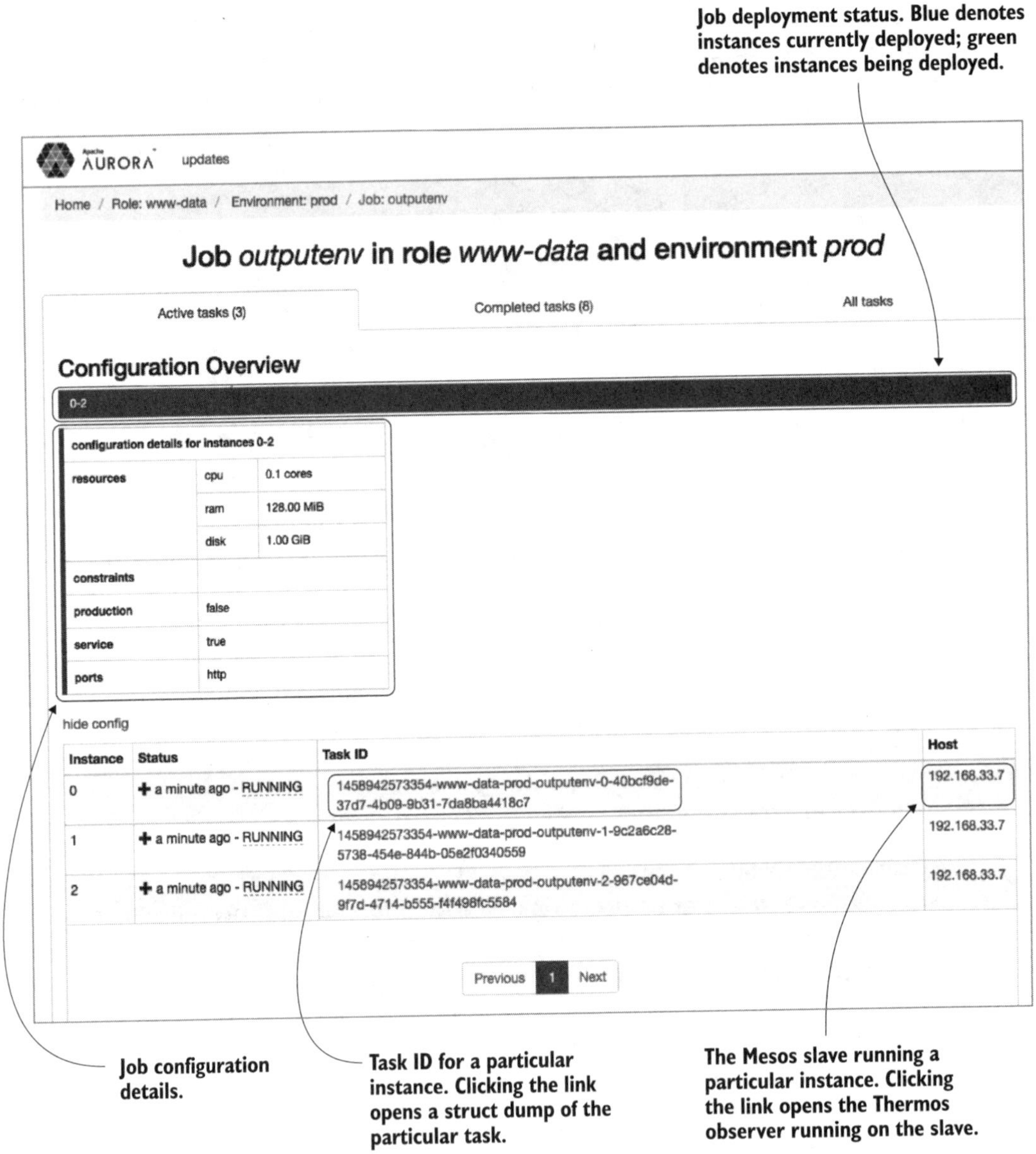

Job deployment status. Blue denotes instances currently deployed; green denotes instances being deployed.

Figure 9.2   Job overview, configuration, and deployment status

running on. Figure 9.3 explains the information available via the Thermos observer in a bit more detail.

The Thermos observer, as shown in figure 9.3, provides information about the running tasks and task configurations. Using this interface, you're able to view the tasks' sandboxes, stdout and stderr log files, and consumed resources.

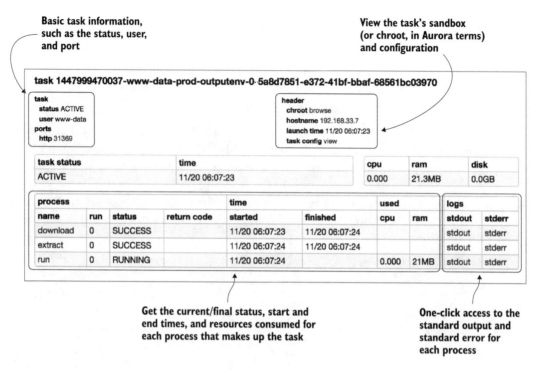

Basic task information, such as the status, user, and port

View the task's sandbox (or chroot, in Aurora terms) and configuration

task 1447999470037-www-data-prod-outputenv-0·5a8d7851-e372-41bf-bbaf-68561bc03970

task
 status ACTIVE
 user www-data
ports
 http 31369

header
 chroot browse
 hostname 192.168.33.7
 launch time 11/20 06:07:23
 task config view

task status	time		cpu	ram	disk
ACTIVE	11/20 06:07:23		0.000	21.3MB	0.0GB

process				time		used		logs	
name	run	status	return code	started	finished	cpu	ram	stdout	stderr
download	0	SUCCESS		11/20 06:07:23	11/20 06:07:24			stdout	stderr
extract	0	SUCCESS		11/20 06:07:24	11/20 06:07:24			stdout	stderr
run	0	RUNNING		11/20 06:07:24		0.000	21MB	stdout	stderr

Get the current/final status, start and end times, and resources consumed for each process that makes up the task

One-click access to the standard output and standard error for each process

Figure 9.3   Thermos observer information for a particular Aurora task

> **TIP**   For more information on service configurations, check out the user guide
> at http://aurora.apache.org/documentation/latest/user-guide.

You'll notice that when deploying this application, the machines in the cluster need to
have a few packages already available: one or more Ruby runtimes and the Bundler
tool that Ruby uses to install application dependencies. In the last few years, Docker
has become a popular way to avoid additional cluster configuration and dependency
conflicts by allowing you to package all of your application code and dependencies
into a single container image.

   Now that you've deployed the OutputEnv application on an Aurora cluster, let's
take a look at deploying Docker containers on Aurora, as well as some of the limitations of Aurora's Docker implementation present in version 0.9.0.

9.3.2   Deploying a Docker-based application

As of this writing, deploying Docker images by using Aurora is an experimental feature. Twitter uses cgroups in its environment, and native Docker support was only
recently introduced in Mesos (version 0.20.0, to be exact). Some basic functionality
that you get with Marathon and Mesos (mapping ports and volumes between the host

and the Docker container) isn't implemented in this version of Aurora, but is planned for a future release.

> **TIP**   There's an effort to expose all of the `DockerInfo` fields from Mesos (`Image`, `Network`, `PortMapping`, and so forth) in Aurora. You can track the progress of this functionality at https://issues.apache.org/jira/browse/AURORA-1396.

For now, if your Docker container runs a service that needs to listen on a network port, your best bet is to have the service within the Docker container listen on an ephemeral port provided by the Mesos resource offer. You might consider building your image in a way that you can set the listening port via an environment variable (such as $PORT), or pass it in as an argument to the script in the container that starts your service. An abbreviated way of doing this in the Aurora DSL might look like the following:

```
p = Process(cmdline='./run_server.py --port {{thermos.ports[http]}}')
t = Task(processes=[p])
jobs = [
    Service(
      task=t,
      container=Container(docker=Docker(image='user/image:version'))
    )
]
```

Another way you could go about launching Docker containers when using Aurora is to skip the built-in Docker functionality altogether, instead opting to use the docker run command directly; after all, it's just another process. Because this method allows you to use all the functionality currently built into Docker, the following listing demonstrates how to do just that.

Listing 9.3   Launching a Docker container by using the Docker CLI

```
docker = Process(
    name='docker-run-nginx',
    cmdline='docker run -p {{thermos.ports[http]}}:80 nginx:1.9'
)

task = Task(
    processes=[docker],
    resources=Resources(cpu=0.1, ram=128*MB, disk=1*GB)
)

jobs = [
    Service(
        cluster='aurora-cluster',
        role='www-data',
        environment='prod',
        name='docker-nginx',
        task=task
    )
]
```

Assuming the code in the listing was saved as docker-nginx.aurora, you can run the following command to launch this container on the cluster:

```
$ aurora job create aurora-cluster/www-data/prod/docker-nginx
➥ docker-nginx.aurora
```

> **NOTE** In this particular example, you're running the Nginx job as the www-data user. If this user isn't already a member of the docker group on the Mesos slaves, you'll get an error that the docker run command couldn't connect to the Docker daemon. You can add the user to the group by running sudo usermod -a -G docker www-data.

If you navigate to the job URL provided by the Aurora client, you should see that the Nginx container is running and Docker is bridging the ephemeral port offered by Mesos to the port exposed by the Nginx container—in this case, port 80.

Deploying applications (or services, in Aurora terms) is half of what it can do. Aurora also provides support for scheduling Cron jobs on a cluster, much like the Chronos framework covered in chapter 8. Let's look at how to manage scheduled tasks in Aurora.

9.4 Managing scheduled tasks

Unlike Chronos, Aurora takes a more traditional approach to running scheduled jobs, commonly referred to as *Cron jobs*. It follows—and builds upon—the familiar Cron schedule, with these additional features:

- *Automatic retry on failure*—If an Aurora Cron job fails, it can be automatically retried a number of times, based on the value provided to a task's max_task _failures attribute.
- *Collision policies*—Control the scheduler's behavior when a new Cron job is attempting to start, but the previous instance hasn't yet finished. This behavior is controlled by setting a task's cron_collision_policy attribute to KILL_ EXISTING or CANCEL_NEW.
- *Time-zone support*—This cluster-wide option is specified as an option to the Aurora scheduler and not an individual job. Therefore, it defaults to UTC, but can be set using the -cron_timezone configuration option.

For more detailed information about Cron jobs within Aurora, including examples, be sure to check out the documentation at http://aurora.apache.org/documentation/latest/cron-jobs. For now, let's cover some basic examples of creating Cron jobs, both standalone and within a Docker container.

9.4.1 Creating a Cron job

In the Aurora DSL, creating a Cron job is similar to creating any other job, with the exception of the few specific Cron attributes just covered. The following listing creates a Cron job that comprises a Process, a Task, and a Job, just as you saw in the previous listing, except that you set a value for the `cron_schedule` attribute in the `Job` object. Let's take a look.

```
sleep = Process(
        name='simple-sleep',
        cmdline="""
        echo "At the tone the time will be: $(date +'%r %Z')"
        echo "Sleeping for 60 seconds."
        sleep 60
        """
)

task = Task(
    processes=[sleep],
    resources=Resources(cpu=0.1, ram=16*MB, disk=1*MB)
)

jobs = [
    Job(
        cluster='aurora-cluster',
        role='www-data',
        environment='prod',
        name='simple-sleep',
        cron_schedule='*/5 * * * *',
        task=task
    )
]
```

Assuming that the code in this listing was saved as simple-sleep-cron.aurora, you can create this Cron job by running the following command:

```
$ aurora cron schedule aurora-cluster/www-data/prod/simple-sleep
➥ simple-sleep-cron.aurora
```

This command creates the Cron job within the Aurora scheduler, and runs the job on the schedule provided (every five minutes). Aurora also allows you to run the job manually using the Aurora command-line client. If you'd like to run the job on demand, you can do so by running the following command:

```
$ aurora cron start aurora-cluster/www-data/prod/simple-sleep
```

Additional Cron subcommands are available in the Aurora client; these include removing Cron jobs and killing the tasks of currently running jobs. For more information on these additional features, run `aurora cron -h`.

9.4.2   *Creating a Docker-based Cron job*

Although I mentioned previously that Docker support is experimental, it's rather straightforward to run a command in a Docker container when using Aurora. Borrowing an example introduced in chapter 8, the following listing shows what it looks like to deploy a Cron job that runs a given command within a Docker container.

Listing 9.5 Creating a Cron job that runs in a Docker container

```
script = 'https://raw.githubusercontent.com/rji/
    ➥ mesos-in-action-code-samples/master/email-weather-forecast.py'

install_python3 = Process(
        name='install_python3',
        cmdline='apt-get update && apt-get -y install python3'
)

download = Process(name='download', cmdline=' '.join(['curl -LO', script]))

run = Process(
        name='run',
        cmdline="""
        export TO_EMAIL_ADDR=user@example.com
        export FROM_EMAIL_ADDR=weather@example.com
        export ZIP_CODE=97201
        export MAIL_SERVER=mail.example.com:25
        export MAIL_USERNAME=weather@example.com
        export MAIL_PASSWORD=ItsTopSecret

        python3 email-weather-forecast.py
        """
)

task = SequentialTask(
    processes=[install_python3, download, run],
    resources=Resources(cpu=0.5, ram=1*GB, disk=768*MB)
)

jobs = [
    Job(
        cluster='aurora-cluster',
        role='www-data',
        environment='prod',
        name='daily-weather-report',
        cron_schedule='0 0 * * *',
        task=task,
        container=Container(docker=Docker(image='python:2.7.10'))
    )
]
```

In this example, I've added a new container attribute to the job, specifying that the SequentialTask that you defined should run within the python:2.7.10 Docker image from Docker Hub. Assuming that the code in this listing was saved as daily-weather-cron.aurora, run the following command to create the job on the Aurora cluster:

```
$ aurora cron schedule aurora-cluster/www-data/prod/daily-weather-report
    ➥ daily-weather-cron.aurora
```

> **WARNING**   Aurora copies `thermos_executor.pex`, which depends on Python 2.7, into the task's sandbox. If Python 2.7 isn't present in the Docker container, the executor will never register with the Mesos slave, and the task will be stuck in the `STAGING` state.

Hopefully, those few examples provided enough information to get started deploying your own applications and Cron jobs on Aurora. As always, the Aurora project maintains a fair amount of documentation, including a complete reference of all possible options and attributes for both services and Cron jobs. For more information, be sure to check out http://aurora.apache.org/documentation/latest/configuration-reference.

9.5   Administering Aurora

Aurora is an opinionated Mesos framework in that it expects to run most, if not all, services on a given Mesos cluster. In some ways, this is a good thing: as a systems administrator, it gives you a single way to maintain user authentication and authorization, set resource quotas, and even influence scheduling decisions so that a Mesos slave can be safely taken offline for maintenance. In the next two sections, I'll cover these features in more detail.

9.5.1   Managing users and quotas

One of Aurora's strengths is its support for multiple users, having grown out of Twitter's need to support a large engineering organization. Aurora integrates with the open source Apache Shiro security framework to provide authentication and authorization for its users. Shiro allows for authentication with a variety of data sources, including support for LDAP and Active Directory out of the box. Its pluggable nature allows you to implement your own as well, if you should need to do so.

As of version 0.9.0, Aurora provides two authentication mechanisms: basic HTTP authentication and Kerberos. To keep things simple throughout this section, I'll limit the scope to basic HTTP authentication and an INI-based authorization file located on the machine running the Aurora scheduler. If you're interested in more-complex authentication and authorization schemes (such as using Kerberos), please refer to aurora.apache.org/documentation/0.9.0/security.

AUTHENTICATION

At its absolute simplest, Aurora's security file contains a Users section that allows you to specify usernames and passwords like this:

```
[users]
alice = topsecretpw
```

> **NOTE**   Aurora's security.ini file stores user credentials in plaintext. Be sure to set the permissions on this file to the least amount required for the scheduler process to read it. There's a ticket open in the Aurora bug tracker to allow for hashed and salted passwords in security.ini; for more information, see https://issues.apache.org/jira/browse/AURORA-1179.

To configure the Aurora command-line clients for basic HTTP authentication, users must create an entry in their ~/.netrc file with Aurora's hostname and your credentials:

```
machine aurora-cluster.example.com
login alice
password topsecretpw
```

The machine name in the .netrc file must match the name or IP address that the Aurora scheduler used to register with the Mesos master. If you have a load balancer in front of Aurora, or refer to the scheduler by a single DNS name, you can set this with the -hostname option when starting the scheduler.

> **TIP** For more information on the .netrc file, see www.gnu.org/software/ inetutils/manual/html_node/The-_002enetrc-file.html.

AUTHORIZATION

Along with user authentication, Aurora allows you to configure arbitrary roles that users may belong to. These roles are based on the roles available via the Aurora Thrift API, whose documentation can found by accessing the Aurora scheduler at http:// aurora.example.com:8081/apiclient/api.html.

In the following example, the user Alice is granted admin-level access to the Aurora cluster, and Bob is granted access to only the accounting role. Carol isn't added to any roles:

```
[users]
alice = secret, admin
bob   = secret, accounting
carol = secret

[roles]
admin      = *
accounting = thirft.AuroraAdmin:setQuota
```

MANAGING RESOURCE QUOTAS

In Aurora, production-level tasks are allowed to preempt nonproduction tasks; a production task can kill a lower-priority nonproduction task if it requires additional cluster resources. This allows various environments within Aurora (development, staging, production, and so on) to safely use the same cluster without running the risk of impacting production workloads.

Resource quotas are required for production jobs and reserve a pool of cluster resources in which that job will run. Two subcommands within the Aurora admin client are used to set and increase quota:

```
aurora-admin set_quota <role> <cpus> <mem> <disk>
aurora-admin increase_quota <role> <cpus> <mem> <disk>
```

If cluster security was set up as mentioned in the Authentication and Authorization sections, you'll need to be in the admin role or the accounting role in order to make changes to resource quotas.

As an Aurora user, you can determine the allocated quota for a specific role, as well as identify production and nonproduction resources being consumed, by using the Aurora user client:

```
aurora quota get devcluster/example_role
```

9.5.2   *Performing maintenance*

One of the administrative features available in Aurora is the ability to perform scheduler-level maintenance on a set of machines in the cluster. This allows you to place a host in maintenance mode, drain the tasks and reschedule them on other nodes in the cluster, perform your maintenance, and return the machine back to normal service.

This functionality is exposed through the Aurora admin client and comprises the following subcommands:

- host_deactivate—Puts a host or set of hosts into maintenance mode. This effectively de-prioritizes the host in scheduling decisions made by Aurora, but tasks may still be scheduled onto a deactivated host depending on available cluster capacity.
- host_drain—Kills the running tasks on a host or set of hosts, and prevents the scheduler from scheduling any new tasks on it. This subcommand is best combined with host_deactivate, where you de-prioritize scheduling on a large set of machines and then use host_drain to perform maintenance in smaller batches.
- host_activate—Removes a host or set of hosts from maintenance mode and resumes normal scheduling.
- host_status—Gets the maintenance status of a host or set of hosts. Will be one of SCHEDULED (host_deactivate), DRAINED (host_drain), or NONE (host_activate).

Using the Aurora admin client, each of these subcommands can be run against a given cluster by using the following format:

```
$ aurora-admin <subcommand> --hosts=host.example.com[, ...] <cluster_name>
```

Some of these subcommands have additional options that you may find helpful. For example, each subcommand mentioned here can take a text file of hosts to place in maintenance mode, and the host_drain subcommand can accept an optional argument to run a script on a host after all its tasks have been drained. For full usage information, run aurora-admin help <subcommand>.

9.6 *Summary*

In this chapter, you learned about deploying applications and scheduled tasks by using the Apache Aurora framework for Mesos. Here are a few things to remember:

- Aurora consists of four main components: a scheduler, an executor, an observer, and a client. The executor and observer are both components of a project known as Thermos, which is included with the Aurora distribution.
- The Aurora scheduler is responsible for accepting and declining resource offers from the Mesos master. It is highly configurable, and launches tasks within the Thermos executor on an available Mesos slave.
- The Thermos observer is a service that runs on the Mesos slave and polls the running executors for task information. It provides one-stop access to a task's logs, sandbox, and resource-consumption statistics.
- The Aurora user client is commonly distributed to individual users and engineers who need to manage services and Cron jobs on an Aurora cluster. For full usage information, run `aurora -h`.
- The Aurora admin client is commonly distributed to systems administrators needing to maintain the cluster, including setting and modifying user quotas and performing host maintenance. For full usage information, run `aurora-admin help`.
- When running services or Cron jobs within a Docker container, ensure that Python 2.7 is present so the Thermos executor can register with the Mesos slave. Otherwise, tasks will get stuck in the `STAGING` state.
- Aurora uses the Apache Shiro security framework for authentication and authorization. Out of the box, Aurora provides support for unauthenticated requests, basic HTTP authentication, and Kerberos.
- Production-level resource quotas can be set on a per-role basis, and will preempt nonproduction tasks if necessary.
- Using the Aurora admin client, you can place hosts in maintenance mode to influence scheduling decisions about a set of hosts in the cluster. Using the various subcommands available, you can drain the tasks from a host before performing maintenance and restore the host to normal service after your infrastructure maintenance is complete.

Because Aurora is a powerful framework that scales to hundreds of users, I couldn't cover every possible feature and configuration in this chapter. Fortunately, the Aurora project provides extensive documentation at http://aurora.apache.org/documentation/0.9.0.

The next (and final) chapter provides a primer on the Mesos API and how to get started developing your own Mesos framework.

Developing a framework

10

This chapter covers

- The components that make up a Mesos framework
- The Mesos Scheduler and Executor APIs
- Writing a framework by using the Python bindings for Mesos

Welcome to the last and final chapter of *Mesos in Action*. Up to this point, I've covered topics such as how Mesos provides a new architecture for datacenter computing, how to deploy Mesos, and how to deploy applications and Cron jobs. This chapter provides a primer on how to start developing your first Mesos framework.

Unlike previous chapters, this chapter is more development-oriented than the operations-oriented material I've presented up to this point. Before we proceed, I'll assume that you have some experience with software development and with reading and writing code in the Python programming language. Although Mesos provides bindings for other languages, such as C++, Java, and Scala, and there are community efforts around bindings for languages such as Erlang and Go, I'm using Python here because it's generally easy to read and understand.

This chapter provides an introduction to the components that make up a Mesos framework, and presents some considerations to keep in mind when writing your own framework. Because of the amount of functionality exposed in the Mesos APIs, it isn't possible to cover everything in this chapter; we'd probably need a separate book dedicated to framework development. After reading this chapter, you should have a better understanding of the Mesos APIs, and should be able to run—and build upon—the example code included here.

Ready? Let's get started.

10.1 Understanding framework basics

Mesos frameworks are distributed systems that use Mesos to receive cluster resources. The term *framework* in Mesos refers to any application that registers with the Mesos master and runs on top of the Mesos cluster. There are two components that make up a Mesos framework—the *scheduler* and the *executor*:

- *Scheduler*—Registers with the Mesos master and implements the logic required for accepting or declining resource offers from the master, and deciding which tasks will use which resources.
- *Executor*—Registers with the Mesos slave and implements the logic for managing a task's lifecycle, including launching and killing the task and providing status updates. When a process first starts, the executor sends an update that the task is running; when it exits, the executor sends an update that the task has finished or failed.

In its most basic form, this interaction between Mesos, the scheduler, and the executor is depicted in figure 10.1.

NOTE This chapter provides information on developing both custom schedulers and executors. It's worth noting early on that you don't necessarily need to write a custom executor to write your own framework; it's perfectly reasonable to execute commands in a shell, using the built-in Mesos `Command-Executor`. I'll discuss both of these approaches a bit later in this chapter.

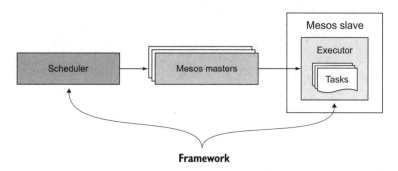

Figure 10.1   The scheduler and executor that make up a framework, in the context of the Mesos master and slave

Let's consider for a moment the lifecycle of a resource offer in the context of the scheduler. In figure 10.2, you can see a cyclical process in which Mesos slaves offer up available resources, and a framework scheduler launches executors using the resource offers.

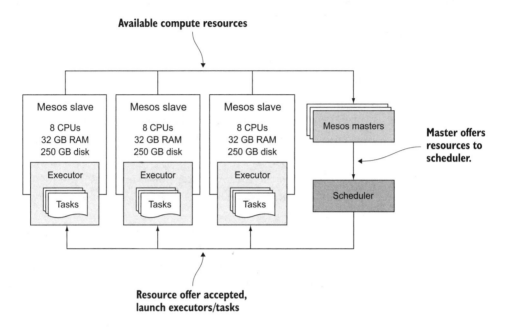

Figure 10.2   **The scheduler launches executors and tasks based on resource offers.**

When Mesos slaves advertise available resources to the master, the master makes some decisions based on the fair share of resources assigned to the registered frameworks. The resources are then offered to a framework's scheduler, which includes the logic for accepting or declining resource offers. If a resource offer is accepted, the scheduler is responsible for launching the executors on the slaves, which in turn launch the framework's tasks.

In addition to the scheduler and executor, there's a third requirement, although this requirement is (potentially) independent of the framework itself: you need a way serve up the custom executor code so that Mesos can use it. Fortunately, you have a few options:

- *HTTP*—If the scheduler can/will run a web server, you can bundle the executor code with the scheduler and serve it over HTTP. The Mesos fetcher will download the code into the sandbox before attempting to call the executor.
- *Network file system*—The Mesos fetcher also supports downloading the executor code from FTP and Amazon's Simple Storage Service (S3).

- *Distributed file system*—Using a distributed file system, such as HDFS, you're able to distribute the executor independently of the scheduler, allowing it to be less coupled.
- *From the slave's local file system, or a mount point*—If you already have a configuration management tool, such as Puppet or Chef, or a common mount point on every slave in the cluster (such as an NFS export), you can reference the executor code as a path on disk. If you decide to go this route, you need to refer to the executor by its absolute path (which must be the same on all hosts), or set the `--frameworks_home` configuration option for the `mesos-slave` daemon and use a relative path to the executor.

10.1.1 *When and why would you write a framework?*

Similar to how the Linux kernel schedules resources (CPU, memory, disk, ports) on a single machine, Mesos is a distributed kernel that schedules resources (CPU, memory, disk, ports) across multiple machines. Instead of applications using the Linux APIs, they use the Mesos APIs. To think about it another way, Mesos provides a common set of primitives for running distributed applications.

With the popularity of Marathon, Chronos, and Aurora, it might make sense to reuse these frameworks for various engineering teams to deploy applications and Cron jobs. But each of these frameworks needs to use the Mesos APIs that you're learning about in this chapter in order to schedule workloads on a Mesos cluster. Because you already know how Marathon, Chronos, and Aurora work, let's consider a couple of services that have been adapted to the Mesos model of resource scheduling:

- *Jenkins*—The team at Twitter wrote a Mesos plugin for Jenkins, the popular continuous integration (CI) system. Because Jenkins distributes its builds to a set of machines attached to a master, it matches quite well with the Mesos model of scheduling resources. The benefit? Jenkins is now able to schedule the CPU, memory, and disk resources it needs alongside other frameworks running on a larger Mesos cluster, instead of requiring its own statically partitioned cluster.
- *HDFS*—The team at Mesosphere maintains many Mesos frameworks, including one for running the Hadoop Distributed File System (HDFS) on top of Mesos. Normally, Hadoop (like Jenkins) would require its own cluster of machines to run. The logic to ensure that the HDFS `NameNodes` start up before the `Data-Nodes`, and that each instance must run on a unique Mesos slave, can all be built into the scheduler, and HDFS can use the storage available on a large fleet of Mesos slaves. Mesos provides primitives out of the box, such as fault tolerance and high availability, ensuring that the HDFS nodes can be rescheduled on a healthy machine in the event one of them fails.

If you're looking to deploy applications and scheduled jobs to a Mesos cluster, you probably don't need to be developing your own framework, opting instead to use an off-the-shelf solution. After all, developing a new distributed system is a nontrivial task, and creating a production-grade framework is even more difficult. But if you're trying to write a new Mesos-native application, port an existing service to Mesos, or your application requires specialized scheduling logic, your best bet is to write your own framework.

10.1.2 *The scheduler implementation*

The scheduler is the component of the framework that's responsible for the following:

- Receiving resource offers from the master
- Accepting a resource offer and launching tasks, or declining the offer
- Receiving and responding to status updates from tasks

Internally, Mesos serializes messages between components by using a system called *protocol buffers*, a project originally developed at Google. Although the full explanation of protocol buffers is outside the scope of this book, using it allowed the Mesos developers to write bindings for Mesos in multiple languages while still conforming to a common message format implemented for the Mesos API. These messages can be found in the Mesos code base at https://github.com/apache/mesos/blob/0.22.2/include/mesos/mesos.proto and are generally well documented.

I've included the most important messages here so that you can get a better understanding of how they work when you're getting ready to write and run your own scheduler. Using mesos.proto as a reference should prove helpful while developing your framework.

RESOURCE OFFERS

Because Mesos is responsible for scheduling cluster compute resources across multiple frameworks, the most logical place to start is with the format of the resource offers themselves. The `Offer` message describes the amount of resources available on a Mesos slave. In addition to listing the available resources, the offer includes the hostname and the unique ID of the Mesos slave:

```
message Offer {
  required OfferID id
  required FrameworkID framework_id
  required SlaveID slave_id
  required string hostname
  repeated Resource resources
  repeated Attribute attributes
  repeated ExecutorID executor_ids
}
```

You might recall from chapter 4 that I covered customizing the resources on a given Mesos slave by using three distinct types: scalars, ranges, and sets. The Resource message, which is part of the Offer, describes these resource types:

```
message Resource {
  required string name
  required Value.Type type
  optional Value.Scalar scalar
  optional Value.Ranges ranges
  optional Value.Set set
  optional string role [default = "*"]
}
```

Because all scheduling depends on resource offers in Mesos, the resourceOffers() method is one of the few methods that you're required to implement in your own scheduler; this is where you'll start implementing your scheduling logic:

```
def resourceOffers(self, driver, offers):
    for offer in offers:
        logging.info("Received offer with ID: {}".format(offer.id.value))
        logging.info("Declining offer ID {}".format(offer.id.value))
        driver.declineOffer(offer.id)
```

The previous code example prints a logging message and declines all offers as they're received. Typically, you'd check a queue of pending work to determine whether the offer could be used and whether it met the needs of the task to be launched. Section 10.2 covers resourceOffers() and the other methods that make up the Scheduler API in more detail.

FRAMEWORK INFO

The FrameworkInfo message is responsible for describing the framework. There are only two required options that you have to specify when creating a framework: the user that it will run as, and the name of the framework:

```
message FrameworkInfo {
  required string user
  required string name
  optional FrameworkID id
  optional double failover_timeout [default = 0.0]
  optional bool checkpoint [default = false]
  optional string role [default = "*"]
  optional string hostname
  optional string principal
  optional string webui_url
}
```

Other options in FrameworkInfo include the hostname that the scheduler is registering as, the principal to identify the framework, and the URL to the scheduler's web interface (if any). If you specify a value for the framework's webui_url, you'll be able to quickly navigate to the scheduler's web interface from within the Mesos UI.

In Python, you'll set each of these options by creating a new instance of Framework-Info() and passing it to the MesosSchedulerDriver, which the next section covers in more detail:

```
framework = mesos_pb2.FrameworkInfo()
framework.user = ''
framework.name = 'ExampleFramework'
framework.checkpoint = True
framework.principal = 'ExampleFramework'
...
driver = MesosSchedulerDriver(..., framework, ...)
...
```

If you specify an empty string for framework.user (as I did previously), Mesos will assume that you meant the user on the system currently running the framework.

SCHEDULER DRIVER

MesosSchedulerDriver is responsible for connecting to and interacting with the Mesos master. After you instantiate the driver, you'll use it to either accept an offer and launch some tasks on a slave by using launchTasks(), or decline the offer with the declineOffer() method if there isn't any work to be done:

```
class ExampleScheduler(mesos.interface.Scheduler):
    ...
    def resourceOffers(self, driver, offers):
        for offer in offers:
            driver.declineOffer(offer.id)
    ...
driver = MesosSchedulerDriver(ExampleScheduler(), framework, master)
driver.run()
```

Section 10.2 covers the various methods that make up the Scheduler API and SchedulerDriver.

10.1.3 *The executor implementation*

The other component that makes up a Mesos framework is the executor. In short, the executor is responsible for the following:

- Launching and killing tasks
- Providing status updates about a task back to the scheduler

Out of the box, Mesos includes a built-in CommandExecutor that launches commands as arguments to /bin/sh, as you might expect if you ran the command from your laptop or from the console of a server directly. In this section, I'll cover the custom executor implementation in Mesos.

Because a shell can launch most processes, you might be wondering why you need to write a custom executor for your framework. Usually, it's a good idea to do this when you need to perform health checks of the task you're launching, when you want to run some code written in your framework's programming language, or when your process needs more setup than simply running in a shell. Building on the health-check scenario, you could send status updates about the task back to the scheduler based on the status of the health checks, thus allowing the scheduler to make additional decisions about how to handle a particular situation.

Because health checks are the first use case that comes to mind and they map nicely with the various task statuses, let's start by going over the `TaskStatus` message.

EXECUTOR TASK STATUS

To update the status of a task, a Mesos executor uses the `TaskStatus` message. At a minimum, a task's status update requires that you specify the task ID and a state for the status:

```
message TaskStatus {
    ...
    required TaskID task_id
    required TaskState state
    optional string message
    optional Source source
    optional Reason reason
    optional bytes data
    optional SlaveID slave_id
    optional ExecutorID executor_id
    optional double timestamp
    optional bytes uuid
    optional bool healthy
}
```

Because task states are used across multiple Mesos components, the possible states a task can be in are defined as a separate `TaskState` message in mesos.proto:

```
enum TaskState {
    TASK_STAGING
    TASK_STARTING
    TASK_RUNNING
    TASK_FINISHED
    TASK_FAILED
    TASK_KILLED
    TASK_LOST
    TASK_ERROR
}
```

The first state, `TASK_STAGING`, should be used only internally by Mesos and shouldn't be used by your framework's status updates. Furthermore, each of the statuses after `TASK_RUNNING` (for example, `TASK_FINISHED`, `TASK_FAILED`, and so forth) is considered to be a *terminal* state. This implies that the task is no longer running and that Mesos should clean up after the task, including scheduling the task's sandbox for garbage collection and offering the consumed resources to another task or framework.

The task ID is available in the executor's `launchTask()` method, which is discussed more in section 10.3. For now, you can see a basic implementation of launching a task and providing a status update in the following code snippet:

```
def launchTask(self, driver, task):
    update = mesos_pb2.TaskStatus()
    update.task_id.value = task.task_id.value
    update.state = mesos_pb2.TASK_RUNNING
    driver.sendStatusUpdate(update)
    ...
```

After sending the initial `TASK_RUNNING` update to the driver, you then perform any of the logic required for running the task, sending additional status when needed.

DEFINING THE EXECUTOR THAT A SCHEDULER WILL USE

A framework's scheduler and executor are loosely coupled, but the scheduler does need to know a bit about the executor that will be launching its tasks. `ExecutorInfo` contains information such as the executor ID, the command to execute, and the resources that will be allocated:

```
message ExecutorInfo {
    required ExecutorID executor_id
    optional FrameworkID framework_id
    required CommandInfo command
    optional ContainerInfo container
    repeated Resource resources
    optional string name
    optional string source
    optional bytes data
    optional DiscoveryInfo discovery
}
```

As part of the `ExecutorInfo` message, there's also `CommandInfo`, which is responsible for describing how a task will be executed:

```
message CommandInfo {
    message URI {
        required string value = 1;
        optional bool executable = 2;
        optional bool extract = 3 [default = true];
    }
    message ContainerInfo {
        required string image = 1;
        repeated string options = 2;
    }
    optional ContainerInfo container = 4;
    repeated URI uris = 1;
    optional Environment environment = 2;
    optional bool shell = 6 [default = true];
    optional string value = 3;
    repeated string arguments = 7;
    optional string user = 5;
}
```

To use a custom executor when launching tasks, you first need to instantiate a new executor based on the `ExecutorInfo` message and pass it to the instance of your scheduler:

```
executor = mesos_pb2.ExecutorInfo()
executor.executor_id.value = 'ExampleExecutor'
executor.command.value = os.path.abspath('./example-executor.py')
executor.name = 'Example Executor'
...
driver = MesosSchedulerDriver(ExampleScheduler(executor) ...)
```

By passing the executor to an instance of your scheduler's class, you'll have access to it when creating tasks (via `TaskInfo`).

> **NOTE** In this example, and in other places throughout this chapter, I've assumed that we're developing this framework in a development environment, with the Mesos master and slave running on the same machine. As such, the scheduler and the executor are both available on the same file system. You may have noticed the uris field in the `CommandInfo` message; to use the Mesos fetcher, check out the method `executor.command.uris.add()`. That method will allow you to download the executor's code into the sandbox by using the various methods described in the beginning of this chapter.

TASK INFO

The `TaskInfo` message describes a task and is a bit different from the other messages I've talked about so far. The task info is passed from the scheduler to the executor (via `driver.launchTasks()`). It requires either `ExecutorInfo` to be set if working with a custom executor, or `CommandInfo` if using the built-in Mesos `CommandExecutor`:

```
message TaskInfo {
  required string name
  required TaskID task_id
  required SlaveID slave_id
  repeated Resource resources
  optional ExecutorInfo executor
  optional CommandInfo command
  optional ContainerInfo container
  optional bytes data
  optional HealthCheck health_check
  optional Labels labels
  optional DiscoveryInfo discovery
}
```

A task is created as the result of a resource offer being received by the scheduler, and the scheduler constructing a task and sending it back to the `MesosSchedulerDriver`:

```
def resourceOffers(self, driver, offers):
    for offer in offers:
        task = mesos_pb2.TaskInfo()
        task_id = str(uuid.uuid4())
```

```
task.task_id.value = task_id
task.slave_id.value = offer.slave_id.value
task.name = "task {}".format(task_id)
task.executor.MergeFrom(self.executor)

cpus = task.resources.add()
. . .

mem = task.resources.add()
. . .

driver.launchTasks(offer.id, [task])
```

Now, when a task is launched on a Mesos cluster, it will launch the custom executor to execute your code, where you have more control over health-checking the service and providing status updates.

More messages for the scheduler and executor are defined in the mesos.proto file, but by this point, you should have an understanding of how Mesos is offering resources and launching tasks to frameworks. You might want to refer back to mesos.proto and the Mesos API for Python during the development process, or use an IDE like IntelliJ IDEA or PyCharm, both available from JetBrains (jetbrains.com), to help with development.

In the next section, you'll apply the knowledge you've gained up to this point while learning to develop a framework of your own.

10.2 *Developing a scheduler*

As you've learned throughout this book, Mesos follows a two-tier scheduling model: the master offers resources to a scheduler, and a scheduler decides to accept or decline the offer based on whether there's any work to be done (tasks to be launched). The scheduler can use the information offered to it as a means to make decisions about when and where to schedule specific workloads; in the case of the HDFS framework, the scheduler was developed in a way that each HDFS DataNode must run on a unique Mesos slave. This ensures that all of the DataNode tasks can't run on a single node, and that HDFS doesn't suffer from an outage should that node go offline.

As mentioned briefly in the last section, the scheduler and executor are connected to Mesos with an abstraction known as a *driver*; there's a separate driver for the scheduler (known as SchedulerDriver) and for the executor (ExecutorDriver). In figure 10.3, you can see how a task launched by the scheduler is launched as a new process on the slave.

The sections that follow demonstrate (with code) how to use the APIs and drivers available in Mesos to launch your own custom scheduler and executor, and run tasks on the cluster. In the interest of brevity, the text covers the minimum viable implementations, implementing only the methods that are required to get the scheduler

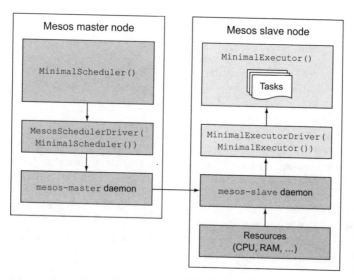

Figure 10.3 Interactions between the scheduler, scheduler driver, executor, and executor driver

working. More complete examples are included with the supplementary code for this book.

10.2.1 Working with the Scheduler API

The Mesos interface predefines several methods that you'll use when developing your own scheduler. These methods, which I refer to as the *Scheduler API*, allow you to either accept the default logic provided by Mesos, or implement your own logic by subclassing mesos.interface.Scheduler and overriding the methods that you wish to reimplement.

You can view the entire interface, along with detailed descriptions of how each method is used (and should be used) by checking out the Mesos source code.[1] For a full working skeleton that you can use as a starting point when developing your own framework, check out the examples located in the chapter10/ directory.

OVERVIEW OF THE SCHEDULER API

Each method in the Scheduler API roughly explains what it's used for, and the data that will be passed in as arguments to the method. Borrowing from (and abbreviating) the source code for the Mesos Python interface, the available methods (and their arguments) in the Scheduler API are as follows:

```
class Scheduler(object)
    def registered(self, driver, frameworkId, masterInfo)
    def reregistered(self, driver, masterInfo)
    def disconnected(self, driver)
```

---

[1] https://github.com/apache/mesos/blob/0.22.2/src/python/interface/src/mesos/interface/ __init__.py#L34-L129

```
def resourceOffers(self, driver, offers)
def offerRescinded(self, driver, offerId)
def statusUpdate(self, driver, status)
def frameworkMessage(self, driver, executorId, slaveId, message)
def slaveLost(self, driver, slaveId)
def executorLost(self, driver, executorId, slaveId, status)
def error(self, driver, message)
```

When a given event occurs, whether the scheduler has registered(), reregistered(), or received a frameworkMessage(), the API allows you to accept the default logic or implement your own. The only method that you're required to implement is resourceOffers().

WRITING YOUR OWN SCHEDULER

The following listing provides a minimal example for developing your own Mesos scheduler. The listing also includes information for using a custom executor, which you'll implement in the next section.

Listing 10.1   Developing a minimal Mesos scheduler

```
from __future__ import print_function
import sys
import uuid
from threading import Thread
from mesos.interface import Scheduler, mesos_pb2
from mesos.native import MesosSchedulerDriver

class MinimalScheduler(Scheduler):
    def __init__(self, executor):
        self.executor = executor

    def resourceOffers(self, driver, offers):
        for offer in offers:
            task = mesos_pb2.TaskInfo()
            task_id = str(uuid.uuid4())
            task.task_id.value = task_id
            task.slave_id.value = offer.slave_id.value
            task.name = "task {}".format(task_id)
            task.executor.MergeFrom(self.executor)
            task.data = "Hello from task {}!".format(task_id)

            cpus = task.resources.add()
            cpus.name = 'cpus'
            cpus.type = mesos_pb2.Value.SCALAR
            cpus.scalar.value = 0.1

            mem = task.resources.add()
            mem.name = 'mem'
            mem.type = mesos_pb2.Value.SCALAR
            mem.scalar.value = 32

            tasks = [task]
            driver.launchTasks(offer.id, tasks)
```

Implement a new class by subclassing mesos.interface.Scheduler.

Accept an ExecutorInfo() object as an argument.

In the MinimalScheduler class, you must implement the resourceOffers() method.

One or more resource offers are available as an array in the method.

Construct a new TaskInfo() object with CPUs, memory, executor, name, and data.

Use a specific offer to launch one or more tasks.

```
def main():
    executor = mesos_pb2.ExecutorInfo()
    executor.executor_id.value = 'MinimalExecutor'
    executor.name = executor.executor_id.value
    executor.command.value = '/path/to/executor-minimal.py'

    framework = mesos_pb2.FrameworkInfo()
    framework.user = ''
    framework.name = 'MinimalFramework'
    framework.checkpoint = True
    framework.principal = framework.name
```

Create a new ExecutorInfo object.

Create a new FrameworkInfo object.

In the previous example, the scheduler accepts every resource offer it receives and uses the offer to launch one or more tasks, with each task allocated 0.1 CPUs and 32 MB RAM. After defining the scheduler logic, the executor and framework objects in `main()` need to be passed to `MesosSchedulerDriver()`, which is responsible for communicating with the Mesos master. I'll cover the `SchedulerDriver` in the next section.

10.2.2 Working with the SchedulerDriver

The Mesos scheduler driver provides an interface for connecting the scheduler code to the Mesos master. It's used to do the following:

- Manage the scheduler lifecycle by using `run()`, `stop()`, and so forth
- Interact with Mesos by using `launchTasks()`, `declineOffer()`, and so forth

In the interest of brevity, this chapter doesn't cover all the details of the scheduler driver. You can learn about the various methods in the interface and detailed descriptions about what they're used for by checking out the relevant code in the Mesos Python bindings:[2]

```
class SchedulerDriver(object)
    def start(self)
    def stop(self, failover=False)
    def abort(self)
    def join(self)
    def run(self)
    def requestResources(self, requests)
    def launchTasks(self, offerIds, tasks, filters=None)
    def killTask(self, taskId)
    def declineOffer(self, offerId, filters=None)
    def reviveOffers(self)
    def acknowledgeStatusUpdate(self, status)
    def sendFrameworkMessage(self, executorId, slaveId, data)
    def reconcileTasks(self, tasks)
```

---

[2] https://github.com/apache/mesos/blob/0.22.2/src/python/interface/src/mesos/interface/__init__.py#L132-L244

Listing 10.2 provides a minimal example for invoking the scheduler driver, which is responsible for registering the scheduler with the master. The scheduler driver can be run from anywhere, provided that the machine running the scheduler has access to the Mesos master, and vice versa. The scheduler driver takes a few arguments, which include the instance of the scheduler subclass, the framework info, and the Mesos master to connect with.

Listing 10.2 Connecting the scheduler to Mesos with the scheduler driver

```
def main():
    ...
    driver = MesosSchedulerDriver(                              Create a new
        MinimalScheduler(executor), framework, 'localhost:5050')   MesosScheduler-
                                                                Driver.
    status = 0 if driver.run() == mesos_pb2.DRIVER_STOPPED else 1   Run the
    driver.stop()                                               MesosScheduler-
    sys.exit(status)              Stop the                      Driver.
                                  driver.
```

It's worth noting that the scheduler driver will block further execution, so it's generally a good idea to run the driver in its own thread. The examples provided in the GitHub repository for this book provide an example of how to do this.

10.3 Developing an executor

When developing your own Mesos framework, writing a custom executor isn't a strict requirement. Instead, your scheduler could use the built-in `CommandExecutor` in Mesos by modifying `TaskInfo()` when the task is created, like this:

```
task.command.value = 'echo "Hello, world!" && sleep 30'
```

The `CommandExecutor` takes the value of the command and appends it to /bin/sh -c, which is probably fine for many cases. But in the interest of completeness, I'll cover the Executor API in this chapter as well.

10.3.1 Working with the Executor API

The Mesos executor interface predefines several methods that you'll use when developing your own scheduler. These methods, which I refer to as the *Executor API*, allow you to either accept the default logic provided by Mesos, or implement your own logic by subclassing mesos.interface.Executor.

You can view the entire interface, along with detailed descriptions about how each method is used (and should be used) by checking out the Mesos source code.[3] For a

---

[3] https://github.com/apache/mesos/blob/0.22.2/src/python/interface/src/mesos/interface/
__init__.py#L246-L310

full working skeleton that you can use as a starting point when developing your own framework, check out the examples located in the chapter10/ directory.

OVERVIEW OF THE EXECUTOR API

Each method name in the Executor API is roughly self-explanatory, as are the arguments that are passed to the method. Borrowing from the source code for the Mesos Python interface, the available methods (and their arguments) in the Executor API are as follows:

```
class Executor(object)
    def registered(self, driver, executorInfo, frameworkInfo, slaveInfo)
    def reregistered(self, driver, slaveInfo)
    def disconnected(self, driver)
    def launchTask(self, driver, task)
    def killTask(self, driver, taskId)
    def frameworkMessage(self, driver, message)
    def shutdown(self, driver)
    def error(self, driver, message)
```

When a given event occurs, whether the executor has registered() or detected that it has disconnected() from the Mesos slave, the API allows you to accept the default logic in Mesos or implement your own.

WRITING YOUR OWN EXECUTOR

The following listing provides a minimal example for developing your own Mesos executor. After the executor is registered, it can be reused across tasks; note that we print the task.data as part of this executor, where task.data is any arbitrary data that's passed in all the way from the scheduler.

Listing 10.3   Developing a minimal Mesos executor

```
from __future__ import print_function        Implement a new
import sys                                    class by subclassing
import time                                   mesos.interface.Executor.
from threading import Thread
from mesos.interface import Executor, mesos_pb2
from mesos.native import MesosExecutorDriver   Implement the
                                               launchTasks() method
class MinimalExecutor(Executor):               to run the task.
    def launchTask(self, driver, task):
        def run_task():                         Provide a status
            update = mesos_pb2.TaskStatus()     update for the task
            update.task_id.value = task.task_id.value   back to the scheduler.
            update.state = mesos_pb2.TASK_RUNNING
            driver.sendStatusUpdate(update)

            print(task.data)                    User-defined code
            time.sleep(30)                       would commonly
                                                 appear here.
            update = mesos_pb2.TaskStatus()
            update.task_id.value = task.task_id.value
```

```
        update.state = mesos_pb2.TASK_FINISHED
        driver.sendStatusUpdate(update)

    thread = Thread(target=run_task, args=())
    thread.start()
```

The task should be run in its own thread or process.

In the previous example, an executor is created for a host and runs a given task. In this case, the executor prints the value of task.data as passed in all the way from the scheduler, when the task was originally created. But to connect this executor with the Mesos slave, you need to invoke the executor driver.

10.3.2 *Working with the executor driver*

The Mesos executor driver provides an interface for connecting the executor code to the Mesos slave. It's used to do the following:

- Manage the executor lifecycle by using run(), stop(), and so forth
- Launch tasks by using launchTask() and provide status updates by using Task-Status()

You can check out the various methods of the interface, including detailed descriptions about what each one does, in the Mesos code base.[4] For now, let's look at the various methods available to the driver:

```
class ExecutorDriver(object)
    def start(self)
    def stop(self)
    def abort(self)
    def join(self)
    def run(self)
    def sendStatusUpdate(self, status)
    def sendFrameworkMessage(self, data)
```

In the following code snippet, I've provided some boilerplate code that can be used to invoke the executor driver, which is responsible for registering the executor to the Mesos slave. This code is part of the executor code, which means it would be executed on the Mesos slave when the scheduler launches a task. The scheduler driver takes one argument—an instance of your custom executor:

Create a new instance of the MesosExecutorDriver.

```
if __name__ == '__main__':
    driver = MesosExecutorDriver(MinimalExecutor())
    sys.exit(0 if driver.run() == mesos_pb2.DRIVER_STOPPED else 1)
```

Run the driver.

---

[4] https://github.com/apache/mesos/blob/0.22.2/src/python/interface/src/mesos/interface/
__init__.py#L314-L367

With a minimal (but working!) implementation of both a scheduler and an executor, let's take a look at how to test out your framework code in a development environment. The next section covers a common Vagrant-based development environment, and some things to keep in mind when creating production-ready frameworks.

10.4 Running the framework

Now that you've had a tour of the Mesos APIs and how to write code against them, let's go over how to run your code in a development environment. Most commonly, you can either build Mesos locally or install it from packages, and run the Mesos master and slave on your laptop. I prefer a more repeatable (and disposable) development environment, which is why I usually develop in a Vagrant environment.

10.4.1 Deploying in development

The team at Mesosphere has a development environment that they've named Playa Mesos. Out of the box, this Vagrant environment installs Mesos, Marathon, Chronos, and Docker, and—fortunately for us—also provides the Mesos native libraries for Python.

BRINGING UP THE VAGRANT ENVIRONMENT

First, you need to install Vagrant and VirtualBox, if you don't already have them installed. Each project is open source and can be downloaded by using the following links:

- www.vagrantup.com
- www.virtualbox.org

Next, clone the Playa Mesos GitHub repository by running the following command:

```
$ git clone https://github.com/mesosphere/playa-mesos
```

By default, Playa Mesos attempts to install the latest packaged version of Mesos from the Mesosphere repositories. For the purposes of this book (which covers Mesos 0.22.2), that might not be desired. To ensure that Mesos 0.22.2 is installed when you're bringing up the Vagrant box, modify the hash in config.json to contain the following line:

```
"mesos_release": "0.22.2-0.2.62.ubuntu1404"
```

Finally, bring up the machine by running the following command:

```
$ vagrant up --provision
```

TESTING OUT THE MINIMAL FRAMEWORK

The provisioning process takes a little while to download and install all of the packages required, so please be patient. After the machine has finished the provisioning process, you should be able to access Mesos by navigating to http://10.141.141.10:5050. If all is well, let's move on.

SSH into the running Vagrant box and clone the Git repository for this book:

```
$ vagrant ssh
vagrant@mesos$ git clone https://github.com/rji/
               ⮡ mesos-in-action-code-samples
vagrant@mesos$ cd mesos-in-action-code-samples/chapter10
```

Now, let's go ahead and run the scheduler:

```
vagrant@mesos$ ./scheduler-minimal.py zk://localhost:2181/mesos
```

OBSERVING OUTPUT

If all is well, the scheduler should have registered with the Mesos master, accepted one or more resource offers, and launched one or more tasks. If you navigate over to the Mesos web interface, you should see that your framework is registered and has been allocated a certain number of resources, as shown in figure 10.4.

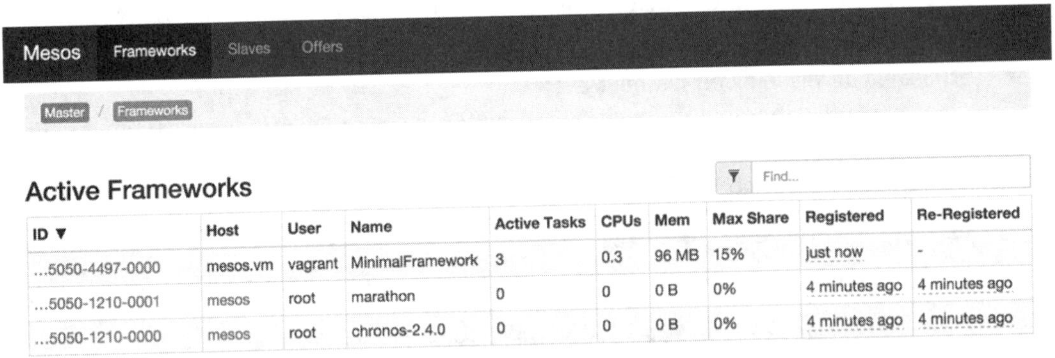

Mesos	Frameworks	Slaves	Offers

Master / Frameworks

Active Frameworks

ID ▼	Host	User	Name	Active Tasks	CPUs	Mem	Max Share	Registered	Re-Registered
...5050-4497-0000	mesos.vm	vagrant	MinimalFramework	3	0.3	96 MB	15%	just now	-
...5050-1210-0001	mesos	root	marathon	0	0	0 B	0%	4 minutes ago	4 minutes ago
...5050-1210-0000	mesos	root	chronos-2.4.0	0	0	0 B	0%	4 minutes ago	4 minutes ago

Figure 10.4   The MinimalFramework is registered with the Mesos master, and three tasks are running.

If you open up the sandbox for a particular task, you should see output similar to the following:

```
Hello from task 2c863b8a-1290-4849-958f-a3f2261e184a!
Hello from task d5aa1d8d-ea07-45f9-a703-d0e57ff88a22!
Hello from task aedc6839-4d44-47ec-8a23-fc7a20f1cd0b!
```

You'll note that you're seeing output from several tasks in the standard output for the executor. Because you're running on only a single node, Mesos has created a single instance of your custom executor, and runs the tasks within it. In our case, because the code is a simple print(task.data), you're seeing the UUID for each task as the standard output for this instance of the executor.

10.4.2 *Considerations for a production deployment*

Although this chapter is just a primer on framework development, I want to leave you with a few parting notes on what you can do to add some production-quality features to your framework. In short, I'll provide a couple of pointers on making your scheduler highly available, and how you can authenticate with a Mesos cluster that has framework authentication enabled. But as I mentioned previously, Mesos frameworks are really distributed systems, and one chapter isn't enough space to cover developing a production-ready framework.

HIGH AVAILABILITY

Although Mesos provides a means for frameworks to reregister with the master using the same framework ID, that alone doesn't mean that a deployed framework is highly available; that logic needs to be built into your own framework before the scheduler driver registers with the master.

One common way to ensure that only one instance of your scheduler is registered is to elect a leading instance by using ZooKeeper. The registered instance persists its framework ID (as assigned by Mesos) into ZooKeeper, and if it fails, a surviving instance can then reregister using the same framework ID, allowing the newly elected instance to connect to the running tasks. You can find more information on the ZooKeeper website (http://zookeeper.apache.org/doc/current/recipes.html#sc_leaderElection).

On the Mesos side of things, you'll need to set a few additional options. Specifically, these include the following:

- Set the framework's `failover_timeout` to a value greater than 0.
- Enable framework checkpointing (`checkpoint=True`).
- When stopping the `MesosSchedulerDriver` for a particular instance, set `failover=True`.

FRAMEWORK AUTHENTICATION

An optional feature of Mesos frameworks is known as *framework authentication*, which you first learned about in chapter 6. Framework authentication allows you to define a principal and a secret for a framework to use when registering with a Mesos master, and gives systems administrators a way to control the frameworks registering with a specific cluster:

```
message Credential {
  required string principal
  optional bytes secret
}
```

If framework authentication is enabled on the cluster, you need to first create a `Credential()` object, and then pass it in as an argument to `MesosSchedulerDriver`, like this:

```
...
credential = mesos_pb2.Credential()
credential.principal = os.getenv('EXAMPLE_PRINCIPAL')
```

```
credential.secret = os.getenv('EXAMPLE_SECRET')
...
driver = MesosSchedulerDriver(
    ExampleScheduler(), framework, master, credential)
driver.run()
```

10.5   *Summary*

In this chapter, you learned about developing a Mesos framework. I covered topics such as why you might want to write your own framework, and the Scheduler and Executor APIs. Here are a few things to remember:

- Mesos frameworks are composed of a scheduler and an executor. The scheduler and executor are implemented by subclassing mesos.interface.Scheduler and mesos.interface.Executor, respectively.

- In the scheduler, the only method that you're required to override is resource-Offers(). This is where the bulk of the scheduling logic will take place.

- In the executor, the only method that you're required to override is launch-Task(). Any code launched in this method should be run in a separate thread or process.

- The custom scheduler and executor are connected to Mesos by using Mesos-SchedulerDriver and MesosExecutorDriver.

- To achieve high availability for your scheduler, consider using the leader election recipe found on the ZooKeeper website. By persisting the framework ID (as assigned by Mesos) into ZooKeeper, another instance of the scheduler can reregister using the same ID in the event a failover occurs.

If you're looking for examples of developing a scheduler and executor in other languages such as C++, Go, Haskell, Java, and Scala, you might want to check out the RENDLER example framework, located at https://github.com/mesosphere/rendler. The Mesos project also maintains some basic framework development documentation, which can be found at http://mesos.apache.org/documentation/latest/app-framework-development-guide.

Well, that's all, folks! Thanks for reading *Mesos in Action*, and I hope that you've found this book helpful in understanding the Mesos architecture, deploying it in your own datacenter, and running applications and Cron jobs on top of it. A list of Mesos frameworks and related tools known at the time of writing, including language bindings, is included in appendix B.

appendix A
Case study: Mesosphere DCOS, an enterprise Mesos distribution

Throughout this book, you've learned about the open source Apache Mesos project and how it enables fine-grained resource scheduling for large clusters of machines in a datacenter. You've also learned about various use cases for Mesos, including the execution of large-scale data-processing jobs, the deployment of applications and containers, and the running of scheduled tasks. But by this point, you may be feeling overwhelmed about the sheer number of moving parts in such a system, and concerned about finding ways to ensure that certain versions of components are compatible with specific versions of others. The ideas and frameworks presented throughout part 3 of this book have been a primer on datacenter operations: application management, load balancing, security and access control, and even an introduction to distributed systems development.

This appendix provides a case study on the Datacenter Operating System (DCOS): an innovative, enterprise-grade, distributed operating system—based on Mesos—being built by Mesosphere. I cover topics such as how DCOS provides a turnkey Mesos solution for organizations of all sizes; how DCOS handles package management for distributed systems; and how you can use Jenkins on DCOS to develop a continuous delivery pipeline for deploying your own applications and containers, thus reducing the time it takes to get changes into production.

A.1 Introduction to DCOS

Although open source adoption within organizations seems to be trending over the past several years, and this book prepares you for deploying a Mesos cluster in your own organization, some enterprises are interested in purchasing turnkey solutions that come with software support contracts. Others are accepting of open source technologies, but don't mind going with an enterprise solution if it offers significant added value. With DCOS, Mesosphere is building enterprise software atop the open source Mesos project to help organizations scale their infrastructure and automate their application deployments, while still providing the comfort and convenience of 24/7 customer support, thoroughly tested components, and convenient tools for users and administrators.

DCOS combines open source projects—several of which I've mentioned throughout this book—and commercial-only components to deliver a Mesos cluster that's easy to manage and deploy, both for on-premises and cloud installations, thus allowing you to quickly deploy applications and containers. In DCOS, these components have all been tested together to ensure a stable platform, and the engineers at Mesosphere have written production-ready configurations for each of them so you don't have to.

> **NOTE**   This appendix covers DCOS 1.4, the current stable version at the time of writing.

Mesosphere offers DCOS in two flavors:

- *Community edition (CE)*—A free version of DCOS that runs on Amazon Web Services (AWS) and is being expanded to additional providers including Microsoft Azure and Google Cloud Platform.
- *Enterprise edition (EE)*—An enterprise version of DCOS that runs on premises or in the cloud, and is billed on a per-node basis. DCOS EE includes additional desirable features such as 24/7/365 support, Kerberos authentication, custom installation and configuration, and even emergency patches (if needed).

Before I get into this book's capstone example of continuous delivery using Jenkins on DCOS, let's go over the details of the DCOS architecture. Having read this book, the concepts and components should, for the most part, already be familiar. I revisit each of them briefly in the next section within the context of DCOS and, in some cases, within the context of Jenkins.

A.1.1   *Understanding the DCOS architecture*

In developing and shipping DCOS, Mesosphere configures Mesos similarly to how I first covered it in chapter 3, with either a single master or with three masters for high availability. In addition to the Mesos master daemon, the DCOS masters also run administrative services that I cover later in this section. Depending on the size of your workloads, you then attach an appropriate number of DCOS agents to the masters. Where this begins to differ from an open source Mesos deployment is that DCOS also includes one or more *public nodes*, configured with the Mesos role `slave_public`.

The role of the public node is to provide you with a means for running reverse proxies, load balancers, and other external-facing services on a dedicated node (or set

Just like Mesos, DCOS can have multiple masters for high availability. Each of the masters runs an instance of Mesos-DNS, ZooKeeper, Marathon, and Admin Router.

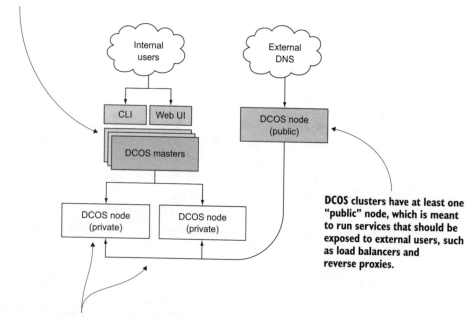

DCOS clusters have at least one "public" node, which is meant to run services that should be exposed to external users, such as load balancers and reverse proxies.

The bulk of the nodes in a DCOS cluster will be "private" nodes, which run your various workloads. Any services you install on DCOS run in containers on the private nodes, not on the masters, and are available via Mesos-DNS.

Figure A.1 High-level representation of a DCOS deployment

of nodes), allowing you to place a public DCOS node in your DMZ to serve user traffic, while the remainder of the cluster—the nodes running your applications—remain private. You can visualize this sort of deployment by taking a look at figure A.1.

Because the public node is sending resource offers to the DCOS master with the role slave_public, the only thing you need to do to run apps on this DMZ node is to add the following field to your application's marathon.json:

```
"acceptedResourceRoles": [ "slave_public" ]
```

Although DCOS has more components than I've depicted in the diagram, you should already be familiar with how Mesos uses ZooKeeper and how Mesos-DNS publishes task information via DNS, so I intentionally left these out of the diagram in the interest of clarity. But the next few sections provide a bit more information on how each of the main components in DCOS—Mesos, Marathon, Mesos-DNS, ZooKeeper, and a reverse proxy called Admin Router—work within the context of DCOS.

MESOS

At the heart of DCOS is Mesos, the distributed systems kernel that I've covered throughout this book. Mesos is responsible for abstracting resources from individual machines and offering them directly to frameworks, but like the kernel of an operating system, it's just one component. Mesosphere is a significant contributor to the open source Apache Mesos project.

MARATHON

In any operating system is a subsystem for managing long-running services. RHEL has systemd; Ubuntu has Upstart; DCOS has Marathon. On DCOS, Marathon runs the various services that you install on the cluster, in addition to any applications you might also deploy. These services, running in containers on one of the private nodes, register themselves to the leading Mesos master (which can be found by querying Mesos-DNS for `leader.mesos`, but I'll get to that in a minute). If an instance of the framework's scheduler happens to crash, or the machine that it's running on fails, Marathon automatically schedules the task on another node and launches the container.

The idea of Mesos frameworks running on top of another Mesos framework might sound a bit confusing, but figure A.2 should help you better understand the concept. Take note of the Jenkins framework running on top of Marathon.

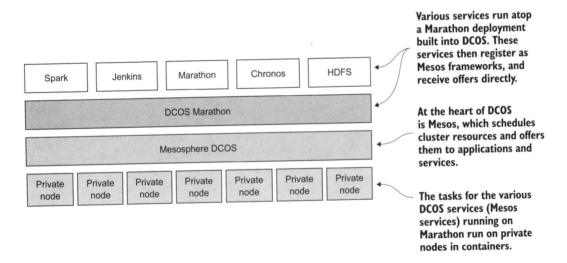

Figure A.2   A built-in Marathon instance runs DCOS services (Mesos frameworks). Individual instances of Marathon can be run atop DCOS Marathon, providing individual teams with dedicated instances on which to deploy their applications.

For Jenkins to be deployed on DCOS, a few things happen:

1 A new Marathon application is created to run the Jenkins master. For this example, let's assume that the Jenkins master will run inside a Docker container.
2 Marathon launches an instance of the Jenkins master on one of the DCOS agents.
3 After Jenkins is up and running, the Mesos plugin registers with the underlying Mesos master, just as if it were running on a dedicated server somewhere else in your infrastructure.
4 After Jenkins is registered, it can accept resource offers and launch tasks on the DCOS agents.

Now, I know this seems like a bit of a high-level scenario; it's all within the context of Marathon. Don't worry about these details for now. I provide additional details on how to install and run Jenkins later in this appendix. For now, let's move on to how DCOS handles service discovery with Mesos-DNS.

MESOS-DNS

I first introduced the problem of service discovery in chapter 7, where applications might not necessarily know which host another, dependent service (such as a database) is running on. Each of the DCOS masters runs an instance of Mesos-DNS, which polls Mesos for information about its running tasks and publishes that information via DNS. Mesos-DNS provides both A records to identify which host a task is running on, and SRV records that include the host IP, protocol, and port number. Because Mesos-DNS connects directly to the leading Mesos master under the hood, and not to a specific Mesos framework, it automatically provides DNS records for tasks running across multiple frameworks.

ZOOKEEPER

Mesos—and as a result, many Mesos frameworks—rely on a ZooKeeper ensemble for leader election, coordination, and to maintain state. Because of these dependencies, which could be owed to ZooKeeper's reputation in distributed systems coordination, DCOS also includes ZooKeeper, but builds upon it by including Exhibitor, the Zoo-Keeper supervisor and configuration manager developed at Netflix that I first introduced in chapter 6. Other than potentially configuring your own framework to work on DCOS, chances are you won't need to interact with the ZooKeeper ensemble all that much.

ADMIN ROUTER

One of the complexities in deploying and administering a Mesos cluster and several frameworks is keeping track of which hosts and ports each of the components is running and listening on. As you may recall from chapter 6, I suggested the possibility of using HAProxy in front of the Mesos masters so that your monitoring systems could use a single DNS name to communicate with the current leader. I suggested a similar approach for Marathon and Chronos in chapters 7 and 8. Admin Router is Mesosphere's solution for this problem.

Admin Router is responsible for acting as a reverse proxy to various DCOS services, but instead of using ports, it uses named URIs. When you install the Jenkins service for DCOS, it will be available at http://dcos.example.com/service/jenkins; there's no need to worry about which port the scheduler is running on! Most user interactions with DCOS will either occur via Admin Router, or at least use it to gather information about the cluster (for SSHing into a specific node, for example). This way, you can limit the number of services that are exposed outside the cluster's network.

> **TIP**   The code for Admin Router is open source and can be found at https://github.com/mesosphere/adminrouter-public.

Although I've talked about how Mesosphere combines these various components to make for a stable and robust Mesos deployment, the real value begins to be apparent when you have clearly defined interaction points with the system for administrators and users alike.

A.1.2   Interacting with DCOS

When you take a moment to consider the base components that you use to interact with a traditional operating system, such as Red Hat Enterprise Linux or Ubuntu, the components can largely be broken down into the following three categories:

- *Package management*—A package format (rpm, deb), package manager (yum, apt), and a set of base repositories (base, main). You may also optionally enable experimental or testing repositories, both from the vendor and from third parties.
- *Command-line interface*—A shell that's launched when a user logs in (bash, sh, zsh) that can be used for interacting with the system.
- *Graphical user interface*—An optional graphical user interface for monitoring and administering the system.

In DCOS, each of these operating system components still exists, but at a different layer of abstraction. Let's take a look at each of these in a bit more detail to understand how they work in a distributed system such as Mesos.

PACKAGE MANAGEMENT

At the time of this writing, Mesosphere provides two package repositories for DCOS, named Universe and Multiverse. These repositories host production-ready and experimental packages, respectively. A package's metadata in one of these repositories is a JSON object that can be processed by the DCOS CLI and understood by Marathon's REST API, which isn't all that different from what you learned about application definitions in Marathon in chapter 7.

Some of the services available for DCOS—Cassandra, HDFS, and Kubernetes, to name a few—require nontrivial amounts of effort to deploy effectively. The team at Mesosphere, using these package repositories, provides and maintains turnkey solutions for deploying these services in your own datacenter in a fully automated, fault-tolerant manner.

The documentation for the Universe repository covers the schema quite nicely, so I won't cover it all here. But if you're interested in creating your own packages for DCOS or understanding this schema in more detail, check out the documentation at http://mesosphere.github.io/universe.

COMMAND-LINE INTERFACE

The DCOS CLI can be installed on your laptop or workstation and interacts with various services in DCOS. It provides functionality for managing packages, services, and nodes in a DCOS cluster. DCOS services are capable of installing their own DCOS subcommands, but a few notable, built-in subcommands are included here:

- `config`—Get and set configuration options for the DCOS CLI.
- `package`—Install, manage, update, and uninstall DCOS packages.
- `node`—List and SSH into the nodes belonging to the DCOS cluster.
- `marathon`—Deploy and manage Marathon applications.

For example, to install the Jenkins package on DCOS using the CLI, you would run the following command:

```
$ dcos package install --yes jenkins
```

That's it! No provisioning additional infrastructure, and no need to know where in the cluster Jenkins will run. Everything else has been taken care of for you by the package's maintainer. For full usage for a given subcommand, run the command `dcos help <subcommand>`.

GRAPHICAL USER INTERFACE

Although the DCOS CLI allows you to fully administer the operating system from the command line, the web interface provides information about the cluster, including installed services, running tasks, and nodes belonging to the cluster. Figure A.3 shows the main dashboard of the DCOS UI, including cluster CPU and memory allocation, task failure rate, service health, running tasks, and the number of connected nodes.

Additional tabs on the left side of the dashboard allow you to explore a service's resource allocation on the cluster, as well as the resource utilization and health of individual nodes.

> **TIP** If you'd like to spin up your own DCOS cluster, you can find more information on how to do so at mesosphere.com/product.

One of the nice things about DCOS is that it gives you the power of Mesos with additional enterprise-ready features on top. Having read through this book, you've not only learned how to deploy and use Mesos, but in a way, also learned a lot about DCOS in the process, perhaps without even realizing it.

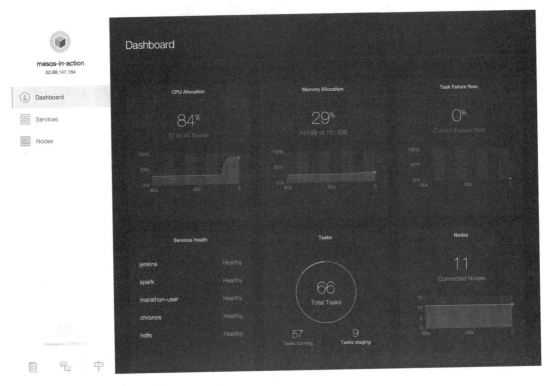

Figure A.3 Overview of the DCOS web interface

Now, as the book winds down, let's go over the final lesson you'll learn in this text: using Jenkins with DCOS (and Mesos and Marathon, for that matter!) to continuously test and deploy changes to an application so that you and your engineering team can ship new features and bug fixes to production, quickly and easily.

A.2   *Continuous deployment with Jenkins and Marathon*

A common theme I've covered throughout this book is how Mesos allows you to simplify operations by abstracting the resources from multiple machines and representing them as a single entity. I've covered application platforms such as Marathon and Aurora and included a few example applications that you could use to try out each of these projects. But up to this point, you haven't been able to use concepts covered in multiple chapters in a cohesive, end-to-end example.

I aim to present a use case for the knowledge you've gained up to this point. By the end of this appendix, you'll explore how to use Jenkins, a popular, open source continuous integration system, along with Mesos, Marathon, and DCOS, to poll for code changes to a Git repository and automatically trigger new builds of Docker images for your software projects. Assuming the build completed successfully, the new Docker image will be pushed up to Docker Hub, and a new version will be deployed to Marathon, and as a result, Mesos. You'll have automated the pain out of your application deployments so that you can focus your time and effort on writing code instead.

If any of that sounds like something you might be interested in, great! Let's get started.

A.2.1 Preparing DCOS for continuous application deployments

Building on what you learned about DCOS previously, this section presents a use case in which you'll use Jenkins running on DCOS to continuously build and deploy changes to an example HTML and CSS application included with this book's supplementary materials. I'll also introduce you to another project named Marathon-LB, which is similar to Marathon's servicerouter.py script that automatically configures and reloads a HAProxy load balancer. Throughout this section, you'll build a small infrastructure in which to host applications and load-balance user traffic, just by running a few commands and writing a Jenkins build script. I've depicted this a bit more clearly in figure A.4.

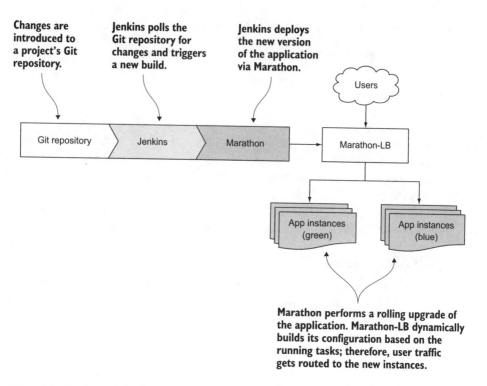

Figure A.4   Continuous deployment pipeline using Git, Jenkins, Marathon, and Marathon-LB

I'm going to demonstrate how to perform this example by using a DCOS cluster for running Jenkins and deploying the example web app. If you'd like to follow along using the Mesos cluster you learned about (and possibly provisioned by reading this book), you should take the time to ensure the following:

- You'll need at least one "public node" that Marathon-LB will run on. Typically, this node would be placed in a DMZ and receive traffic from the public internet (or from your internal users). For this, I recommend a dedicated Mesos slave, configured with `--default_role=slave_public`.
- You'll need to have Marathon and Mesos-DNS installed on the Mesos masters. Although this isn't strictly required, you might consider deploying Marathon as a means to run other Mesos frameworks, including one or more instances of Marathon.
- You should have the DCOS CLI installed on your workstation. Note that DCOS CLI also works with open source Mesos deployments. Configuration instructions for this are available in the project's README file, located at https://github.com/mesosphere/dcos-cli.

After configuring the DCOS CLI with your cluster's URL, use it to install the Marathon, Marathon-LB, and Jenkins packages by running the following commands:

```
$ dcos package update
$ dcos package install --yes marathon
$ dcos package install --yes marathon-lb
$ dcos package install --yes jenkins
```

After a short time, each of these services will be visible via the DCOS Marathon instance. New instances of Jenkins and Marathon will be running on top of the Marathon instance built into DCOS, and Marathon-LB will be running on the public node. After Jenkins has finished coming up, you'll see it listed in the Services pane of the DCOS UI.

  With your infrastructure ready to handle the task at hand, let's go ahead and create the Jenkins job that will deploy the application to Marathon.

A.2.2 Configuring Jenkins

To keep this example clear and concise, I'm going to present the various build steps (poll for changes, build the project, run the tests, deploy the app) that you'd normally see in a continuous delivery pipeline within the context of a single Jenkins job. To do so, I've included a simple static HTML and CSS web page in this book's GitHub repository that can be served to users with the Nginx web server.

> **NOTE** I'm assuming that you already have a Docker Hub account and access to a Git repository. If not, you can create a free account for Docker Hub at hub.docker.com, and for GitHub at github.com.

To set up this build-and-deploy job within Jenkins, you need to navigate to the Jenkins web interface. In DCOS, you can access Jenkins from the main Dashboard page, under Services. In Mesos, you can access Jenkins by navigating to the Frameworks tab and clicking the link to the framework's web URL.

After you've reached the Jenkins web interface, perform the following steps:

1 Create a new Jenkins job and name it accordingly. For this example, let's assume the job is called "demo-app-build-and-deploy."

2 Within the job configuration page, configure the Git plugin to poll your application's repository for changes. (Feel free to copy the example code for this appendix from this book's GitHub repo into a GitHub repo of your own to test it out.)

3 Create a new build step that executes a shell script. Here, you'll want to write a build script that builds the Docker image, pushes it to Docker Hub, and then updates your Marathon application with the new Docker image tag. I've included an example in the Git repo, and personally, I prefer to keep this build script in version control alongside my application's code.

4 Optional: configure Jenkins to send an email or chat notifications when the job has started and when it has finished. This way, you and the members of your team know that a change is being deployed.

After creating the Jenkins job with the URL to your Git repository, polling schedule, and build script, you can either wait for it to run or manually trigger a build.

A.2.3 *Continuous deployment in action*

Without thinking too much about it, the Jenkins job cloned your code repository, built a new Docker image, pushed it to Docker Hub, and deployed the new version of your application to Marathon. Marathon then performed a rolling upgrade of the application, taking the new version and deploying it alongside the old one. Once the health checks for the new version started passing, Marathon began tearing down the old instances.

While all of this was occurring, Marathon-LB, running on the public node, was subscribed to Marathon's event stream, which is accessible via an API endpoint. While new instances of the app were coming online and old instances were being torn down, the load balancer was updating its HAProxy configuration to ensure that requests were being routed to healthy instances of the app. All of this was possible after running a few commands from the DCOS CLI.

I understand that the example presented here might be basic, and that in reality CI and CD pipelines are usually more complex and applications have different dependencies that need to be brought in; that's fine. Go build upon this example to suit your needs and the needs of your application.

A.3   *Summary*

In this appendix, you learned how Mesosphere is providing an enterprise-grade Mesos distribution. You also learned how Jenkins, Marathon, and Mesos are capable of automatically deploying changes to an application without the need for human intervention. Here are a few things to remember:

- The Mesosphere DCOS is an enterprise-grade distribution built on top of the Mesos distributed systems kernel. DCOS provides a turnkey solution to enterprises wanting to deploy application containers at scale.
- Nodes in a DCOS deployment are divided into two classifications: public and private. Whereas private nodes make up the bulk of the cluster, a small number of public nodes can run external-facing services such as reverse proxies and load balancers.
- Mesosphere engineers maintain a growing number of distributed services for DCOS, including Cassandra, Chronos, HDFS, Jenkins, Kafka, Marathon, and Spark, among others. In essence, any Mesos framework can also be run on DCOS.
- By installing the Jenkins and Marathon services on DCOS, you can continuously build, test, and deploy new instances of your applications in a fully automated fashion. The Jenkins framework dynamically launches container-based build slaves when needed, and destroys them when they're no longer in use.
- By using Jenkins and Marathon to deploy your applications, you can continuously deploy updates to your application when your CI pipeline completes successfully. Marathon-LB subscribes to Marathon's event stream and automatically updates your load balancer's configuration file and reloads the service.

The next appendix provides a list of Mesos frameworks known—and maintained—as of this writing. Each of these frameworks can be deployed onto a Mesos cluster of your own, and some are already available for DCOS, thanks to the efforts of the Mesosphere engineering team.

appendix B
List of Mesos frameworks and tools

Mesos was designed to run multiple frameworks on a single cluster of computers, thereby improving overall resource utilization. Various community efforts have arisen around running existing applications on Mesos.

In this appendix, I provide a list of the Mesos frameworks known and actively being maintained as of publishing time. I also include references to Mesos language bindings, which will allow you to write your own frameworks in languages other than C++, Java, Scala, and Python. Finally, I cover tools in the community that can be used for configuration management, monitoring, service discovery, and load balancing.

B.1 Mesos frameworks

At publishing time, several open source Mesos frameworks are available. Some of these are purpose-built—such as Aurora, Chronos, and Marathon—whereas others are existing distributed services that work well with the Mesos model; these include (but aren't limited to) Cassandra, Jenkins, and Spark. This section covers Mesos frameworks that you can immediately begin using with your cluster.

B.1.1 Application management and batch scheduling

One of the mainstream uses of Mesos is to deploy long-running applications on a Mesos cluster, effectively using Mesos as a way to distribute and run containers. This section covers frameworks that can be used for deploying applications and batch jobs on a Mesos cluster, similar to the topics covered in chapters 7 through 9.

Name	Description	More info
Aurora	Apache Aurora is a framework developed by Twitter for managing long-running services and scheduled jobs.	https://aurora.apache.org
Chronos	Chronos is a framework developed by Airbnb to run scheduled data-processing jobs in a fault-tolerant manner. Supports ISO 8601–based schedules and job dependencies.	http://mesos.github.io/chronos
Cloud Foundry	Huawei has developed a Mesos framework for running the open source Cloud Foundry PaaS as a service on a Mesos cluster.	https://github.com/mesos/cloudfoundry-mesos
Docker Swarm	Swarm, the container clustering and orchestration tool developed by Docker, can be configured to use a Mesos cluster for managing compute resources.	https://github.com/docker/swarm/blob/v1.0.1/cluster/mesos/README.md
Jenkins	Jenkins is an open source continuous integration and deployment tool for software development and application management. Using the Mesos plugin, Jenkins can scale its build infrastructure elastically on a Mesos cluster.	https://github.com/jenkinsci/mesos-plugin
Kubernetes	Mesosphere has developed a framework for running Google's open source container scheduler on top of a Mesos cluster. This allows you to run Kubernetes alongside other Mesos frameworks such as Spark.	https://github.com/mesosphere/kubernetes-mesos
Marathon	Marathon is an open source framework for Mesos developed and maintained by Mesosphere. It deploys applications and long-running services on top of Mesos.	http://mesosphere.github.io/marathon
PaaSTA	PaaSTA is a platform developed by Yelp for running services and scheduled jobs on Mesos. It's built upon several other open source projects, including Marathon, Chronos, and Docker.	https://github.com/Yelp/paasta
Singularity	Singularity is a framework developed at HubSpot for launching long-running, scheduled, and one-off tasks on a Mesos cluster.	https://github.com/HubSpot/Singularity

B.1.2 *Data processing*

The first uses for Mesos, as specified in its original research paper, were data-processing tasks. In fact, the Apache Spark project began with some of the same members of the original Mesos project, to prove a hypothesis that specialized data-processing frameworks were more valuable than general-purpose frameworks. This section covers popular data-processing frameworks, providing a description and project URL for each.

Name	Description	More info
Cook	Cook is a batch scheduler for Mesos developed at Two Sigma. It was designed to support multiple users and preempt low-priority tasks, and can provide a multitenant environment for running Spark jobs.	https://github.com/twosigma/cook
DPark	DPark is a Python clone of Apache Spark and includes built-in support for running jobs on a Mesos cluster.	https://github.com/douban/dpark
Hadoop	Apache Hadoop is a popular data-processing framework and ecosystem. It was among the first applications ported to Mesos and is widely cited in the original Mesos paper.	https://github.com/mesos/hadoop
Kafka	Apache Kafka is a distributed, high-throughput publish-subscribe (pubsub) messaging system. By running Kafka on Mesos, you can scale Kafka elastically alongside other frameworks that consume streaming data, such as Apache Spark.	https://github.com/mesos/kafka
Myriad	Apache Myriad, a project currently in the Apache Incubator, enables Hadoop YARN (MapReduce v2) to run on a Mesos cluster. By running YARN on Mesos, YARN applications are able to share the same physical infrastructure as other Mesos frameworks.	https://myriad.incubator.apache.org
Spark	Apache Spark is a popular, open source data-processing framework and was the first purpose-built data-processing framework for Mesos. In contrast to Hadoop's disk-based map/reduce paradigm, Spark can load data sets into memory and, in some cases, has shown a 10× performance improvement over Hadoop.	https://spark.apache.org
Storm	Apache Storm is an open source stream-processing system that focuses on real-time computation.	https://github.com/mesos/storm

B.1.3 *Distributed databases and storage*

Distributed databases and filesystems, like Cassandra and HDFS, handle their own clustering and replication. Typically these services would run on dedicated sets of machines. Because Mesos provides primitives for distributed computing, various efforts have arisen to run these distributed systems in a fully automated fashion on a single general-purpose Mesos cluster. This section provides a list of distributed databases and filesystems that run on Mesos as of publishing time.

Name	Description	More info
ArangoDB	ArangoDB is an open source, distributed NoSQL database that can handle JSON documents, graphs, and key/value pairs.	https://github.com/arangodb/arangodb-mesos
Cassandra	Apache Cassandra is a scalable NoSQL database used for managing large amounts of data. It's used in production at organizations including Apple, CERN, and Netflix.	http://mesosphere.github.io/cassandra-mesos
Ceph	Ceph is a fault-tolerant, self-healing distributed filesystem. The Big Data Analytics team at Intel has created a Mesos framework for scaling Ceph clusters on Mesos.	https://github.com/Intel-bigdata/ceph-mesos
Elasticsearch	Elasticsearch is an open source, distributed search and analytics server developed by Elastic and based on Apache Lucene.	https://github.com/mesos/elastic-search
Etcd	Etcd is a distributed key/value store developed by CoreOS.	https://github.com/mesosphere/etcd-mesos
HDFS	The Hadoop Distributed File System (HDFS) is a distributed, fault-tolerant filesystem designed to run on commodity hardware.	https://github.com/mesosphere/hdfs
MemSQL	MemSQL is a distributed, in-memory SQL database.	https://github.com/memsql/memsql-mesos
Riak KV	Riak KV is a robust key/value store developed by Basho.	https://github.com/basho-labs/riak-mesos

B.2   Mesos-related tools

Mesos provides a drastically different approach to traditional datacenter architecture, allowing you to schedule resources across many machines instead of dedicating individual machines (or sets of machines) to an application. When you know the individual hostnames that an application is running on, configuring load balancers or connecting web applications to databases is relatively easy. But when the applications can be running on any one of tens, hundreds, or even thousands of nodes, things become a bit more complicated.

This section presents some tools you can use in your own environment. These include language bindings for developing your own Mesos frameworks, load-balancing and service-discovery solutions, monitoring and configuration management scripts, and a few Vagrant development environments.

B.2.1   Language bindings

Language bindings for Mesos allow you to write Mesos frameworks in your language of choice. Some of these bindings—I refer to them as *native bindings*—are maintained and distributed with Mesos itself. Others are developed and maintained by the community, and allow you to write frameworks in a language that you or your development team is more comfortable with.

MESOS NATIVE

As I covered in chapter 10, Mesos allows you to write frameworks in C++, Java, Scala, and Python, right out of the box. Here are some online resources:

- http://mesos.apache.org/api/latest/c++
- http://mesos.apache.org/api/latest/java
- https://github.com/apache/mesos/blob/0.22.2/src/python/interface/src/mesos/interface/__init__.py

In addition, be sure to check out the Mesos framework development guide, located at http://mesos.apache.org/documentation/latest/app-framework-development-guide, and the RENDLER example, located at https://github.com/mesosphere/rendler.

COMMUNITY MAINTAINED

Some of the members and organizations in the Mesos community have created and maintain language bindings, which allow you to write Mesos frameworks in your language of choice:

- Clojure—https://github.com/dgrnbrg/clj-mesos
- Erlang—https://github.com/mdevilliers/erlang-mesos
- Haskell—https://github.com/iand675/hs-mesos
- Pure Java—https://github.com/groupon/jesos
- Go—https://github.com/mesos/mesos-go
- Perl—https://github.com/mark-5/perl-mesos
- Pure Python—https://github.com/wickman/pesos
- Rust—https://github.com/spacejam/mesos-rs

B.2.2 Load balancing and service discovery

Because you don't always know which machines are running a particular application or service, you'll need a way to discover and connect to them by using the information that Mesos (or your Mesos framework) already has about the running tasks.

Name	Description	More info
Aurproxy	Aurproxy is a load balancer for Apache Aurora. It generates configurations for Nginx and gracefully reloads the service when changes occur.	https://github.com/tellapart/aurproxy
Bamboo	Bamboo is a load balancer for Marathon that configures HAProxy based on the state available via the Marathon API. It also includes a user interface and API for defining HAProxy ACLs.	https://github.com/QubitProducts/bamboo

Name	Description	More info
Marathon-LB	Marathon-LB is a load balancer for Marathon, developed by Mesosphere. It can pull state from the Marathon API or subscribe to Marathon's event stream to dynamically build HAProxy configurations and gracefully reload the service.	https://github.com/mesosphere/marathon-lb
Mesos-Consul	Mesos-Consul polls Mesos for information about running tasks across all frameworks and publishes the information to Consul, which then makes it available via DNS and the Consul HTTP API.	https://github.com/CiscoCloud/mesos-consul
Mesos-DNS	Mesos-DNS is a stateless DNS server that polls Mesos for information about running tasks across all frameworks. It then provides this service information via its built-in DNS server and HTTP API.	https://mesosphere.github.io/mesos-dns

B.2.3 *Monitoring and management*

When deploying any new service into your environment, especially one as critical as Mesos, it's important to know what options exist for monitoring the health of the service and managing and deploying changes to the service's configuration. This section describes tools that can be used to monitor the health of your Mesos cluster, and add-ons for today's three most popular configuration management tools.

MONITORING

For monitoring Mesos services and frameworks, you can typically use whatever monitoring tools you already have in place. For example, you can use the Elasticsearch, Logstash, and Kibana (ELK) stack or Splunk for centralized log management across the cluster, and you can use Nagios, Icinga, or another third-party monitoring tool for overall monitoring and alerting. Here are a few additional open source projects that you might be interested in:

- Collectd plugin for Mesos—https://github.com/rayrod2030/collectd-mesos
- Exhibitor (a supervisor for ZooKeeper)—https://github.com/Netflix/exhibitor
- Nagios checks for Mesos—https://github.com/opentable/nagios-mesos
- Nagios checks for ZooKeeper—https://github.com/apache/zookeeper/tree/trunk/src/contrib/monitoring
- Prometheus exporter for Mesos—https://github.com/prometheus/mesos_exporter
- Satellite (monitoring service for Mesos)—https://github.com/twosigma/satellite

CONFIGURATION MANAGEMENT

In many organizations and environments, configuration management tools enable systems administrators to manage machines in a many-to-one fashion. As of this writing, three popular configuration management tools are in this space: Ansible, Chef, and Puppet. Community members have written code in order to use these tools to provision Mesos and ZooKeeper clusters, and I'd like to highlight some of the better-known projects here.

Ansible is a configuration management tool and orchestration engine that allows you to deploy changes to machines over SSH, without needing to run an agent on the machine being managed. The following two playbooks will allow you to provision Mesos and ZooKeeper clusters:

- https://github.com/AnsibleShipyard/ansible-mesos
- https://github.com/AnsibleShipyard/ansible-zookeeper

Chef allows systems administrators to declare the desired state of their infrastructure by using a domain-specific language, or DSL. These two Chef cookbooks will allow you to provision Mesos and Zookeeper clusters:

- https://supermarket.chef.io/cookbooks/mesos
- https://supermarket.chef.io/cookbooks/zookeeper

Puppet also allows administrators to declare the desired state of their infrastructure by using a DSL. These two Puppet modules in particular will allow you to provision and manage the configuration of Mesos and ZooKeeper clusters:

- https://forge.puppetlabs.com/deric/mesos
- https://forge.puppetlabs.com/deric/zookeeper

B.2.4 Vagrant environments

A couple of Vagrant environments are available that allow you to provision a Mesos cluster right on your laptop. These two in particular will install Mesos, Marathon, and Docker:

- https://github.com/mesosphere/playa-mesos
- https://github.com/tayzlor/vagrant-puppet-mesosphere

index